THE PROSE WORKS OF DANTE ALIGHIERI

THE PROSE WORKS OF DANTE ALIGHIERI

VOLUME I
THE ITALIAN WORKS

Preface & Introductions by Joe Carlson

ROMAN ROADS CLASSICS

Also in the Roman Roads Classics series:

Inferno: Book One of the Divine Comedy, by Dante Alighieri, translated by Joe Carlson

Purgatorio: Book Two of the Divine Comedy, by Dante Alighieri, translated by Joe Carlson

Paradiso: Book Three of the Divine Comedy, by Dante Alighieri, translated by Joe Carlson

The Iliad, by Homer, a new rendering by Wesley Callihan

The Odyssey, by Homer, a new rendering by Wesley Callihan

On Duties, by Cicero, translated by Walter Miller, introduction by Wesley Callihan

———————————————

The Prose Works of Dante: Volume 1, The Italian Works, by Dante Alighieri
With preface and introductions by Joe Carlson

Original Italian texts by Dante Alighieri, 1265–1321.

Translators:
The Vita nuova (1895) — Charles Eliot Norton (1827-1908)
The Convivio (1903) — Philip H Wicksteed (1844-1927)

Published by Roman Roads Press,
Moscow, Idaho
RomanRoadsPress.com / permissions: info@romanroadspress.com

General Editor: Joe Carlson
Preface and Introductions: Joe Carlson
Editor: Carissa Hale
Cover Design and Interior Layout: Carissa Hale

The Prose Works of Dante: Volume 1, The Italian Works, by Dante Alighieri
Roman Roads Press / Roman Roads Classics

ISBN: 978-1-963505-14-6

Version 1.0.1 • March 2025

CONTENTS

A BRIEF WORD FROM THE PUBLISHER

The Prose Works of Dante: Vols. I & II present the complete prose works of Dante Alighieri, the poet primarily known for the *Divine Comedy*. While the *Comedy* is certainly his most important contribution to what C. S. Lewis called "Old Western Culture,"[1] Dante's other works brilliantly attest to his extensive reading and learning, his tremendous ability to digest and synthesize the teachings of others, his innate skill as a rhetorician, and his singularly inquisitive mind. Dante is a *sui generis*, if ever there was one. We have divided the works into two volumes, separating those written in Italian (Volume I) from those written in Latin (Volume II). The only work of his not included in these volumes (besides the *Comedy*) is a collection of Dante's numerous lyric poems, often titled simply *Rime*. However, Dante himself never collected these shorter poems into a single volume, and a number of those attributed to him are of questionable authenticity. Moreover, many of the more significant lyric poems in that collection are already found in the *Vita nuova* and *Convivio*.[2] Therefore, we have felt justified in limiting our scope to those works, finished and unfinished, Dante produced in prose.

To better understand the works, a brief sketch is here given of both Dante's life and the various contexts in which the works were written. At the beginning of each individual work, we have provided concise introductions that draw attention to that work's major themes, structure, and relation to Dante's entire oeuvre, including the *Comedy*. It is our desire that these volumes will encourage the

---

1   C. S. Lewis, "De Descriptione Temporum."

2   Two notable exceptions to this are the Rime Petrose (lyrics addressed to a lady named Petra) and the Latin eclogues (a description of which will be found at the end of the preface). However, these are readily available in translation to any student of Dante who wishes to study them.

reader to take seriously the intellect and affections of a Christian man who lived to love God and to know His world so that he might love God better, the same man who once said,

> Therefore, reader, raise with me your vision
> to the high wheels, directly to that part
> where the one and the other motion strike;
> and there begin to lovingly admire
> the Master's art: He loves it, in Himself,
> such that from it He never takes His eye.
> *Par.* X.7–12

PREFACE

Dante in Florence
(*Vita nuova*)

Late in the Spring of 1265, Dante Alighieri was born into a semi-noble Florentine family of little to no consequence. Not much is known of his early life, other than in 1274 he first laid his eyes on Beatrice. This singular event (which is told in some detail in *Vita nuova* II) would throw the young boy onto the path of destiny. The fourteenth-century Italian author Boccaccio describes the scene in the earliest biography of Dante we have. It is worth quoting in full:

> In that season wherein the sweetness of heaven reclothes the earth with its adornments, making her all to smile with diversity of flowers mingled amongst green leaves it was the custom both of men and women in our city, each in his district, to hold festival, gathering together in their several companies; wherefore it chanced that Folco Portinari, amongst the rest, a man in those days much honoured of the citizens, had gathered his neighbours round about, to feast them in his house on the first day of May. Now amongst them was that Alighieri already spoken of; and thither (even as little lads are wont to go about with their fathers, especially to places of festivity) Dante, whose ninth year was not yet ended, had accompanied him. And here, mingling with the others of his age—for in the festal house were many of them, boys and girls—the first tables being served, he abandoned himself with the rest to children's sports, so far as the compass of his small years would extend. There was amongst the throng of young ones a little daughter of the aforesaid Folco, whose name was Bice (though he himself always called her by the original of the name, to wit, Beatrice), whose age was some eight years; right gracious after

her childish fashion, and full gentle and winning in her ways, and of manners and speech far more sedate and modest than her small age required; and besides this the features of her face full delicate, most excellently disposed, and replete not only with beauty but with such purity and winsomeness, that she was held of many to be a kind of little angel. She then, such as I am painting her, or may be far more beauteous yet, appeared before the eyes of our Dante at this festival, not I suppose for the first time, but for the first time with power to enamour him; and he, child as he still was, received her fair visage into his heart with such affection, that, from that day forth, never, so long as he lived, was he severed therefrom.[3]

According to Dante's own testimony, he did not see her again until nine years later in 1283. As the story goes, she was walking with two friends when, glancing at Dante, their eyes met and she greeted him with a nod. This produced in the young man such feelings of rapture and beatitude he went home, fell into a vision, and wrote his first recorded poem: "To every captive soul and gentle heart" (see *Vita nuova* III). Trying to mask his deep and intense affection for her, Dante paid particular attention to another lady in society, which led directly to Beatrice never again blessing him with her greeting. She was married in 1287 and died three years later, plunging Dante into the deepest grief. The story of *Vita nuova* chronicles this journey of the soul, in which the stricken poet turns from his meditations on earthly love to spiritual and heavenly love. He famously concludes this first published work with the promise of another, greater poem in which Beatrice would be properly magnified:

After this sonnet, a wonderful vision appeared to me, in which I saw things which made me resolve to speak no more of this blessed one, until I could more worthily treat of her. And to attain to this, I study to the utmost of my power, as she truly knows. So that, if it shall please Him through whom all things live, that my life be prolonged for some years, I hope to say of her what was never said of any woman. And then may it please

---

3   Boccaccio, *Life of Dante*, trans. Philip H. Wicksteed (Cambridge, MA: Riverside Press, 1904), 17–18.

> Him who is the lord of Grace, that my soul may go to behold
> the glory of its lady, namely, of that blessed Beatrice, who in
> glory looks upon the face of Him *qui est per omnia saecula benedic-*
> *tus* [who is through all ages blessed]. (*Vita nuova* XLII)

It would not be until nearly fifteen years later that Dante began to fulfil his promise with the writing of the *Inferno*, the first canticle of the *Comedy*.

The year before Beatrice died, when he was 24, Dante fought at the battle of Campaldino, in which the Guelphs defeated the Ghibellines, restoring Guelph dominance in Florence. Three to four years after distinguishing himself on the battlefield, he published his first work, *Vita nuova*, a prosimetric frame story (see the Introduction to the work below) in which he includes many of the poems he had composed since first seeing Beatrice a decade earlier. Following this, Dante enrolled in the Guild of Physicians and Apothecaries, a necessary first step toward a career in politics. From 1296 to 1300, we have a few records of his civic contributions, showing how he acted as an ambassador or delegate to various meetings and councils, speaking successfully on behalf of Florence. It was during this time he also attended the three religious schools in Florence, studying both religion and philosophy with the Augustinians, the Dominicans, and the Franciscans.[4] Then, in the late spring of 1300, he was elected to serve, for a two-month term, as one of the six Priors, the highest office in the independent republic of Florence. Though it would seem ascendency to this position of authority would have been remembered with affection and pride, Dante would later write: "All my woes and all my misfortunes had their origin and commencement with my unlucky election to the priorate." Why? To understand this statement, we must turn to the second, and far more significant half of Dante's life.

---

4   See *Conv.* II.xii.5–7.

Dante in Exile

(*Convivio, De vulgari eloquentia, De monarchia, Epistolae, Questio de aqua et terra*)

> As Hippolytus was torn from Athens
> by his cruel and treacherous stepmother,
> so too you must needs be torn from Florence.
> This is willed and is already being planned,
> and soon will be managed by one who schemes,
> there where every day Christ is bought and sold.
> The blame will follow the injured party
> in fame, as usual; but the vengeance
> will witness to the truth that metes it out.
> You will need to abandon everything
> most dearly beloved; this is the arrow
> the bow of your exile will first let fly.
> You will prove how the bread of another
> tastes of salt, and how it is a hard path,
> the down and up of another man's stair.
> And what will burden your shoulders the most
> will be the base and brainless company
> that will fall with you into this valley;
> for all ungrateful, impious, and mad
> will they be against you; but very soon
> their temples, not yours, will redden for it.
> Of their savagery, their own progression
> will be the proof; such that it will be well
> to have made for yourself your own party.
> *Par.* XVII.46–69

In October 1301, Dante Alighieri was sent by the priors of Florence as part of an embassy to Rome in order to convince Pope Boniface VIII not to send Charles of Valois (the younger son of Philip III of France) to Florence. The pope's stated reason for doing so was to bring order to the fractious and unstable political climate that then existed in Dante's hometown. Underneath this, however, was a desire for more direct papal control over the affluent and influential city-state. Designated as "papal vicar," Charles could be the long arm of Boniface, allowing the pope to interfere in Florentine politics. Dante and his fellow White Guelphs (who were currently in power) thought this was a bad idea, while their political opponents, the Black Guelphs, welcomed the oversight of both the French king and the Pope. The Blacks claimed the Whites had unjustly persecuted their party and were looking for vengeance. They, therefore, needed the strong arm of foreign powers to achieve their own plans for dominance and retribution. While Boniface had agreed to receive the embassy, his intention was always to invade Florence, which he did through Charles' army in November 1301. The French prince immediately brought back the more ferocious Black party members that had been exiled by Dante's party. What began was nothing less than a coup. Members of the White party were killed or exiled, and their property was destroyed or confiscated. Naturally, political power was transferred back to the Black party, who maintained control for several decades. Charles had served his purpose: Boniface now had a party loyal to himself installed in Florence, with all dissenters either killed or neutralized.

But what of Dante? All this took place while he was in Rome, believing Boniface's good-faith pledge to consider the arguments of the White party. The betrayal was deeply painful and set Dante on a course that would change his life (and the world) forever. Being a member of the White party (who were accused of corruption by the Blacks), Dante was banished for two years, fined 5000 florins, and permanently banned from holding public office. This decree was made on January 27, 1302. On March 10 of the same year, having failed to appear before the council to receive his sentence, Dante was condemned to death should he ever return to Florence. His permanent exile from Florence had begun.

For a couple of years, Dante entertained hopes that the Florentine government would reconsider their unjust accusations and pronouncements. During this season he wrote a letter to Cardinal Nicholas of Prato, who had been sent by Boniface's successor to restore order to Florence (see *Epistle* I). However, it soon became clear Florence would remain in the grip of partisan politics for quite some time without any hope of the kind of restoration of truth and justice that would allow Dante to return home. He resigned himself to the life of a writer in exile.

In a passage early in the *Convivio*, Dante describes his condition:

> Since it was the pleasure of the citizens of the most beauteous
> and the most famous daughter of Rome, Florence, to cast me
> forth from her most sweet bosom, wherein I was born and
> nurtured until the culmination of my life (wherein I was born,
> and nurtured until the culmination of my life, wherein with
> their good leave, I long with all my heart to repose my wearied
> mind and end the time which is granted me), through well-nigh
> all the regions whereto this tongue extends, a wanderer, almost
> a beggar, have I paced, revealing against my will the wound
> of fortune, which is often wont to be unjustly imputed to him
> who is wounded.
>
> Verily have I been a ship without sail and without helm,
> drifted upon diverse ports and straits and shores by the dry
> wind that grievous poverty exhales. And I have seemed cheap
> in the eyes of many who perchance had conceived of me in
> other guise by some certain fame; in the sight of whom not
> only has my person been cheapened, but every work of mine,
> already accomplished or yet to do, has become of lower price.[5]

The tenor of this passage proves its early composition (somewhere between 1302 and 1304), when he was still hoping to regain
the city. Over the course of his remaining years, that tone would
change to frank vitriol and scorn (see *Inferno* XXVI.1–3: "Rejoice,
Florence! For you are so august, / that you beat your wings over sea
and land, / and your name spreads itself abroad through Hell!").
Seeking patronage and hospitality, he travelled from Siena to Forlì
to Verona to Lunigiana, back to Verona, and finally to Ravenna,
where he was laid to rest and his grave stands to this day. De-
pendent on others, he used his skill as a writer to earn whatever
living he could. There are rumors that he visited Paris (and even
Oxford!) during this time, but it is impossible to know for sure, as
the records of an exile's aimless wanderings are not always clearly
recorded for posterity.

During the first six years of his exile, he began at least two
projects which were ultimately abandoned: *Convivio* and *De vulgari
eloquentia*. Begun primarily to reestablish his reputation as an author, the first is a commentary (*comento*) in which Dante reinter-
preted three of his own canzoni. It can be described in a number

---

5   *Conv.* I.iii.4–5.

of ways (see the Introduction to the work below), but probably most helpfully as a philosophical treatise in the form of an intellectual banquet (*convivio*) of wisdom. While somewhat speculative, there are indications that Books I–III were written in 1302–1304, with Dante returning to Book IV in 1307–1308. In between Book III and Book IV, Dante probably began (and also abandoned) the one and a half books of *De vulgari eloquentia*, or *On the Eloquence of the Vernacular*. Briefly, this latter work was intended to persuade writers of prose and verse that the vernacular language (Italian in particular) was not only sufficient but preferable to Latin for the communication of certain truths. Ironically, this work was itself written in Latin.

Both these works were left unfinished because sometime around 1308 Dante began the work he would become known for the world over: *La commedia*, or as we know it, the *Divine Comedy*. This work would be his magnum opus, a beautiful, richly-layered consummation of his extensive learning and experience. But it did not stop him from writing other things. Likely after the completion of *Purgatorio* in 1315–1316, he began (and this time finished!) another prose work, in which he argued that monarchy (and by extension, world empire) was the only God-ordained system of government. *De monarchia* (*On Monarchy*) further argued that the emperor (Caesar) and the pope (Peter) had authority only within their own spheres of governance (the State and Church, respectively), a conviction that eventually got the book banned by the Vatican.

Dante also wrote letters, thirteen of which survive. We know of at least two others that are now lost, both referenced in an early biography of Dante by Leonardo Bruni (1370–1444). One letter, known only by its Latin invocation (*"Popule mi quid feci tibi?"* [Oh my people, what have I done to you?]), he wrote to the people of Florence, seeking restoration. Of the second, only a fragment survives. That fragment, however, is extremely interesting. Dante writes,

> All my woes and all my misfortunes had their origin and commencement with my unlucky election to the priorate; of which priorate, although I was not worthy in respect of worldly wisdom, yet in respect of loyalty and of years I was not unworthy of it; inasmuch as ten years had passed since the battle of

> Campaldino, where the Ghibelline party was almost entirely broken and brought to an end, on which occasion I was present, not inexperienced in arms, and was in great fear, and afterwards greatly exultant, by reason of the varying fortunes of that battle.[6]

Here Dante locates the source of all his troubles not to his exile but to his "unlucky election to the priorate" in June 1300. This becomes significant because the fictional pilgrimage of the *Comedy* is set three months prior, in March.[7] Why is this important? It means the trials and tribulations represented by the dark wood in *Inferno* I are not the pains and terrors of exile, but the avaricious and strife-filled atmosphere of Florence.[8]

Finally, in the year before he died, Dante gave a philosophical lecture on the relationship between the sea and land, the tension between Aristotle and Genesis 1 with regard to creation, and the scientific assumptions governing early fourteenth-century Europe. *Questio de aqua et terra* is the least studied of Dante's works, probably due to its narrow focus and obsolete scientific theories. Still, in the words of one Dante scholar, the *Questio* represents a "final testimony to the passionate interest in philosophy nurtured by its author, who in its concluding paragraph describes himself as 'the least among true philosophers'"[9] (see §24 of the *Questio*).

What I have described here is not the full extent of what Dante wrote, either before or after his exile. My focus in these two volumes, as noted above, is his prose works (including the epistles) as they grant significant insight into the mind of the greatest poet of all time. In addition to these works, however, Dante also composed over a hundred shorter lyric poems (sonnets, ballatas, and canzoni), all of which were completed before he began the *Commedia*, as well as two Latin eclogues in poetic conversation with Giovanni del Virgilio (a professor at Bologna) and a fellow Floren-

---

6 *Life of Dante*, 94.

7 It is commonly held that the pilgrim woke up in the dark wood during the night of Maundy Thursday, March 25, 1300.

8 I discuss this at length in the opening lecture of *The Dante Lectures* video series, also published by Roman Roads Press.

9 John A. Scott, *Understanding Dante* (Notre Dame: University of Notre Dame Press, 2004), 348.

tine exile in Ravenna (probably one Dino Perini). These last two, written in imitation of Vergil's *Bucolics*, are the first pastoral eclogues written in over a thousand years.[10] In them, Dante defends his decision to write the *Comedy* in Italian (contrary to the exhortation of Giovanni, who believed the then popular Latin verse to be more worthy of Dante's themes), and expresses his confidence that they will bring him glory.

Instead of producing a new translation of each of the works in these volumes, we have compiled the excellent translations of Charles Eliot Norton (*Vita nuova*), Philip H. Wicksteed (*Convivio, De vulgari eloquentia,* and *Questio*), Aurelia Henry Reinhardt (*De monarchia*), and Paget Toynbee (*Epistolae*), only lightly editing their work when absolutely necessary. However, we have taken the liberty to reorganize their texts to conform them to the modern reference systems, and include footnotes indicating the references to the many authors/authorities Dante loves to quote. Most of the footnotes were culled from the original editions represented here (*The New Life of Dante Alighieri*, Houghton, Mifflin and Company, 1896; *The Convivio of Dante Alighieri*, J. M. Dent, 1903; *A Translation of the Latin Works of Dante Alighieri*, J. M. Dent, 1904; *The De Monarchia of Dante Alighieri*, Houghton, Mifflin and Company, 1904; *The Letters of Dante*, Oxford, 1920), to which I added a number of intertextual allusions to the *Comedy*. All quotations from the *Comedy* in this preface and in the introductions that follow are taken from my own translations, also published by Roman Roads Press.

Joe Carlson
Moscow, ID, Epiphany 2025

---

10   Scott, *Understanding Dante*, 351.

VITA NUOVA

(NEW LIFE)

translated by Charles Eliot Norton

INTRODUCTION

Dante's earliest published work, the *Vita nuova* (*New Life*) combines thirty-one poems and accompanying prose to tell the story
of Dante's love for Beatrice and the new life into which that love
brought him. As in the *Comedy*, Dante the author/poet narrates
the events of Dante the main character, taking the history of his
interactions with Beatrice and his reaction to her early death as his
subject matter. But more than simply an autobiographical account
of the events, Dante uses the medium of prose interwoven with
poetry (known as *prosimetrum*) to establish himself as a poet of the
first rank and bring into maturity the burgeoning "*dolce stil novo*"
(sweet new style), a style of poetry that greatly contributed to Dante's pre-exilic fame and notoriety. The now famous phrase is first
found in *Purgatorio* when the pilgrim is talking with the spirit of the
Tuscan poet, Bonagiunta, about the very poetry Dante developed
in the *Vita nuova*:

> But tell me if I see here the one who
> innovated the new rhyme, beginning
> *'Ladies who have intelligence of love.'*"
> And I to him, "I am one who takes note
> when Love breathes on me, and in the manner
> he speaks within, I go on transcribing."
> "My brother," he said, "I now see the knot
> that kept Notaro, Guittone, and me
> on this side of the sweet new style (*dolce stil novo*) I hear!
> *Purg.* XXIV.49 57

The canzone, "Ladies who have intelligence of love," is found in
chapter XIX of *Vita nuova* at a crucial turning point in the story.
In chapter XVIII, Dante comes to the realization that the poems

in which he had praised "his lady" had been too subtle, such that no one knew what he was actually talking about. Realizing with shame that his deep and intense love for Beatrice has been obscured by timidity, he vows "to take up a new theme, and one more noble than the foregoing" (XVII). Thus, this canzone begins a new chapter in the *Vita nuova* and, according to Bonagiunta in *Purgatorio*, a new chapter in Italian poetry as well. But what makes this *stil novo* so important? Previously, the vernacular poetry of Italy was largely in imitation of the French Troubadors of the twelfth and thirteenth centuries. Bonagiunta, Giacomo da Lentini ("Notaro"), and Guittone d'Arezzo were of this school. With the *Vita nuova*, and this canzone in particular, Dante begins to use the formulas of Troubadorean love poetry to raise the eyes of the reader beyond the object of love into a meditation on Love Himself. Praise of the beloved became a gateway to praise of the Beloved. This is the miracle of Beatrice's beauty: the spiritual power to generate love for God. From this moment on, Beatrice becomes more and more of a Christ-figure; Dante lifts her out of the mundane history of the 1280s and into the realm of Christian allegory.

Dante attributes this new style of poetry to his role as Love's stenographer. Love, a thinly veiled personification representing Christ, "breathes on" him and Dante simply transcribes. These heavenly missives lead the poet to praise Beatrice with greater and greater intensity, attributing to her beauty (specifically her eyes and her smile) a miraculous power to transform the beholder, bringing him into a state of grace. This new attitude toward the beloved would eventually find its fullest expression in *Paradiso*, where Beatrice becomes a literal means of spiritual transformation and renewal:

> My enamored mind, always speaking love
> to my lady, burned now more than ever
> to limit the scope of my sight to her;
> and if nature or art ever made bait
> to catch the eyes so as to catch the mind,
> whether in human flesh or in paintings,
> all together they would seem as nothing
> to the divine delight that shone on me
> when I turned around to her smiling face.

> And the power that gaze granted to me
> pulled me out of Leda's beautiful nest
> and thrust me into the swiftest Heaven…
> But she, who was seeing my desire, began,
> smiling at me with so much happiness
> that God seemed to be the joy in her face…
>   *Par.* XXVII.88–99, 103–105

While the temptation is understandable, the sensitive Christian should be hesitant to cry "Blasphemy!" Dante is speaking allegorically. Especially in the *Comedy*, but even as early as the *Vita nuova*, Dante reads a deeper significance into people and events than we moderns typically do. For this poet of the *dolce stil novo*, any object could become a means of remembering, understanding, and loving Christ, the Lord of Love. The beloved, with her ability to draw the affections of the heart, was an especially potent image of God's redeeming power, such that the beloved herself became a symbol of salvation. Symbolic allegory may not be everyone's cup of tea, but we should not cast stones at those who find in it great devotional power. We must always read with charity.

One of the more complicated forms of symbolic allegory found in *Vita nuova* is Dante's insistence that Beatrice was the number nine. He explains:

> One reason why this number was so friendly to her may be this: since, according to Ptolemy and according to the Christian truth, there are nine heavens which move, and, according to the common astrological opinion, the said heavens work effects here below according to their respective positions, this number was her friend to the end that it might be understood that at her generation all the nine movable heavens were in most perfect relation. This is one reason thereof; but considering more subtly and according to the infallible truth, this number was she herself; I mean by similitude, and I intend it thus: the number three is the root of nine, for, without any other number, multiplied by itself it makes nine, as we see plainly that three times three make nine. Therefore, since three is the factor by itself of nine, and the Author of miracles by himself is three, namely, Father, Son, and Holy Spirit, who are three and one, this lady was accompanied by the number

nine, that it might be understood that she was a nine, that is, a miracle, whose only root is the marvellous Trinity. Perchance even a more subtle reason might be seen herein by a more subtle person; but this is that which I see for it, and which best pleases me.[1]

This might seem a little strange to the reader unfamiliar with medieval numerology. However, I bring it up here in the Introduction so that you are prepared to encounter it, starting on the very first page. At the root of this rich symbolism is the active recognition of a cosmic harmony that reflects the harmony of the Triune God of Scripture. That harmony, according to Dante, can be seen anywhere and everywhere, though to different degrees.[2] The cosmos is alive, tangibly alive, with the refulgent glory of God. His glory "penetrates the universe," as Dante says at the opening of *Paradiso*. Every square inch is alive with his Beauty, His truth, His goodness. His harmony, represented in the number nine, is the power that gives structure and meaning to everything that exists. Therefore, because this world bears the imprint of its Maker, any object can lead us to praise Him, to meditate on His beauty and grace. This helps to explain how the beloved becomes a symbol of the Beloved, her own love a gateway to His. Beatrice was a symbol of this harmony, this reality. But this is where Dante distinguishes himself from every poet that came before: Beatrice was also an actual lady who walked the streets of Florence. Her reality was not limited to the lines of a poet's verse. Dante's poetry (from the early canzoni in *Vita nuova* to the *Comedy*) does not bind her to the page, but instead gives allegorical meaning and symbolic power to the flesh and blood girl he loved from afar. Beatrice is no poetic ideal that lives only in the abstract; she is a living, breathing *specula Christi*, "mirror of Christ," made in the image of God to reflect His goodness and love.

The structure of the *Vita nuova* also reflects Dante's emphasis on the number nine. The collection of poems and the prose that elucidates their meaning and setting is organized around nine direct visions of Beatrice with a tenth instance describing her in-

---

1   See chapter XXX.

2   See *Par.* I.1–3.

effability following her death and ascension into Heaven.[3] Interestingly, this anticipates the 9+1 structure so prevalent in the *Comedy*.[4] Consider the following outline:

1)   The first meeting (when they are both nine years old) is recorded in chapter II; Dante sees Beatrice from a distance, and is immediately struck by her beauty.

2)   In chapter III, nine years later, Dante and Beatrice meet again on the street, and she greets him.

3)   After this meeting, also in chapter III, Dante falls asleep filled with rapture from her "sweet salutation" and has a vision of Beatrice taken up in the arms of Love. This intense vision, which involves the figure of Love holding Dante's burning heart and feeding it to Beatrice, leads to the first poem of *Vita nuova*: "To every captive soul and gentle heart."

4)   In chapter V, Dante sees her again in church, though his long, loving gaze is interpreted by others to be aimed at another lady, a mistake Dante will use to conceal his love for Beatrice. This will backfire on the poet, as is seen in the next encounter.

5)   In chapter X, Dante, meeting Beatrice again on the street, seeks to gain another "sweet salutation" but this time is denied, due to the rumors of the other lady Dante was said to be looking at.

6)   In chapter XIV, Dante is taken to a wedding by a friend where he sees Beatrice. He is overcome with trembling, undone by her presence.

7)   Later, in chapter XXIII, having been confined to his rooms with illness, Dante's fancy begins to wander and he

---

3   See Robert Hollander's article, "*Vita Nuova*: Dante's Perceptions of Beatrice," *Dante Studies*, no. 92 (1974), 1–18, for a more detailed account.

4   Robert Hollander, "Dante's Perceptions of Beatrice," note 30. See also Janet Levarie Smarr, "Celestial Patterns and Symmetries in the *Vita Nuova*," *Dante Studies*, no. 98 (1980), 145–150.

imagines (as in a fever dream) that Beatrice has died; he watches as her still form is covered with a white veil. This vision is recounted in the central canzone of the work.

8)   In the following chapter, XXIV, Dante sees from afar a lady known to all as Primavera (Spring) walking in front of another lady, who turns out to be Beatrice. He begins to think of Primavera as the one who comes first (*prima verra*), with all the connotations of John the Baptist, which strengthens the Christological symbolism Dante attributed to Beatrice.

9)   After this final encounter, Beatrice dies. Over a year later, Dante's strong imagination presents him with the image of Beatrice as he first saw her as a child (chapter XXX-IX). He repents of his faithlessness to her memory.

10) Finally, in the last chapter (XLII), Dante has a vision "in which I saw things which made me resolve to speak no more of this blessed one, until I could more worthily treat of her. And to attain to this, I study to the utmost of my power, as she truly knows. So that, if it shall please Him through whom all things live that my life be prolonged for some years, I hope to say of her what was never said of any woman."

Thus we have a 9+1 structure on which Dante draps the story of his persevering love for Beatrice, a love that would transcend the woman herself and raise Dante up to the highest spheres of Heaven. The poetry and prose, interacting with each other to propel the story forward, unpack both the turmoil of infatuation and the ennoblement of true love. Importantly, this is the story written in "the book of [Dante's] memory," remembered with the rich resonance of the deeper meaning inherent to physical manifestations of God's eternal love.

In this Introduction, I have not touched on certain important plot points (for instance, the death of Beatrice's father, or the consolation Dante finds in the eyes of another woman following the death of Beatrice) but instead have focused on the underlying themes that give the *Vita nuova* its importance, especially in relation to the *Comedy*. To be sure, more could be said, as is true of all the Introductions that follow. If I have adequately set the stage and whet the appetite for more, then I will have accomplished my goal.

For Further Reading:

Harrison, Robert Pogue. "Approaching the Vita Nuova," in *The Cambridge Companion to Dante*, edited by Rachel Jacoff. Cambridge, MA: Cambridge University Press, 1993.

Musa, Mark. *Dante's Vita Nuova: A Translation and Essay*. Bloomington: Indiana University Press, 1973.

Scott, John A. *Understanding Dante*. Notre Dame: University of Notre Dame Press, 2005. See chapter 1.

VITA NUOVA

(1292–1293)

Proem

In that part of the book of my memory before which little can be read is found a rubric which says: *Incipit Vita Nova* [The New Life begins]. Under which rubric I find the words written which it is my intention to copy into this little book—and if not all of them, at least their meaning.

Chapter II

Nine times now, since my birth, the heaven of light had turned almost to the same point in its own gyration, when the glorious Lady of my mind, who was called Beatrice by many who knew not what to call her, first appeared before my eyes. She had already been in this life so long that in its course the starry heaven had moved toward the region of the East one of the twelve parts of a degree; so that at about the beginning of her ninth year she appeared to me, and I near the end of my ninth year saw her. She appeared to me clothed in a most noble color, a modest and becoming crimson, and she was girt and adorned in such wise as befitted her very youthful age. At that instant, I say truly that the spirit of life, which dwells in the most secret chamber of the heart, began to tremble with such violence that it appeared fearfully in the least pulses, and, trembling, said these words: *Ecce deus fortior me, qui veniens dominabitur mihi* [Behold a god stronger than I, who coming shall rule over me].

At that instant the spirit of the soul, which dwells in the high chamber to which all the spirits of the senses carry their perceptions, began to marvel greatly, and, speaking especially to the spirit of the sight, said these words: *Apparuit jam beatitudo vestra* [Now has appeared your bliss].

At that instant the natural spirit, which dwells in that part where our nourishment is supplied, began to weep, and, weeping, said these words: *Heu miser! quia frequenter impeditus ero deinceps* [Woe is me, wretched! because often from this time forth shall I be hindered].

I say that from that time forward Love lorded it over my soul, which had been so speedily wedded to him: and he began to exercise over me such control and such lordship, through the power which my imagination gave to him, that it behoved me to do completely all his pleasure. He commanded me ofttimes that I should seek to see this youthful angel; so that I in my boyhood often went seeking her, and saw her of such noble and praiseworthy deportment, that truly of her might be said that word of the poet Homer, "She seems not the daughter of mortal man, but of God." And though her image, which stayed constantly with me, gave assurance to Love to hold lordship over me, yet it was of such noble virtue that it never suffered Love to rule me without the faithful counsel of the reason in those matters in which it were useful to hear such counsel. And since to dwell upon the passions and actions of such early youth seems like telling an idle tale, I will leave them, and, passing over many things which might be drawn from the original where these lie hidden, I will come to those words which are written in my memory under larger paragraphs.

Chapter III

When so many days had passed that nine years were exactly complete since the above-described apparition of this most gentle lady, on the last of these days it happened that this admirable lady appeared to me, clothed in purest white, between two gentle ladies who were of greater age; and, passing along a street, turned her eyes toward that place where I stood very timidly; and by her ineffable courtesy, which is to-day rewarded in the eternal world, saluted me with such virtue that it seemed to me then that I saw all the bounds of bliss. The hour when her most sweet salutation reached me was precisely the ninth of that day; and since it was the first time that her words came to my ears, I took in such sweetness, that, as it were intoxicated, I turned away from the folk; and, betaking myself to the solitude of my own chamber, I sat myself down to think of this most courteous lady.

And thinking of her, a sweet slumber overcame me, in which a marvellous vision appeared to me; for methought I saw in my chamber a cloud of the color of fire, within which I discerned a shape of a Lord of aspect fearful to whoso might look upon him; and he seemed to me so joyful within himself that a marvellous thing it was; and in his words he said many things which I understood not, save a few, among which I understood these: *Ego Dominus tuus* [I am thy Lord]. In his arms meseemed to see a person sleeping, naked, save that she seemed to me to be wrapped lightly in a crimson cloth; whom I, regarding very intently, recognized as the lady of the salutation, who had the day before deigned to salute me. And in one of his hands it seemed to me that he held a thing which was all on fire; and it seemed to me that he said to me these words: *Vide cor tuum* [Behold thy heart]. And when he had remained awhile, it seemed to me that he awoke her that slept; and he so far prevailed upon her with his craft as to make her eat that thing which was burning in his hand; and she ate it timidly. After this, it was but a short while before his joy turned into the most bitter lament; and as he wept he gathered up this lady in his arms, and with her it seemed to me that he went away toward heaven. Whereat I felt such great anguish, that my weak slumber could not endure it, but was broken, and I awoke. And straightway I began to reflect, and found that the hour in which this vision had appeared to me had been the fourth of the night; so that, it plainly appears, it was the first hour of the nine last hours of the night.

And thinking on what had appeared to me, I resolved to make it known to many who were famous poets at that time; and since I had already seen in myself the art of discoursing in rhyme, I resolved to make a sonnet in which I would salute all the liegemen of Love, and, praying them to give an interpretation of my vision, would write to them that which I had seen in my slumber. And I began then this sonnet:—

> To every captive soul and gentle heart
>   Unto whose sight may come the present word,

> That they thereof to me their thoughts impart,
>   Be greeting in Love's name, who is their Lord.
> Now of those hours well-nigh one third had gone
>   What time doth every star appear most bright,
>   When on a sudden Love before me shone,
>   Remembrance of whose nature gives me fright.
> Joyful to me seemed Love, and he was keeping
>   My heart within his hands, while on his arm
>   He held my lady, covered o'er, and sleeping.
> Then waking her, he with this flaming heart
>   Did humble feed her fearful of some harm.
>   Thereon I saw him thence in tears depart.

This sonnet is divided into two parts. In the first part I offer greeting, and ask for a reply; in the second I signify to what the reply is to be made. The second part begins here: *Now of.*

To this sonnet reply was made by many, and of diverse opinions. Among those who replied to it was he whom I call first of my friends, and he then wrote a sonnet which begins, *All worth, in my opinion, thou hast seen.*[1] And this was, as it were, the beginning of the friendship between him and me, when he knew that I was he who had sent it to him.

The true meaning of this dream was not then seen by any one, but now it is plain to the simplest.

Chapter IV

After this vision my natural spirit began to be hindered in its operation, for my soul was wholly given over to the thought of this most gentle lady; whereby in brief time I fell into so frail and feeble a condition, that my appearance was grievous to many of my friends; and many full of envy eagerly sought to know from me that which above all I wished to conceal from others. And I, perceiving their evil questioning, through the will of Love, who commanded me according to the counsel of reason, replied to them

---

1   Guido Cavalcanti (1258–1300) was a slightly older poet from the Florentine aristocracy. He and Dante exchanged many sonnets during this time. See *Inf.* X.51–72 for a depiction of Guido's father (Cavalcante) in Hell, asking about his son. Both father and son were Epicureans and, therefore, not Christians.

that it was Love who had brought me to this pass. I spoke of Love, because I bore on my face so many of his signs that this could not be concealed. And when they asked me: "For whom has Love thus wasted thee?" I, smiling, looked at them and said nothing.

Chapter V

One day it happened that this most gentle lady was sitting apart, where words concerning the Queen of Glory were to be heard; and I was in a place from which I saw my bliss. And in the direct line between her and me sat a gentle lady of very pleasing aspect, who often looked at me, wondering at my gaze, which seemed as if it ended upon her; so that many observed her looking. And such note was taken of it, that, as I departed from this place, I heard say near me: "Behold how that lady wastes the life of this man;" and naming her, I understood that they spoke of her who had been in the path of the straight line which, parting from the most gentle Beatrice, had ended in my eyes. Then I took great comfort, being sure that my secret had not been communicated to others on that day through my eyes; and at once I thought to make of this gentle lady a screen of the truth; and in a short time I made such show of it that many persons who held discourse about me believed that they knew my secret.

With this lady I dissembled for some months and years; and in order to establish in others a firmer credence, I wrote for her certain trifles in rhyme, which it is not my intention to transcribe here, save in so far as they might serve to treat of that most gentle Beatrice; and therefore I will leave them all, save that I will write something of them which seems to be praise of her.

Chapter VI

I say that, during the time while this lady was the screen of so great a love as possessed me, the will came to me to record the name of that most gentle one, and to accompany it with many names of ladies, and especially with the name of this gentle lady; and I took the names of sixty of the most beautiful ladies of the city where my lady had been placed by the Most High Lord, and I composed an epistle in the form of a *serventese*, which I will not transcribe; and of which I would not have made mention, but for the sake of telling this which fell out marvellously in its composition, namely, that in no other place did the name of my lady endure to stand, but as the ninth in number among the names of these ladies.

Chapter VII

The lady with whom I had so long concealed my will was obliged to depart from the above-mentioned city, and go to a very distant place; whereat I, well-nigh dismayed by reason of the fair defence which had failed me, did more discomfort me than I myself would beforehand have believed. And, thinking that if I did not speak somewhat grievingly of her departure people would sooner become acquainted with my secret, I resolved to make some lament for it in a sonnet, which I will transcribe because my lady was the immediate occasion of certain words which are in the sonnet, as is evident to whoever understands it; and then I devised this sonnet:

> O ye who turn your steps along Love's way,
>> Consider, and then say,
>> If there be any grief than mine more great;
>> That ye to hear me deign, I only pray;
>> Then fancy, as ye may,
>> If I am every torment's inn and gate.
> 'T was not my little goodness to repay,
>> But bounty to display,
>> Love gave me such a sweet and pleasant fate,
>> That many times I heard behind me say,
>> "Ah, through what merit, pray,
>> Hath this man's heart become so light of late?"
> But now is wholly lost my hardihead,
>> Which came from out a treasure of Love's own,
>> And I stay poor alone,
>> So that of speech there cometh to me dread.
> Thus wishing now to do like unto one
>> Who, out of shame, concealeth his disgrace,

I wear a joyful face,
While in my heart I waste away and groan.

This sonnet has two principal parts; for in the first I intend to cry to the liegemen of Love with those words of Jeremy the prophet: *O vos omnes qui transitis per viam, attendite et videte, si est dolor sicut dolor meus* [All ye that pass by, behold, and see if there be any sorrow like unto my sorrow]; and to pray them to deign to listen to me. In the second I relate where Love had set me, with other intent than that which the last parts of the sonnet indicate; and I tell that which I have lost. The second part begins here: *'T was not my*.

Chapter VIII

After the departure of this gentle lady it pleased the Lord of the Angels to call unto His glory a lady young and of exceeding gentle aspect, who had been very lovely in the above-mentioned city; whose body I saw lying without its soul, in midst of many ladies who were weeping very pitifully. Then, remembering that formerly I had seen her in company with that most gentle one, I could not restrain some tears; nay, weeping, I resolved to say some words about her death, in guerdon for that I had seen her sometimes with my lady. And thereon I touched somewhat in the last part of the words that I said of her, as plainly appears to him who understands them. And I devised then these two sonnets; the first of which begins, *Lovers, lament*; the second, *Discourteous death*:

Lovers, lament, since Love himself now cries,
    Hearing what cause 't is maketh him to weep.
    Love seeth ladies mourn in sorrow deep,
    Showing their bitter grieving through their eyes;
Because discourteous Death, on gentle heart
    Working his cruel, unrelenting ways,
    Hath all despoiled which in the world wins praise
    For gentle dame, excepting honor's part.
Hear ye what honor Love to her did pay;
    For him in real form I saw lament
    Above the lovely image of the dead;

And often toward the heaven he raised his head,
  Whereto the gentle soul had made ascent
  Which had been mistress of a shape so gay.

This first sonnet is divided into three parts. In the first, I call and solicit the liegemen of Love to weep; and I say that their Lord weeps, and that, hearing the cause why he weeps, they should be the more ready to listen to me. In the second, I relate the cause. In the third, I speak of certain honor that Love paid to this lady. The second part begins here: *Love seeth*; the third, here: *Hear ye*.

Discourteous Death, of clemency the foe,
  Mother from old of woe,
  Thou judgment irresistible, severe,
  Since sorrow to this heart thou dost not spare,
  Therefore in grief I go,
  And blaming thee my very tongue outwear.
And since I wish of grace to strip thee bare,
  Behoves me to declare
  The wrong of wrongs in this thy guilty blow;
  Not that the folk do not already know,
  But to make each thy foe,
  Who henceforth shall be nurtured with Love's care,
From out the world thou courtesy hast ta'en,
  And virtue, which in woman is to praise;
  And in youth's gayest days
  The charm of love thou hast untimely slain.
Who is this lady I will not declare,
  Save as her qualities do make her known;
  Who merits heaven, alone
  May have the hope her company to share.

This sonnet is divided into four parts. In the first I call Death by certain names proper to her; in the second, speaking to her, I tell the reason why I am moved to reproach her; in the third, I revile her; in the fourth, I turn to speak to an indefinite person, although definite as regards my meaning. The second part begins here: *Since sorrow*; the third, here: *And since I wish*; the fourth, with *Who merits*.

Chapter IX

Some days after the death of this lady, a thing happened wherefore it behoved me to leave the above-mentioned city, and to go toward those parts where that gentle lady was who had been my defence, though the end of my journey was not distant so far as she was. And notwithstanding I was outwardly in company with many, the journey displeased me, so that hardly could sighs relieve the anguish which the heart felt, because I was going away from my bliss. And then that most sweet Lord, who was lording it over me through virtue of the most gentle lady, appeared in my imagination like a pilgrim lightly clad and in mean raiment. He seemed disheartened, and was looking upon the ground, save that sometimes it seemed to me his eyes were turned upon a beautiful, swift, and very clear stream which was flowing along by the road upon which I was.

It seemed to me that Love called me, and said to me these words: "I come from that lady who has been so long thy defence, and I know that she will not come back; and therefore that heart which I made thee keep with her I have it with me, and I carry it to a lady who will be thy defence, as this one was;" and he called her by name, so that I knew her well. "But, however, of these words which I have spoken unto thee, if thou shouldst tell any of them, tell them in such wise that the feigned love which thou hast shown for this lady, and which it will behove thee to show for another, shall not be revealed through them." And when he had thus spoken, all this my imagination disappeared of a sudden, through the exceeding great part of himself which, it seemed to me, Love bestowed on me. And, as if changed in my aspect, I rode that day very pensive and accompanied by many sighs. The next day I began this sonnet:

> As I the other day rode far from glad
>> Along a way it pleased me not to take,
>> I came on Love, who did his journey make,
>> In the light garment of a pilgrim clad.
> His countenance, it seemed to me, was sad,
>> As if he grieved for his lost lordship's sake;

> Pensive he came, and forth his sighs did break;
>   Not to see folk, his head bowed down he had.
> When me he saw, by name he called to me,
>   And said, "I come from that far distant part
>   Where through my will thy heart did dwell of late.
> I bring it now on new delight to wait."
>   Thereon I took of him so great a part
>   That quick he vanished; how, I did not see.

This sonnet has three parts. In the first part I tell how I found Love, and what he seemed to me; in the second, I tell that which he said to me, though not completely, through the fear that I had of disclosing my secret; in the third, I tell how he disappeared. The second begins here: *When me he saw*; the third, here: *Thereon I took*.

Chapter X

After my return, I set myself to seek out that lady whom my Lord had named to me on the road of sighs. And to the end that my speech may be more brief, I say that in short time I made her my defence to such degree, that very many people spoke of it beyond the terms of courtesy; wherefore many times it weighed heavily upon me. And on this account, namely, because of this injurious talk, which seemed to impute vice to me, that most gentle lady, who was the destroyer of all the vices and the queen of the virtues, passing by a certain place, denied me her most sweet salute, in which lay all my bliss. And departing a little from the present subject, I will declare that which her salutation with its virtue wrought in me.

Chapter XI

I say that, whenever she appeared in any place, in the hope of her marvellous salutation there no longer remained to me an enemy; nay, a flame of charity possessed me, which made me pardon every one who had done me wrong; and had any one at that time questioned me of anything, my only answer would have been "Love," and my face would have been clothed with humility And when she was about to salute me, a spirit of Love, destroying all the other spirits of the senses, urged forth the feeble spirits of sight, and said to them, "Go and do honor to your lady," and he remained in their place. And whoever had wished to know Love might have done so by looking at the trembling of my eyes. And when this most gentle lady saluted me, Love was no such mediator that he had power to shade for me the insupportable bliss, but he, as if through excess of sweetness, became such that my body, which was wholly under his rule, oftentimes moved like a heavy, inanimate thing. Hereby it plainly appears that in her salutation abode my bliss, which oftentimes surpassed and overflowed my capacity.

Chapter XII

Now returning to my subject, I say that, after my bliss was denied to me, such grief came to me that, withdrawing from folk, I went into a solitary place to bathe the earth with most bitter tears. And when this weeping was a little assuaged, I betook myself to my chamber, where I could lament without being heard. And here, calling upon the lady of courtesy for pity, and saying, "Love, help thy liegeman!" I fell asleep, like a beaten child, in tears.

It happened, about the middle of my sleep, that I seemed to see in my chamber a youth sitting at my side, clothed in whitest raiment, and very thoughtful in his aspect. He was looking upon me where I lay; and when he had looked upon me for some time, it seemed to me that, sighing, he called me and said to me these words: *Fili mi, tempus est ut prætermittantur simulata nostra* [My son, it is time that our feignings be given up]. Then it seemed to me that I recognized him, since he called me even as he had many times before called me in my slumbers.

And, looking at him, it seemed to me that he wept piteously, and it seemed that he waited for some word from me. Wherefore, taking heart, I began to speak thus with him: "Lord of nobleness, why dost thou weep?" And he said to me these words: *Ego tanquam centrum circuli, cui simili modo se habent circumferentiæ partes; tu autem non sic* [I am as the centre of a circle to which the parts of the circumference bear an equal relation; but thou art not so.] Then, thinking on his words, it seemed to me that he had spoken to me very obscurely, so that I forced myself to speak, and said to him these words: "What is this, Lord, which thou sayest to me with such obscurity?" And he said to me in the common tongue: "Ask no more than may be useful to thee."

And therefore I began to discourse with him of the salutation which had been denied me, and I asked of him the reason; whereupon in this wise he replied to me: "This our Beatrice heard from certain persons who talked of thee, that the lady whom I named to thee on the road of sighs was receiving from thee some harm. And therefore this most gentle lady, who is adverse to every harm, did not deign to salute thy person, fearing lest it should be harmful. Wherefore, to the end that the truth of thy long-kept secret may be somewhat known to her, I will that thou say certain words in rhyme, in which thou shalt set forth the power that I hold over thee through her, and how thou wert straightway hers even from thy boyhood; and for this, call as a witness him who knows it, and also do thou pray him that he should tell it to her. And I, who am he, willingly will speak to her of it; and through this she shall understand thy will, and, understanding it, shall interpret aright the words of the deceived. Make, as it were, a mediator of these words, so that thou speak not to her directly, for this is not befitting. And without me send them nowhere where they might be heard by her; but take care to adorn them with sweet harmony, wherein I shall be whenever there be need."

And having said these words he disappeared, and my sleep was broken. Then I, remembering myself, found that this vision had appeared to me in the ninth hour of the day; and before I went out from that chamber I resolved to make a ballad in which I would execute that which my Lord had laid upon me, and I made this ballad:

> Ballad, I send thee forth upon Love's trace,
>   For thou must him before my Lady bring,
>   So that of my excuse, which thou dost sing,
>   My Lord may then with her speak face to face.
> Such courteous aspect, Ballad, thou dost show,
>   That all alone, indeed,
>   Thou oughtest not in any place to fear;
>   But if securely thou dost wish to go,

> First to find Love is need,
>   For ill it were without Him to appear;
>   Seeing that she who ought thy words to hear,
>   If she be angry, as I think, with me,
>   And thou with Him companioned should not be,
>   Might lightly make thee fall into disgrace.
> With dulcet sound, when with Him thou mayst be,
>   Begin with words like these,
>   First begging her that she would pity take:
>   "Lady, he who to you now sendeth me
>   Wills, when to you it please,
>   That his excuse you deign to hear me make.
>   Love is that one who, for thy beauty's sake,
>   Makes him, as He doth will, his looks to change;
>   Then why He made his eyes on others range.
>   Think you, since in his heart no change hath place."
> Tell her: "O Lady, this his heart is stayed
>   With faith so firmly just,
>   Save to serve you, it hath no other care.
>   Early 't was yours, and never hath it strayed."
>   But if she thee distrust,
>   Say, "Ask of Love, who will the truth declare."
>   And at the end, beg her, with humble prayer,
>   That if it trouble her to pardon give,
>   She then should bid that I no longer live,
>   Nor shall she see her servant sue for grace.
> And say to Him who is compassion's key,
>   Ere from her thou depart,
>   That He may tell her of my reason fair,
>   "Through favor unto my sweet melody,
>   Stay with her where thou art,
>   And of thy servant, what thou wilt, declare,
>   And if she grant forgiveness through thy prayer,
>   Make peace on her fair countenance to shine."
>   When it may please thee, gentle Ballad mine,
>   Honor to win, go forth upon thy race.

This ballad is divided into three parts. In the first, I tell it whither it is to go, and encourage it that it may go the more assured; and I tell whose company it is to seek, if it wishes to go securely and without any danger. In the second, I tell that which it is beholden to make known. In the third, I give it leave to go when it will, commending its going to the arms of fortune. The second part begins, *With dulcet sound*; the third, *When it may please thee*. Some man may object against me and say that he understands not to whom my speech in the second part is addressed, since the ballad is nought else but these words which I am speaking; and therefore I say that I intend to solve and clear up this doubt in this little book, even in a more difficult passage; and then he who may here be in doubt, or who may choose to object after that fashion, will understand.

Chapter XIII

After this above-described vision, having now spoken the words that Love had imposed on me to speak, many and diverse thoughts began to assail and to try me, and against each I was as it were without defence. Among which thoughts four chiefly hindered the repose of my life. One of them was this: "The lordship of Love is good, in that it withdraws the inclination of his liegeman from all vile things." The next was this: "The lordship of Love is not good, because the more fidelity his liegeman bears to him, so much the heavier and more grievous trials he must needs endure." The next was this: "The name of Love is so sweet to hear, that it seems to me impossible that his effects in most things should be other than sweet, seeing that names follow the things named, as it is written, *Nomina sunt consequentia rerum*" [Names are consequences of things]. The fourth was this: "The lady through whom Love thus binds thee is not as other ladies that her heart may be lightly moved." And each thought so assailed me that it made me stand like one who knows not by which way to take his journey, and who desires to go, and knows not whither he should go. And if I thought of desiring to seek a way common to them, namely, that wherein all would accord, this way was very hostile to me, namely, to call upon and put myself in the arms of Pity. And while I abode in this condition, the will came to me to write some rhymed words thereon, and I devised then this sonnet:

All of my thoughts concerning Love discourse,
    And have in them so great variety,
    That one to wish his sway compelleth me,
    Another argues evil of his force;
One, hoping, sweetness doth to me impart,
    Another makes me oftentimes lament;
    Only in craving Pity they consent,
    Trembling with fear that is within my heart.
Thus know I not from which my theme to take;
    I fain would speak, and know not what to say;
    In such perplexities of love I live:
And if with all to make accord I strive,
    I needs unto my very foe must pray,
    My Lady Pity, my defence to make.

This sonnet may be divided into four parts. In the first, I say and declare that all my thoughts are concerning Love: in the second, I say that they are diverse, and I relate their diversity: in the third, I say in what they all seem to accord: in the fourth, I say that, wishing to speak of Love, I know not from which to take my theme, and if I wish to take it from them all, I needs must call upon my foe, my Lady Pity. I say *my Lady*, as it were in a scornful mode of speech. The second begins here: *And have in them*; the third, *Only in craving*; the fourth, *Thus know I.*

Chapter XIV

After the battle of the diverse thoughts, it happened that this most gentle lady went to a place where many gentle ladies were assembled; to which place I was conducted by a friendly person, who thought to give me a great pleasure in leading me where so many ladies were displaying their beauties. Wherefore I, hardly knowing whereunto I had been led, and trusting myself to the person who had conducted his friend to the verge of life, said: "Wherefore are we come to these ladies?" Then he said to me: "To the end that they may be worthily served."

And the truth is, that they were met together here to attend on a gentle lady who was married that day; and therefore, according to the custom of the above-mentioned city, it behoved them to bear her company at her first sitting at table in the house of her new-made husband. So that I, believing to do the pleasure of this friend, determined to stand in company with him at the service of the ladies. And as soon as I had thus resolved, I seemed to feel a wonderful tremor begin in my breast on the left side, and extend suddenly through all the parts of my body. Then I say that, dissembling, I leaned against a painting which ran around the wall of this house, and fearing lest my trembling should be observed by others, I lifted mine eyes, and, looking at the ladies, saw among them the most gentle Beatrice. Then were my spirits so destroyed by the force that Love acquired, on seeing himself in such neighborhood to this most gentle lady, that none remained alive except the spirits of the sight, and even these remained outside of their instruments, because Love wished to stand in their most noble place to look upon this marvellous lady. And although I was other than at first, I grieved much for these little spirits, who were lamenting bitterly, and saying, "If he so like a thunderbolt had not smitten us from our place, we might stand to gaze upon the marvel of this lady, as do the others our peers."

I say that many of these ladies, perceiving my transfiguration, began to wonder; and, talking, make a mock of me with this most gentle lady. Thereupon my friend, who in good faith had been deceived, took me by the hand, and, leading me out from the sight of these ladies, asked me what ailed me. Then, having somewhat reposed, and my dead spirits having risen again, and those that were driven out having returned to their possessions, I said to this my friend these words: "I have held my feet on that part of life beyond which no man can go with intent to return."

And leaving him, I returned to the chamber of tears, in which, weeping and ashamed, I said within myself, "If this lady knew my condition, I do not believe that she would thus have made mock of my person; nay, I believe that she would feel much pity therefor." And being in this grief, I resolved to say some words in which, speaking to her, I would explain the cause of my transfigurement, and would say that I know well that it is not known, and that, were it known, I believe that it would move others to pity; and I resolved to say them, desiring that peradventure they might come to her hearing. And then I devised this sonnet:

> With other ladies you make mock of me,
>   And think not, Lady, of the reason why
>   So strange a shape I offer to your eye,
>   Whene'er it hap that I your beauty see.
> If this you knew, your pity could not hold
>   Longer against me its accustomed guise;
>   For when so near you Love doth me surprise,
>   He courage takes and such assurance bold,
> He smites among my spirits chilled with fear,
>   And some he slays, and some he doth expel,
>   So he alone remains to look on you;
> Hence I another's form am changed into,
>   Yet not so changed but even then full well
>   The grievous cries of those expelled I hear.

This sonnet I do not divide into parts, because the division is made only for the sake of disclosing the meaning of the thing divided; therefore, since, through what has been said of its occasion, it has been made sufficiently plain, there is no need of division. It is true that among the words whereby the occasion of this sonnet is set forth, certain ambiguous words are found; namely, when I say that Love slays all my spirits, and only those of vision remain alive, and even they outside of their instruments. And this ambiguity it were impossible to solve to one who is not in like degree the liegeman of Love; and to such as are so, that is already plain which would solve these ambiguous words; and therefore it is not well for me to explain this ambiguousness, since my speech would be vain or superfluous.

Chapter XV

After this strange transfiguration, a strong thought came to me which seldom left me, nay, rather continually recurred to me, and held this discourse with me: "Since thou presentest so contemptible an appearance when thou art near this lady, why then seekest thou to see her? Behold, if she were to ask thee this, what wouldst thou have to answer? supposing that all thy faculties were free, so that thou couldst answer her." And to this another humble thought replied, and said: "If I lost not my faculties and were free so that I could answer, I should say to her that so soon as I picture to myself her marvellous beauty, so soon a desire to see her comes to me, which is of such great virtue that it slays and destroys in my memory that which might rise against it; and therefore past sufferings hold me not back from seeking the sight of her." Wherefore, moved by such thoughts, I resolved to say certain words, in which, excusing myself to her from blame on this account, I would also set down what befell me in her presence; and I devised this sonnet:

> That which opposeth in my mind doth die
>> Whene'er I come to see you, beauteous Joy!
>> And I hear Love say, when to you I 'm nigh,
>> "Begone, if death be unto thee annoy."
> My face the color of my heart displays,
>> Which, fainting, nay chance support doth seek;
>> And as I tremble in my drunken daze,
>> "Die! die!" the very stones appear to shriek.
> He who may then behold me doeth ill,
>> If my affrighted soul he comfort not,
>> Showing at least that me he pitieth,
> Through that compassion which your scorn doth kill,
>> And which is by the lifeless look begot
>> Of eyes which have a longing for their death.

This sonnet is divided into two parts. In the first, I tell the reason why I abstain not from seeking the presence of this lady; in the second, I tell that which befalls me when I draw nigh to her, and this part begins here: *And I hear Love*. And this second part is also divided into five, according to the five different facts related; for in the first I tell that which Love, counselled by the reason, says to me when I am near her; in the second, I set forth the state of my heart by the example of my face; in the third, I tell how every reliance fails me; in the fourth, I say that he sins who shows not pity for me, inasmuch as this would be some comfort to me; in the last, I tell why others ought to have pity, namely, because of the piteous look which comes into my eyes, which piteous look is destroyed, that is, is not apparent unto others, on account of the derision of this lady which draws to the like disposition those who perchance might see this woe. The second part begins here: *My face*; the third, *And as I tremble*; the fourth, *He who may then*; the fifth, *Through that compassion.*

Chapter XVI

After I had devised this sonnet, a wish moved me to say also some words in which I would tell four things further in regard to my state, which it seemed to me had not yet been made manifest by me. The first of which is, that ofttimes I grieved when my memory excited my fancy to imagine what Love did to me; the second is, that ofttimes Love assailed me on a sudden with such force that nought remained alive in me save a thought which spoke of my lady; the third is, that, when this onset of Love thus attacked me, I went, almost quite without color, to look on this lady, believing that the sight of her would be my defence from this attack, forgetting that which befell me in approaching gentleness so great; the fourth is, how this sight not only defended me not, but finally discomfited my little remaining life. And therefore I devised this sonnet:

> The dark condition Love doth on me lay
>> Many a time occurs unto my thought,
>> And then comes pity, so that oft I say,
>> Ah me! to such a pass was man e'er brought?
> For on a sudden Love with me doth strive,
>> So that my life almost abandons me;
>> One spirit only doth escape alive,
>> And that remains because it speaks of thee.
> Then to mine aid I summon up my strength,
>> And so, all pale, and empty of defence,
>> I seek thy sight, thinking to be made whole;
> And if to look I lift mine eyes at length,
>> Within my heart an earthquake doth commence,
>> Which from my pulses driveth out the soul.

This sonnet is divided into four parts, inasmuch as four things are related in it; and since these are spoken of above, I concern myself only to distinguish the parts by their beginnings; wherefore I say that the second part begins here: *For on a sudden*; the third, here: *Then to mine aid*; the fourth: *And if to look*.

Chapter XVII

After I had devised these three sonnets, in which I had spoken to this lady, since they left little of my condition untold, thinking to be silent and to say no more of this, because it seemed to me that I had sufficiently disclosed myself, although ever afterwards I should abstain from addressing her, it behoved me to take up a new theme, and one more noble than the foregoing. And because the occasion of the new theme is pleasant to hear, I will tell it as briefly as I can.

Chapter XVIII

Inasmuch as through my looks many persons had learned the secret of my heart, certain ladies who were met together, taking pleasure in one another's company, were well acquainted with my heart, because each of them had witnessed many of my discomfitures. And I, passing near them, as chance led me, was called by one of these gentle ladies; and she who had called me was a lady of very pleasing speech; so that, when I drew nigh to them, and saw plainly that my most gentle lady was not among them, reassuring myself, I saluted them, and asked what might be their pleasure. The ladies were many, and certain of them were laughing together. There were others who were looking at me, awaiting what I might say. There were others who were talking together, one of whom, turning her eyes toward me, and calling me by name, said these words: "To what end lovest thou this thy lady, since thou canst not sustain her presence? Tell it to us, for surely the end of such a love must be most strange." And when she had said these words to me, not only she, but all the others, began to await with their looks my reply. Then I said to them these words: "My ladies, the end of my love was formerly the salutation of this lady of whom you perchance are thinking, and in that dwelt the beatitude which was the end of all my desires. But since it has pleased her to deny it to me, my lord Love, through his grace, has placed all my beatitude in that which cannot fail me."

Then these ladies began to speak together: and as sometimes we see rain falling mingled with beautiful snow, so it seemed to me I saw their words issue mingled with sighs. And after they had somewhat spoken among themselves, this lady who had first spoken to me said to me yet these words: "We pray thee that thou tell us wherein consists this beatitude of thine." And I, replying to her, said thus: "In those words which praise my lady." And she replied; "If thou hast told us the truth, those words which thou hast said to her, setting forth thine own condition, must have been composed with other intent."

Then I, thinking on these words, as if ashamed, departed from them, and went saying within myself: "Since there is such beatitude in those words which praise my lady, why has my speech been of aught else?" And therefore I resolved always henceforth to take for theme of my speech that which should be the praise of this most gentle one. And thinking much on this, I seemed to myself to have undertaken a theme too lofty for me, so that I dared not to begin; and that I tarried some days with desire to speak, and with fear of beginning.

Chapter XIX

Then it came to pass that, walking on a road alongside of which was flowing a very clear stream, so great a desire to say somewhat in verse came upon me, that I began to consider the method I should observe; and I thought that to speak of her would not be becoming unless I were to speak to ladies in the second person, and not to every lady, but only to those who are gentle, and are not women merely. Then I say that my tongue spoke as if moved of its own accord, and said, *Ladies who have intelligence of Love*. These words I laid up in my mind with great joy, thinking to take them for my beginning; wherefore then, having returned

to the above-mentioned city, after some days of thought I began a
canzone with this beginning, arranged in the mode which will be
seen below in its division.

> Ladies who have intelligence of Love,
>   I of my lady wish with you to speak;
>   Not that I can believe to end her praise,
>   But to discourse that I may ease my mind.
>   I say that when I think upon her worth,
>   So sweet doth Love make himself feel to me,
>   That if I then should lose not hardihood,
>   Speaking, I should enamour all mankind.
>   And I wish not so loftily to speak
>   As to become, through fear of failure, vile;
>   But of her gentle nature I will treat
>   In manner light compared with her desert,
>   Ye loving dames and damosels, with you,
>   For 't is not thing of which to speak to others.
> An angel crieth in the mind divine,
>   And saith: "O Sire, on earth is to be seen
>   A miracle in action, that proceeds
>   From out a soul which far as here doth shine.
>   Heaven, which hath not any other defect
>   Save want of her, demands her of its Lord,
>   And every Saint doth for this favor beg."
>   Only Compassion our part defendeth;
>   And thus speaks God, who of my lady thinks:
>   "O my elect, now suffer ye in peace
>   That, while it pleaseth me, your hope abide
>   There, where is one who dreads the loss of her:
>   And who shall say in hell to the foredoomed,
>   'I have beheld the hope of those in bliss.'"
> My lady is desired in highest heaven;
>   Now will I of her virtue make you know.
>   I say: Whoso would seem a gentle dame
>   Should go with her; for when she goes her way
>   Love casts a frost upon all caitiff hearts,
>   So that their every thought doth freeze and perish.
>   And who can bear to stay on her to look
>   Will noble thing become, or else will die.
>   And when one finds that he may worthy be

To look on her, he doth his virtue prove;
    For that arrives to him which gives him health,
    And humbles him till he forgets all wrong.
    Yet hath God given her for greater grace,
    That who hath spoke with her cannot end ill.
Love saith concerning her: "How can it be
    That mortal thing be thus adorned, and pure?"
    Then, gazing on her, to himself he swears
    That God in her a new thing means to make.
    Color of pearl so clothes her as doth best
    Become a lady, nowise in excess.
    Whate'er of good Nature can make she is,
    And by her pattern beauty tries itself.
    From out her eyes, howe'er she moveth them,
    Spirits inflamed of love go forth, which strike
    The eyes of him who then may look on them,
    And enter so that each doth find the heart.
    Love you behold depicted in her smile,
    Whereon no one can look with steadfast gaze.
I know, Canzonè, thou wilt go to speak
    With many ladies, when I send thee forth.
    And now I bid thee, having bred thee up
    As young and simple daughter unto Love,
    That where thou comest thou shouldst praying say:
    "Direct me on my way, for I am sent
    To her with praise of whom I am adorned."
    And if thou wishest not to go in vain,
    Make thou no stay where villain folk may be;
    Endeavor, if thou mayst, to be acquaint
    Only with lady or with courteous man,
    Who thee shall guide along the quickest way.
    Thou wilt find Love in company with her;
    Commend me to him as behoveth thee.

In order that this canzone may be better understood, I shall divide it more elaborately than the other preceding things, and therefore I make of it three parts. The first part is a proem to the words which follow; the second is the subject treated of; the third is, as it were, a handmaid to the words which precede. The second begins here: *An angel crieth*; the third here: *I know, Canzonè*. The first part is divided into four; in the first, I tell to whom I wish to speak of my lady, and wherefore I wish to speak; in the second, I tell what she seems to myself, when I think upon her worth, and how I would speak if I lost not hardihood; in the third, I tell how I think to speak in order that I may not be hindered by faintheartedness; in the fourth, repeating yet once more to whom I intend to speak, I tell the reason why I speak to them. The second begins here: *I say*; the third, here: *And I wish not*; the fourth here: *Ye loving dames.*

Then when I say, *An angel crieth*, I begin to treat of this lady, and this part is divided into two; in the first, I tell what is comprehended of her in heaven; in the second, I tell what is comprehended of her on earth,—here: *My lady is desired.*

This second part is divided into two; for in the first, I speak of her in respect of the nobility of her soul, recounting some of the virtues which proceed from her soul; in the second, I speak of her in respect of the nobility of her body, recounting some of her beauties,—here: *Love saith concerning her.* This second part is divided into two; for in the first, I speak of some of the beauties which belong to her whole person; in the second, I speak of some of the beauties which belong to special parts of her person,—here: *From out her eyes.* This second part is divided into two; for in one, I speak of the eyes which are the beginning of Love; in the second, I speak of the mouth which is the end of Love. And in order that every evil thought may be removed hence, let him who reads remember what is written above, that the salutation of this lady, which was an action of her mouth, was the end of my desires so long as I was able to receive it.

Then when I say, *I know, Canzonè*, I add a stanza, as if for a handmaid to the others, in which I tell what I desire of this my canzone. And since this last part is easy to be understood, I do not trouble myself with more divisions.

I say, indeed, that to make the meaning of this canzone more clear, it might be needful to employ more minute divisions; but nevertheless it will not displease me that he who has not wit enough to understand it by means of those already made should let it alone; for surely I fear I have communicated its meaning to too many even through these divisions which have been made, if it should happen that many should hear it.

Chapter XX

After this canzone had been somewhat divulged to the world, inasmuch as one of my friends had heard it, a desire moved him to beg me that I should tell him what Love is, entertaining perhaps through the words he had heard a hope of me beyond my desert. Wherefore I, thinking that after such a treatise it were beautiful to treat somewhat of Love, and thinking that my friend was to be served, resolved to speak words in which I would treat of Love, and then I devised this sonnet:

> Love is but one thing with the gentle heart,
> As in the saying of the sage we find;
> Thus one from other cannot be apart,
> More than the reason from the reasoning mind.
> When Nature amorous becomes, she makes
> Love then her Lord, the heart his dwelling-place,
> Within which, sleeping, his repose he takes,
> Sometimes for brief, and sometimes for long space.
> Beauty in lady sage doth then appear
> Which pleaseth so the eyes, that in the heart
> Desire for the pleasing thing hath birth;
> And sometimes it so long abideth there,
> It makes Love's spirit wide awake to start:
> The like in lady doth a man of worth.

This sonnet is divided into two parts. In the first, I tell of him in respect of what he is potentially; in the second, I tell of him in respect to his potentiality being brought into act. The second begins here: *Beauty in lady sage*. The first is divided into two; in the first, I tell in what subject this potentiality exists; in the second, I tell how this subject and this potentiality are brought together into being, and how one is related to the other, as form to matter. The second begins here: *When Nature*. Then, when I say: *Beauty in lady*, I tell how this potentiality is brought into act; and first, how it is brought in man, then, how it is brought in woman, here: *The like in lady*.

Chapter XXI

After I had treated of Love in the above rhyme, the will came to me to speak further in praise of this most gentle lady words by which I would show how this Love is awakened by her, and how she not only awakens him there where he is sleeping, but there where he is not potentially she, marvellously working, makes him come; and I devised then this sonnet:

Within her eyes my lady beareth Love,
    So that whom she regards is gentle made;
    All toward her turn, where'er her steps are stayed,
    And whom she greets, his heart doth trembling move;
So that with face cast down, all pale to view,
    For every fault of his he then doth sigh;
    Anger and pride away before her fly:
    Assist me, dames, to pay her honor due.
All sweetness truly, every humble thought,
    The heart of him who hears her speak doth hold;
    Whence he is blessed who hath seen her erewhile.
What seems she when a little she doth smile
    Cannot be kept in mind, cannot be told.
    Such strange and gentle miracle is wrought.

This sonnet has three parts. In the first, I tell how this lady reduces this potentiality into act, as respects that most noble part, her eyes; and in the third, I tell how this same thing is effected as respects that most noble part, her mouth. And between the first and the third is a little part, which beseeches aid, as it were, for the preceding part and for the following, and begins here: *Assist me, dames.* The third begins here: *All sweetness.* The first is divided into three; for in the first I tell how she with power makes gentle that which she looks upon; and this is as much as to say that she brings Love potentially there where he is not. In the second, I tell how she brings Love into act in the hearts of all those upon whom she looks. In the third, I tell that which she then effects with power in their hearts. The second begins, *All toward;* the third, *And whom she greets.*

When afterward I say, *Assist me, dames,* I indicate to whom it is my intention to speak, calling upon these ladies to aid me to pay her honor. Then when I say, *All sweetness,* I tell the same thing as has been said in the first part, according to two acts of her mouth, one of which is her most sweet speech, and the other her marvellous smile, except that I do not tell of this last how it works in the hearts of others, because the memory cannot retain it, nor its effects.

Chapter XXII

Not many days had passed after this, when it pleased the Lord of Glory, who refused not death for himself, that he who had been the begetter of such a marvel as this most noble Beatrice was seen to be, departing from this life, should go verily unto the eternal glory. Wherefore, inasmuch as such a departure is grievous to those who remain and have been friends of him who is gone—and there is no friendship so intimate as that of a good father with a good child, and of a good child with a good father; and this lady had been of the highest degree of goodness, and her father, as is believed by many, and is true, had been good in a high degree—it is plain that this lady was most bitterly full of grief.

And inasmuch as, according to the custom of the above-mentioned city, ladies assemble with ladies, and men with men, in such affliction, many ladies assembled where this Beatrice was weeping piteously. Wherefore, seeing certain of them returning from her, I heard them speak of this most gentle lady, how she was lamenting. Among their words I heard how they said: "Truly, she so weeps that whoever should behold her must die of pity." Then these ladies passed on; and I remained in such grief that some tears bathed my face, so that, often putting my hands before mine eyes, I covered it. And had it not been that I expected to hear further of her, for I was in a place where most of the ladies who came from her passed by, I should have hidden myself as soon as the tears had assailed me.

And, therefore, still tarrying in the same place, more ladies passed near me, who went along talking together, and saying: "Who of us should ever be joyful, since we have heard this lady speak so piteously?" After these, others passed, who said, as they went by: "This one who is here is weeping neither more nor less than if he had seen her as we have." And then others said of me: "Behold, this man is become such that he seems not himself." And thus these ladies passing by, I heard speech of her and of myself after this fashion which has been told.

Wherefore, afterwards musing, I resolved to speak words in verse, inasmuch as I had fit occasion to speak, in which I would include all that I had heard from these ladies. And since I would willingly have questioned them, had it not been for blame to me, I treated my theme as if I had questioned them, and they had replied to me. And I made two sonnets; and in the first, I question, in the way in which the desire came to me to question; and in the other, I tell their answer, taking that which I heard from them as if they had said it in reply to me. And I began the first, *Ye who a semblance*; the second, *Art thou then he.*

> Ye who a semblance so dejected bear,
>   And who with eyes cast down your trouble show,
>   Whence do ye come, that thus your color now
>   Appears like that which pity's self doth wear?
> Our gentle lady truly have ye seen,
>   Bathing her face with tears of loving woe?
>   Tell me, ye ladies; my heart tells me so,
>   Since I behold you going with grave mien.
> And if ye come from sight of grief so great,
>   Be pleased to stay a little here with me,
>   And hide not from me what may be her state.
> For in your eyes such trace of tears I see,
>   And ye return with such a mournful gait,
>   That my heart trembles, thus beholding ye.

This sonnet is divided into two parts. In the first, I call upon and ask these ladies if they come from her, saying to them that I believe it, because they return as if ennobled. In the second, I pray them to tell me of her; and the second begins here: *And if ye come.*

> Art thou then he who oft discourse did hold
>   Of this our lady unto us alone?
>   Thy voice resembles his indeed in tone,

> But thy form seems to us of other mould.
> Ah! wherefore weep'st thou so without control,
>> Thou makest us to feel a pity keen?
>> And hast thou then, forsooth, her weeping seen,
>> So thou canst not conceal thy grieving soul?
> Leave tears to us, and let us sadly go,
>> (He doeth ill who seeketh us to aid,)
>> For we have heard her speak in tearful woe;
> And on her face such sorrow is displayed,
>> That who had wished to gaze upon her so,
>> Before her would in death be weeping laid.

This sonnet has four parts, according to the four fashions of speech of the ladies for whom I reply. And because these are sufficiently shown above, I do not concern myself to tell the purport of the parts, and therefore I only mark them. The second begins here: *Ah! wherefore weep'st thou*; the third: *Leave tears to us*; the fourth: *and on her face.*

Chapter XXIII

A few days after this it fell out that a grievous infirmity came upon me in a certain part of my body, from which I suffered for many days most bitter pain, which brought me to such weakness that I was forced to lie as one who cannot move. I say that on the ninth day, feeling almost intolerable pain, a thought came to me which was of my lady. And when I had thought somewhat of her, I returned in thought to my enfeebled life, and seeing how slight was its duration, even were it sound, I began lamenting within myself at such wretchedness. Wherefore, sighing deeply, I said within myself: "It must needs be that the most gentle Beatrice shall at some time die."

And thereupon a strong bewilderment so overcame me, that I closed my eyes, and began to be distracted like a person in a frenzy, and to imagine in this wise: that, at the beginning of the wandering which my fancy made, certain faces of ladies with hair dishevelled appeared to me, and they said to me: "Thou too shalt die." And after these ladies, there appeared to me certain strange faces, and horrible to behold, which said to me: "Thou art dead."

Thus my fancy beginning to wander, I was brought to such a pass that I knew not where I was; and it seemed to me that I saw ladies with hair dishevelled go by, weeping, marvellously sad; and it seemed to me that I saw the sun grow dark, so that the stars showed themselves of such a color as to make me deem they wept; and it seemed to me that the birds as they flew fell dead, and that there were very great earthquakes. And in this fantasy, marvelling and much afraid, I imagined that a certain friend came to me to say: "Dost thou then not know? thine admirable lady is departed from this world." Then I began to weep very piteously; and wept not only in my imagination, but wept with my eyes, bathing them with real tears.

I imagined that I looked toward heaven, and it seemed to me that I saw a multitude of angels, who were returning upwards, and had before them a little cloud of exceeding whiteness; and it seemed to me that these angels sang gloriously, and the words of their song it seemed to me were these: *"Osanna in excelsis!"*—and aught else meseemed not to hear. Then it seemed to me that the heart wherein was so much love said to me: "True is it that our lady lies dead." And forthwith it seemed to me that I went to behold the body in which that most noble and blessed soul had dwelt. And so strong was the erring fancy, that it showed to me this lady dead; and it seemed to me that ladies had covered her head with a white veil, and it seemed to me that her face had such an aspect of humility that it seemed to say: "Now do I behold the beginning of peace."

In this imagination there came to me such humility through seeing her, that I called upon Death, and said: "Most sweet Death, come unto me, and be not discourteous to me; for thou oughtest to be gentle, in such place hast thou been. Come then unto me, who greatly desire thee; and thou seest it, for I already wear thy color." And when I had seen all the mournful ministries completed which are wont to be rendered to the bodies of the dead, it seemed to me that I returned to my chamber; and here it seemed to me that I looked toward heaven, and so strong was my imagination that, weeping, I began to say with my real voice: "O most beautiful soul, how blessed is he who sees thee!" And as I said these words, with a grievous sob of weeping, and called upon Death to come to me, a young and gentle lady, who was at the side of my bed, believing that my weeping and my words were lamentation on account of the pain of my infirmity, with great fear began to weep. Wherefore other ladies who were in the chamber became aware that I was weeping, through the tears they saw her shed; wherefore making her, who was connected with me in the nearest kingship, depart from me, they drew towards me to wake me, believing that I had been dreaming, and said to me: "Sleep no more, nor be discomforted." And as they thus spoke to me, the strong fantasy ended at the moment when I was about to say: "O Beatrice, blessed be thou!" And I had already said, "O Beatrice," when, arousing myself, I opened my eyes and saw that I had been deluded. And although I had uttered this name, my voice was so broken by sobs that those ladies had not been able to understand me. And notwithstanding I was sore ashamed, nevertheless, by some admonition of Love, I turned me to them. And when they saw me, they began to say: "He seems far gone"; and to say each to other: "Let us try to comfort him." Thereupon they said many words to comfort me; and then they asked me of what I had been afraid. Wherefore I, being somewhat comforted, and having recognized the falsity of my imagining, replied to them, "I will tell you what has ailed me." Then, beginning at the beginning, I told them even to the end that which I had seen, keeping silent the name of this most gentle lady.

Wherefore afterwards, being healed of this infirmity, I resolved to speak concerning that which had befallen me, since it seemed to me that it would be a thing delightful to hear; and so I devised this canzone concerning it:

> A lady, pitiful, and young in years,
>> Adorned full well with human gentilesse,
>> Who present was where oft I called on Death,
>> Seeing my eyes to be filled up of woe,
>> And hearing the vain words that fell from me,
>> Was by her fear impelled to weep aloud;
>> And other ladies who were thus made ware
>> Of me, through her who with me there was weeping,
>> Made her go away,
>> While they drew near to cause me to awake.

One said: "No longer sleep;"
And one: "Why art thou so discomforted?"
Thereon the novel fantasy I left
In giving utterance to my lady's name.
So mournful was my voice, and broken so
By anguish and by tears, that I alone
The name within my heart did understand.
And thereon, with the look of utter shame,
Which had gained full possession of my face,
Love did compel me unto them to turn.
And such my color was to look upon,
As made these others to discourse of death.
"Ah! let us comfort him,"
One lady to the other humbly prayed;
And oftentimes they said:
"What hast thou seen that thou no strength has left?"
And when a little I was comforted,
"Ladies," I said, "I will tell it to you.
While I was thinking of my fragile life,
And saw how slight continuance it hath,
Love wept within my heart, where he abides;
Whereby, indeed, my soul was so dismayed,
That then I, sighing, said within my thought:
'Sure it must be my lady too shall die.'
Then into such bewilderment I fell,
I closed my eyes that basely were weighed down;
And consternated so
My spirits were, that each went straying off.
And then imagining,
Bereft of consciousness alike and truth,
Ladies with looks of wrath appeared to me,
Who said to me: 'Thou too shalt die, shalt die.'
Then saw I many fearful things within
The false imagining wherein I lay;
Meseemed to be I know not in what place,
And to see ladies pass dishevelled by,
Some weeping and some uttering laments,
So that the fire of sadness they shot forth.
Then, as it seemed, I by degrees beheld
The sun grow dark, and then the star appear,
And he and she to weep;
The birds in their mid-flight through air fell down,

> And the earth seemed to shake;
> And I beheld a man pale-faced and hoarse,
> Who said: 'What ails thee? Knowst thou not the news?
> Dead is thy lady, she that was so fair.'
> I raised my eyes which with my tears were bathed,
> And saw what seemed to be a rain of manna:
> The Angels, who to heaven were returning,
> And had in front of them a little cloud,
> Following which, they all 'Hosanna!' sang;
> Had they said more, to you I would it tell.
> And then Love said: 'No more I hide from thee;
> Come thou to see our lady where she lies.'
> The false imagining
> Conducted me to see my lady dead;
> And, as I looked, I saw
> That ladies with a veil were covering her;
> And she had a humility so true,
> It seemed as if she said, 'I am in peace.'
> So humble in my sorrow I became
> Seeing in her such humbleness displayed,
> That I said: 'Death, thee very sweet I hold;
> Thou oughtest now to be a gentle thing,
> Since thou within my lady hast abode,
> And thou shouldst pity have, and not disdain.
> Behold! I am so eager among thine
> To be, that I resemble thee in truth.
> Come! my heart calleth thee.'
> Then I departed, the sad rites complete;
> And when I was alone,
> Looking unto the realm on high, I said,
> 'Blessèd is he who sees thee, beauteous soul!'
> Ye called me thereupon, thanks be to you."

This canzone has two parts. In the first, I tell, speaking to an undefined person, how I was roused from a vain fantasy by certain ladies, and how I promised them to tell it. In the second, I tell how I told it to them. The second begins here: *While I was thinking*. The first part is divided into two; in the first, I tell that which certain ladies, and that which one alone, said and did on account of my fantasy, before I had returned to true consciousness; in the second, I tell that which these ladies said to me after I left this frenzy, and this part begins here: *So mournful was my voice.* Then when I say, *While I was thinking*, I tell how I told them this my imagination, and of this I make two parts. In the first, I tell this imagination in its order; in the second, telling at what point they called me, I thank them at the close; and this part begins here: *Ye called me.*

Chapter XXIV

After this my vain imagination, it came to pass one day that, as I sat thoughtful in a certain place, I felt a trembling begin in my heart, just as if I had been in the presence of this lady. Then I say that an imagination of Love came to me; for it seemed to me that I saw him coming from that place where my lady dwelt; and it seemed to me that he joyfully said to me in my heart: "Mind thou bless the day on which I took possession of thee, for thou oughtest so to do." And of a truth it seemed to me that my heart was so gladsome, that it did not seem to me to be my heart, because of its new condition.

And a little after these words which my heart had said to me with the tongue of Love, I saw coming toward me a gentle lady who was famous for her beauty, and who had now long been the lady of him my first friend. And the name of this lady was Joan, but on account of her beauty, as some believe, the name of Primavera [Spring] had been given to her, and thus she was called. And behind her, as I looked, I saw coming the marvellous Beatrice. These ladies passed near me thus one after the other; and it seemed to me that Love spoke to me in my heart, and said: "This first is called Primavera solely because of this coming of to-day; for I moved the giver of the name to call her Primavera, that is to say, *prima verrà* [she will come first] on the day that Beatrice shall show herself after the imagination of her vassal. And if thou wilt further consider her original name, it means the same as Primavera, because her name, Joan, is derived from that John who preceded the true Light, saying, *Ego vox clamantis in deserto: Parate viam Domini* [I am the voice of one crying in the wilderness: Prepare ye the way of the Lord]." And also it seemed to me that after these he said to me other words, namely: "He who should consider subtly would call that Beatrice

Love, because of the great likeness she has to me." Wherefore I, then thinking this over, resolved to write of it in rhyme to my first friend (keeping silent certain words which it seemed should be kept silent), for I believed that his heart still admired the beauty of this gentle Primavera. And I devised this sonnet:

> An amorous spirit in my heart that lay
>> I felt awaken from his slumber there;
>> And then I saw Love come from far away,
>> But scarce I knew him, for his joyous air.
> "Honor to me," he said, "think now to pay,"
>> And with his every word did smiles appear.
>> Then did my Lord a little with me stay,
>> And from that part wherefrom he came whilere
> I Lady Joan and Lady Bicè see,
>> Unto the place approaching where I was;
>> One marvel following the other came;
> And, as my mind reporteth unto me,
>> Love said, "This one is Spring, and this, because
>> She so resembleth me, hath Love for name."

This sonnet has many parts; the first of which tells how I felt the wonted tremor awake in my heart, and how it seemed that Love appeared to me joyous from afar; the second tells how it seemed to me that Love spoke to me in my heart, and what he seemed to me; the third tells how, after he had been thus with me for some time, I saw and heard certain things. The second part begins here: *Honor to me*; the third, here: *Then did my Lord*. The third part is divided into two; in the first, I tell that which I saw; in the second, I tell that which I heard, and it begins: *Love said*.

Chapter XXV

It may be that some person, entitled to have every doubt cleared away, may here be perplexed at my speaking of Love as if it were a thing in itself, and not only an intellectual substance, but as if it were a corporeal substance. The which thing, in truth, is false, for Love exists not in itself as substance, but is an accident in substance. And that I speak of it as if it were a body, and, further, as if it were a man, appears from three things which I say of it. I say that I saw it come from far off; wherefore, since coming implies a local motion, and, according to the Philosopher, only a body is locally movable in itself, it appears that I assume Love to be a body. I say further of it that it laughed, and also that it spoke, which things appear to be properties of man, especially the faculty of laughing, and thus it appears that I assume that it is a man.

To explain this matter so far as is meet for the present occasion, it must first be understood that formerly there were no rhymers of Love in the vulgar tongue, but certain poets in the Latin tongue were rhymers of Love; among us, I mean, although perchance among other people it happened, and still happens that, as in Greece, not the vulgar but the lettered poets treated of these things. And no great number of years have passed since these poets in the vulgar tongue first appeared; for to write in rhyme in the vulgar is, after a manner, the same thing as to write in verse in Latin. And the proof that it is but a short time is that if we undertake to search in the tongue of the *oco*, and in the tongue of the *sì*, we do not find anything written more than a hundred and fifty years before the present time. And the reason why some illiterate persons acquired the fame of skill in writing verse is that they were, so to speak, the first who wrote in the tongue of the *sì*. And the first who began to write as a poet in the vulgar tongue was moved to do so because he wished to make his words intelligible to a lady who could not easily understand Latin verses. And this is against those who rhyme on any other theme than Love, since this mode of speech was from the beginning invented in order to speak of Love.

It follows that, since a greater license of speech is granted to poets than to writers of prose, and these writers in rhyme are no other than poets using the vulgar tongue, it is fitting and reasonable that greater license of speech should be permitted to them than to the other writers in the vulgar tongue; hence, if any figure or rhetorical coloring is allowed to poets, it is allowed also to the rhymers. Therefore, if we see that the poets have spoken of inanimate things as if they had sense and reason, and have made them speak together, and not only real things but also things not real (that is, that they have said of things which have no existence that they speak, and have often made contingent things speak as if they were substances and human beings), it is fitting that the writer in rhyme should do the like, not, indeed, without some reason, but with a reason which it may be possible afterwards to explain in prose.

That the poets have thus spoken as has been said, appears from Virgil, who says that Juno, that is, a goddess hostile to the Trojans, spoke to Aeolus, lord of the winds, here, in the first of the *Aeneid*: *Aeole, namque tibi*, etc. [Aeolus, for to thee, etc.]; and that this lord replied to her, here: *Tuus, O regina, quid optes*, etc. [Thine, O queen, what thou askest, etc.]. In this same poet the inanimate thing speaks to the animate thing, in the third of the *Aeneid*, here: *Dardanidæ duri*, etc. [Ye hardy Trojans, etc.]. In Lucan the animate thing speaks to the inanimate here: *Multum, Roma, tamen debes civilibus armis* [Much dost thou owe, O Rome, to civic arms]. In Horace a man speaks to his own knowledge as to another person; and not only are they the words of Horace, but he says them as the interpreter of the good Homer, here, in his book on Poetry: *Dic mihi, Musa, virum*, etc. [Tell to me, Muse, of the man, etc.]. In Ovid, Love speaks as if he were a human person, at the beginning of the book of the Remedy for Love, here: *Bella mihi, video, bella parantur, ait* [Wars against me, I see, wars are preparing, he says].

And by this the matter may now be clear to any one who is perplexed in any part of this my little book.

And in order that no uncultured person may derive any over-boldness herefrom, I say, that the poets do not speak thus without reason, and that those who rhyme ought not to speak thus, unless they have some reason for what they say; since it would be a great disgrace to him who should rhyme anything under the garb of a figure or of rhetorical coloring, if afterward, being asked, he should not be able to denude his words of this garb, in such wise that they should have a true meaning. And my first friend and I are well acquainted with those who rhyme thus foolishly.

Chapter XXVI

This most gentle lady, of whom there had been discourse in the preceding words, came into such favor among the people, that when she passed along the way, persons ran to see her; which gave me wonderful joy. And when she was near any one, such modesty came into his heart that he dared not raise his eyes, or return her salutation; and of this many, as having experienced it, could bear witness for me to whoso might not believe it. She, crowned and clothed with humility, took her way, showing no pride in that which she saw and heard. Many said, when she had passed: "This is not a woman; rather she is one of the most beautiful angels of heaven." And others said: "She is a marvel. Blessed be the Lord who can work thus admirably!" I say that she showed herself so gentle and so full of all pleasantness, that those who looked on her comprehended in themselves a pure and sweet delight, such as they could not after tell in words; nor was there any who might look upon her but that at first he needs must sigh. These and more admirable things proceeded from her admirably and with power. Wherefore I, thinking upon this, desiring to resume the style of her praise, resolved to say words in which I would set forth her admirable and excellent influences, to the end that not only those who might actually behold her, but also others should know of her whatever words could tell. Then I devised this sonnet:

> So gentle and so gracious doth appear
> > My lady when she giveth her salute,
> > That every tongue becometh, trembling, mute;
> > Nor do the eyes to look upon her dare.
> Although she hears her praises, she doth go
> > Benignly vested with humility;
> > And like a thing come down, she seems to be,
> > From heaven to earth, a miracle to show.
> So pleaseth she whoever cometh nigh,
> > She gives the heart a sweetness through the eyes.
> > Which none can understand who doth not prove.
> And from her countenance there seems to move
> > A spirit sweet and in Love's every guise,
> > Who to the soul, in going, sayeth: Sigh!

This sonnet is so easy of understanding, through that which has been told, that it has no need of any division; and therefore, leaving it, I say that this my lady reached such favor that not only was she honored and praised, but through her were many ladies honored and praised. Wherefore I, seeing this, and wishing to manifest it to whoever saw it not, resolved further to say words in which this should be set forth; and I devised then this other sonnet, which relates how her virtue wrought in other ladies:

All welfare hath he perfectly beheld
    Who amid ladies doth my lady see;
    And they who go with her are all compelled
    Grateful to God for this fair grace to be.
Her beauty of such virtue is indeed,
    That it no envy doth in others move;
    Rather she makes them with her to proceed,
    Clothed on with gentleness and faith and love.
Her sight creates in all humility,
    And maketh not herself to please alone,
    But each gains honor who to her is nigh.
So gentle in her every act is she,
    That she can be recalled to mind by none
    Who doth not, in Love's very sweetness, sigh.

This sonnet has three parts: in the first, I tell among what people this lady appeared most admirable; in the second, I tell how gracious was her company; in the third, I tell of those things which she wrought with power in others. The second begins here: *And they who go*; the third, here: *Her beauty of such virtue.* This last part is divided into three: in the first, I tell that which she wrought in ladies, namely, as regards themselves; in the second, I tell that which she wrought in them in respect to others; in the third, I tell how she wrought not only in ladies but in all persons, and how she marvellously wrought not only in presence but also in memory. The second begins here: *Her sight*; the third, here: *So gentle.*

Chapter XXVII

After this I began to think one day upon what I had said of my lady, that is, in these two preceding sonnets; and seeing in my thought that I had not spoken of that which at the present time she wrought in me, it seemed to me that I had spoken defectively; and therefore I resolved to say words in which I would tell how I seemed to myself to be disposed to her influence, and how her virtue wrought in me. And not believing that I could relate this in the brevity of a sonnet, I began then a canzone which begins:

> So long hath Love retained me at his hest,
>   And to his sway hath so accustomed me,
>   That as at first he cruel used to be,
>   So in my heart he now doth sweetly rest.
>   Thus when by him my strength is dispossessed,
>   So that the spirits seem away to flee,
>   My frail soul feels such sweetness verily,
>   That with it pallor doth my face invest.
>   Then Love in me doth with such power prevail,
>   He makes my sighs in words to take their way;
>   And they go forth to pray
>   My lady that she give me grater hale.
>   Where'er she sees me, this to me occurs;
>   Nor can it be believed what humbleness is hers.

Chapter XXVIII

Quomodo sedet sola civitas plena populo! facta est quasi vidua domina gentium [How doth the city sit solitary, that was full of people! How is she become as a widow! she that was great among the nations].

I was yet full of the design of this canzone, and had completed this above-written stanza thereof, when the Lord of Justice called this most gentle one to glory, under the banner of that Holy Queen Mary, whose name was ever spoken with greatest reverence by this blessed Beatrice.

And although perchance it might be pleasing, were I now to treat somewhat of her departure from us, it is not my intention to treat of it here for three reasons. The first is, that it is no part of the present design, if we consider the proem which precedes this little book. The second is, that, supposing it did belong to the present design, still my pen would not be sufficient to treat thereof as were meet. The third is, that, supposing both the one and the other, it is not becoming in me to treat thereof, since, in so doing, it would be needful for me to praise myself—a thing altogether blameworthy in whosoever does it—and therefore I leave this theme to some other interpreter.

Nevertheless, since the number nine has often found place among the preceding words, which it seems cannot be without some reason, and in her departure this number seems to have occupied a large place, it is befitting to say something on this point, inasmuch as it seems to befit my design. Wherefore I will first tell how it had place in her departure, and then I will assign some reason wherefore this number was so friendly to her.

Chapter XXIX

I say that, according to the mode of reckoning in Arabia, her most noble soul departed in the first hour of the ninth day of the month; and, according to the reckoning in Syria, she departed in the ninth month of the year, since the first month there is Tisrin, which with us is October. And according to our reckoning, she departed in that year of our indiction, that is, of the years of the Lord, in which the perfect number was completed for the ninth time in that century in which she had been set in this world: and she was of the Christians of the thirteenth century.

One reason why this number was so friendly to her may be this: since, according to Ptolemy and according to the Christian truth, there are nine heavens which move, and, according to the common astrological opinion, the said heavens work effects here below according to their respective positions, this number was her friend to the end that it might be understood that at her generation all the nine movable heavens were in most perfect relation. This is one reason thereof; but considering more subtly and according to the infallible truth, this number was she herself; I mean by similitude, and I intend it thus: the number three is the root of nine, for, without any other number, multiplied by itself it makes nine, as we see plainly that three times three make nine. Therefore, since three is the factor by itself of nine, and the Author of miracles by himself is three, namely, Father, Son, and Holy Spirit, who are three and one, this lady was accompanied by the number nine, that it might be understood that she was a nine, that is, a miracle, whose only root is the marvellous Trinity. Perchance even a more subtle reason might be seen herein by a more subtle person; but this is that which I see for it, and which best pleases me.

Chapter XXX

After the most gentle lady had departed from this world, all the above-mentioned city remained as if a widow, despoiled of every dignity, wherefore I, still weeping in this desolate city, wrote to the chief personages of the land somewhat of its condition, taking that beginning of Jeremiah the prophet, *Quomodo sedet sola civitas!* [How doth the city sit solitary!] And this I tell in order that others may not wonder why I have cited it above, as if for an entrance to the new theme that comes after. And if any one should choose to blame me because I do not write here the words which follow those cited, my excuse is, that from the first it was my design to write nothing except in the vulgar tongue; wherefore, since the words which follow those which have been cited are all Latin, it would be contrary to my design if I should write them; and I know that he, my first friend, for whom I write this, had a similar understanding, namely, that I should write to him only in the vulgar tongue.

Chapter XXXI

After my eyes had wept for some time, and were so wearied that I could not give vent to my sadness, I thought to try to give vent to it with some words of grief; and therefore I resolved to make a canzone, in which, lamenting, I would discourse of her for whom such grief was wasting my soul; and I began then, *The eyes that grieve*, etc.

In order that this canzone may seem to remain the more a widow after its end, I will divide it before I write it out; and this mode I shall follow henceforth. I say that this poor little canzone has three parts: the first is the proem; in the second, I discourse of her; in the third, I speak pitifully to the canzone. The second begins here: *To the high heaven*; the third, here: *Sad song of mine*. The first is divided into three: in the first, I tell wherefore I am moved to speak; in the second, I tell to whom I wish to speak; in the third, I tell of whom I wish to speak. The second begins here: *And since I do remember*; the third, here: *And then, lamenting.* Then when I say, *To the high heaven hath Beatricè gone*, I discourse of her; and of this I make two parts. First, I tell the reason wherefore she was taken from us; then I tell how others mourn her departure; and this part begins here: *Departed from.* This part is divided into three: in the first, I tell who does not mourn for her; in the second, I tell who mourns for her; in the third, I tell of my own condition. The second begins here: *But he hath grief and woe*; the third, *Great anguish.* Then when I say, *Sad song of mine*, I speak to this my canzone, pointing out to it the ladies to whom it is to go, and with whom it is to stay.

The eyes that grieve with pity for the heart
    Have of their weeping borne the penalty,
    So that they now remain as if subdued.
    Wherefore if I would to the grief give vent,
    Which by degrees conducts me unto death,
    Me it behoves to tell my woe in speech.
    And since I do remember that I spoke
    Of her, my lady, while she was alive,
    Ye gentle ladies, willingly with you,
    I will not speak of her,
    Save only to a lady's gentle heart.
    And then, lamenting, I will tell of her,
    That she to heaven suddenly hath gone,
    And hath left Love behind in grief with me.
To the high heaven hath Beatricè gone,
    Unto that realm where peace the angels have,
    And dwells with them; you, ladies, hath she left.
    No quality of cold 't was took her there,
    Nor yet of heat, such as affecteth others,
    But 't was her great benignity alone.

Because the light of her humility
Passed through the heavens with power so great,
It made to marvel the Eternal Lord;
So that a sweet desire
Upon Him came to summon such salvation;
And from below He made her come to Him,
Because He saw that this distressful life
Unworthy was of such a gentle thing.
Departed from her person beautiful,
The gentle soul replete with every grace
Now dwelleth glorious in a fit abode.
Who weeps her not when he doth speak of her
Hath heart of stone so vile and so perverse
Spirit benign can never enter there.
Nor is there wit so high of villain heart
That aught concerning her it can conceive,
Therefore to it comes not the wish to weep.
But he hath grief and woe,
With sighing and with weeping unto death,
And of all comfort is his soul bereft,
Who sometimes in his thought considereth
What she was, and how from us she is taken.
Great anguish do my sighs give unto me,
Whene'er my thought unto my heavy mind
Doth bring her to me who hath cleft my heart.
And thinking oftentimes concerning death,
There comes to me so sweet desire therefor
That it transmutes the color in my face.
When this imagination holds me fixed,
Such pain assaileth me on every side,
That then I tremble with the woe I feel;
And such I do become
That from the people shame takes me away:
Then, alone, weeping, I lamenting call
On Beatrice, and say: "Art thou, then, dead?"
And while I call her I am comforted.
The tears of grief, and sighs of agony,
Lay waste my heart whene'er I am alone,
So he would sorrow for it who might see.
And what indeed my life hath been since she,
My lady, to the new world went away.
No tongue there is that could know how to tell.

And therefore, ladies mine, e'en though I wished,
I could not truly tell you what I am.
To me this bitter life such travail brings,
And it is so abased,
That every man who sees my deathlike look
Appears to me to say, "I cast thee off."
But what I am, that doth my lady see,
And thereof I yet hope reward from her.
Sad song of mine, now weeping go thy way,
And find again the dames and damosels
To whom thy sisters all
Were wont to be the bearers of delight;
And thou who art the daughter of despair,
Go forth disconsolate to dwell with them.

Chapter XXXII

After this canzone was devised, there came to me one who, according to the degrees of friendship, was my friend next in order after the first; and he was so near in blood to this lady in glory that there was none nearer.[2] And after talking with me, he prayed me to write for him something on a lady who was dead; and he dissembled his words, so that it might seem that he was speaking of another lady who had lately died; but I, aware that he spake only of that blessed one, told him I would do that which his prayer begged of me. Wherefore, after thinking thereupon, I resolved to make a sonnet in which I would somewhat bewail myself, and to give it to this my friend, that it might seem that I had made it for him; and I devised then this sonnet which begins: *To hearken now*, etc.

This sonnet has two parts: in the first, I call upon the liegemen of Love to hearken to me; in the second, I describe my wretched condition. The second begins here: *Sighs, which their way*:

To hearken now unto my sighs come ye,
O gentle hearts! for pity wills it so;
Sighs, which their way disconsolately go,
And were they not, I dead of grief should be:

---

2   Likely Manetto Portinari, brother of Beatrice, but certainly one of her five brothers.

Because my eyes would debtors be to me
   For vastly more than they could ever pay;
   To weep, alas! my lady in such way,
   That, weeping her, my heart relieved might be.
Oft you shall hear them calling unto her,
   My gentle lady, who from us is gone
   Unto the world deserving of her worth;
And then, in scorn of this life, making moan,
   As though the grieving soul itself they were,
   Abandoned by its welfare upon earth.

Chapter XXXIII

After I had devised this sonnet, reflecting who he was to whom I intended to give it as if made for him, I saw that the service appeared to me poor and bare for a person so close akin to this lady in glory. And therefore, before I gave him the above-written sonnet, I composed two stanzas of a canzone, the one really for him, and the other for myself; although both the one and the other may appear to him who does not regard subtly as if written for one person. But he who looks at them subtly sees well that different persons speak; in that the one does not call her his lady, and the other does so, as is plainly apparent. This canzone and this sonnet I gave to him, saying that I had made them for him alone.

The canzone begins, *As often as*, and has two parts. In one, that is, in the first stanza, this my dear friend, her kinsman, bewails himself; in the other, I bewail myself, that is, in the second stanza, which begins, *And there is intermingled*. And thus it appears that in this canzone two persons bewail themselves, one of whom bewails himself as a brother, the other as a vassal.

As often as, alas! I call to mind
   That I can nevermore
   The lady see for whom thus sad I go,
   My grieving mind doth cause so great a grief
   To gather round my heart,
   I say, "My soul, why goest thou not away,
   Seeing the torments thou wilt have to bear,
   In this world so molestful now to thee,

Make me foreboding with a heavy fear?"
And therefore upon Death
I call, as to my sweet and soft repose,
And say, "Come thou to me," with such desire
That I am envious of whoever dies.
And there is intermingled with my sighs
A sound of wofulness,
Which evermore goes calling upon Death.
To her were all of my desires turned
When that the lady mine
Was overtaken by her cruelty;
Because the pleasure of her beauteousness,
Taking itself away from out our sight,
Became a spiritual beauty great,
Which through the heaven spreads
A light of love that doth the angels greet,
And makes their high and keen intelligence
To marvel, of such gentleness is she.

Chapter XXXIV

On that day on which the year was complete since this lady was made one of the denizens of life eternal, I was seated in a place where, having her in mind, I was drawing an angel upon certain tablets. And while I was drawing it, I turned my eyes and saw at my side men to whom it was meet to do honor. They were looking on what I did, and, as was afterwards told me, they had been there already some time before I became aware of it. When I saw them I rose, and, saluting them, said, "Another was just now with me, and on that account I was in thought." And when they had gone away, I returned to my work, namely, that of drawing figures of angels; and, while doing this, a thought came to me of saying words in rhyme, as if for an anniversary poem of her, and of addressing those persons who had come to me. And I devised then this sonnet that begins, "The gentle lady," the which has two beginnings; and therefore I will divide it according to one and the other.

I say that, according to the first, this sonnet has three parts: in the first, I tell that this lady was already in my memory; in the second, I tell what Love thereupon did to me; in the third, I tell of the effects of Love. The second begins here: *Love, who*; the third, here: *Lamenting they from out.* This part is divided into two: in the one, I say that all my sighs went forth speaking; in the other, I tell how some said certain words different from the others. The second begins here: *But those.* In this same way it is divided according to the other beginning, except that in the first part I tell when this lady had so come to my mind, and this I do not tell in the other.

FIRST BEGINNING

The gentle lady to my mind had come,
    Who, for the sake of her exceeding worth,
    Had by the Lord Most High been ta'en from earth
    To that calm heaven where Mary hath her home.

SECOND BEGINNING

That gentle lady to my mind in thought
    Had come, because of whom Love's tears are shed,
    Just at the time when, by her influence led,
    To see what I was doing ye were brought.
Love, who within my mind did her perceive,
    Was wakened up within my wasted heart,
    And said unto my sighs, "Go forth! depart!"
    Whereon each one in sorrow took its leave.
Lamenting they from out my breast did go,
    And uttering a voice that often led
    The grievous tears unto my saddened eyes;
But those which issued with the greatest woe,
    "O high intelligence!" they, going, said,
    "To-day makes up the year since thou to heaven didst rise."

Chapter XXXV

Some time afterwards, happening to be in a place where I was reminded of the past time, I stood deep in thought, and with such doleful thoughts that they made me exhibit an appearance of terrible distress. Wherefore I, becoming aware of my woe-begone look, lifted up my eyes to see if any one saw me; and I saw a gentle lady, young and very beautiful, who was looking at me from a window with a face full of compassion, so that all pity seemed gathered in it. Wherefore, since the wretched, when they see the compassion of others for them, are the more readily moved to weep, as if taking pity on themselves, I then felt my eyes begin to desire to weep; and therefore, fearing lest I might display my abject life, I departed from before the eyes of this gentle one; and I said then within me: "It cannot be but that with that compassionate lady should be a most noble love." And therefore I resolved to devise a sonnet in which I would speak to her, and would include all that is narrated in this account. And since this account is manifest enough, I will not divide it.

> Mine eyes beheld how you were wont to show
>   Great pity on your face, what time your sight
>   Fell on the actions and the wretched plight
>   To which I ofttimes was reduced by woe.
> Then was I ware that you did meditate
>   Upon the nature of my darkened years,
>   So that within my heart were wakened fears
>   Lest that mine eyes should show my low estate.
> And then I took myself from you, perceiving
>   That tears from out my heart began to move,
>   Which by your look had been thus deeply stirred.
> Thereon in my sad soul I said this word:
>   "Ah! surely with that lady is that love
>   Which maketh me to go about thus grieving.'

Chapter XXXVI

It came to pass afterwards that, wherever this lady saw me, she became of a compassionate aspect and of a pallid color, even as that of love; wherefore I was often reminded of my most noble lady, who had ever showed herself to me of a like color. And ofttimes, in truth, not being able to weep, nor to give vent to my sadness, I sought to see this compassionate lady, who seemed by her look to draw the tears out from my eyes. And therefore the will came to me furthermore to say certain words, speaking to her; and I devised this sonnet which begins, *Color of Love*, and which is plain without division, through the preceding account.

> Color of Love and semblance of compassion
>> Never so wondrously possession took
>> Of lady's face, through turning oft her look
>> On gentle eyes and grievous lamentation,
> As now, forsooth, of yours they do, whene'er
>> You see my countenance with grief o'erwrought;
>> So that through you comes something to my thought
>> Which, lest it break my heart, I greatly fear.
> I have no power to keep my wasted eyes
>> From looking oft on you, with the desire
>> That gaineth them to let their tears o'erflow.
> And you increase their wish in such a wise
>> That with the longing they are all on fire,
>> But how to weep before you do not know.

Chapter XXXVII

I was brought to such a pass by the sight of this lady, that my eyes began to delight too much in seeing her; whereas I was often angry with myself, and esteemed myself mean enough. And many a time I cursed the vanity of my eyes, and said to them in my thought: "But late ye were wont to make those weep who saw your sad condition, and now it seems that ye wish to forget it by reason of this lady who looks upon you, and who does not look upon you save as she grieves for the lady in glory for whom ye are wont to weep. But whatever ye have power to do, do; for, accursed eyes, very often will I remind you of her; for never, except after death, ought your tears to be stayed." And when I had thus spoken within me to my eyes, very deep and distressful sighs assailed me. And in order that this battle which I had with myself might not remain known only to the wretched one who experienced it, I resolved to make a sonnet, and to include in it this horrible condition; and I devised this which begins, *The bitter tears*.

The sonnet has two parts: in the first, I speak to my eyes as my heart spoke within me; in the second, I remove a difficulty, showing who it is that thus speaks; and this part begins here: *Thus saith*. It might indeed receive still further divisions, but this would be needless, since it is clear by reason of the preceding account.

> The bitter tears that shed by you have been,
>   Ye eyes of mine, so long a season now,
>   Have made the tears of other folk to flow,
>   Out of compassion, as yourselves have seen,
> That you would this forget, it now appears,
>   If on my part so traitorous I should be
>   As not to trouble you continually
>   With thought of her to whom belong your tears.
> Your vanity doth care in me beget,
>   And so alarms me, that I greatly dread
>   Sight of a dame who on you turns her eyes.
> Never should you, until that ye be dead,
>   Our gentle lady who is dead forget:
>   Thus saith my heart, and thereupon it sighs.

Chapter XXXIII

The sight of this lady brought me into so strange a condition, that many a time I thought of her as of a person who had pleased me exceeding much. And I thought of her thus: "This is a gentle, beautiful, young, and discreet lady, and she has appeared perchance through the will of Love, in order that my life may find repose." And oftentimes I thought more lovingly, so that my heart consented thereto, that is, unto its reasoning. And when it had thus consented, I took thought again, as if moved by the reason, and I said to myself: "Ah! what thought is this which in so vile a way seeks to console me, and scarcely leaves me any other thought?" Then another thought rose up and said: "Now that thou hast been in so great tribulation, why dost thou not wish to withdraw thyself from such bitterness? Thou seest that this is an inspiration which brings the desires of Love before us, and proceeds from a place no less gentle than the eyes of the lady who has shown herself so compassionate unto thee." Wherefore I, having thus ofttimes been at strife within me, wished anew to say some words thereof;

and since, in the battle of the thoughts, those had conquered that spoke on her behalf, it seemed to me befitting to address her, and I devised this sonnet which begins, *A gentle thought*; and I said gentle inasmuch as I was speaking to a gentle lady, for otherwise it was most vile.

In this sonnet I make two parts of myself, according as my thoughts had twofold division. The one part I call heart, that is, the appetite; the other soul, that is, the reason; and I tell how one speaks to the other. And that it is fitting to call the appetite the heart, and the reason the soul, is sufficiently plain to those to whom it pleases me that this should be disclosed. It is true that in the preceding sonnet I take the part of the heart against the eyes, and that seems contrary to what I say in the present; and therefore I say that also there I mean by the heart the appetite, since my desire still to remember me of my most gentle lady was greater than to see this one, although I had had truly some appetite therefor, but it seemed slight; wherefore it appears that the one saying is not contrary to the other.

This sonnet has three parts: in the first, I begin with saying to this lady how my desire turns wholly toward her; in the second, I say how the soul, that is, the reason, speaks to the heart, that is, to the appetite; in the third, I say how this replies. The second begins here: *Who then is this*; the third, here: *O saddened soul!*

A gentle thought that of you holds discourse
    Cometh now frequently with me to dwell,
    And with such sweetness it of Love doth tell,
    My heart to yield unto him it doth force.
"Who then is this," the soul saith to the heart,
    "Who cometh to bring comfort to our mind,
    And who hath virtue of so potent kind,
    That other thoughts he maketh to depart?"
"O saddened soul," the heart to her replies,
    "This is a little spirit fresh from Love,
    And to my presence his desires he brings.
His very life and all his influence move
    From out of the compassionating eyes
    Of her who sorroweth for our sufferings.'

Chapter XXXIX

Against this adversary of the reason there arose one day, about the hour of nones, a strong imagination within me; for I seemed to see this glorified Beatrice in those crimson garments in which she had first appeared to my eyes, and she seemed to me young, of the same age as when I first saw her. Then I began to think of her; and calling her to mind according to the order of the past time, my heart began bitterly to repent of the desire by which it had so vilely allowed itself for some days to be possessed, contrary to the constancy of the reason; and this so wicked desire being expelled, all my thoughts returned to their most gentle Beatrice. And I say that thenceforth I began to think of her with my heart so all ashamed, that oftentimes my sighs manifested it; for almost all of them told, as they went forth, that which was discoursed of in my heart, to wit, the name of that most gentle one and how she had departed from us. And many times it came to pass, that some one thought had such anguish in itself that I forgot it and the place where I was. By this rekindling of sighs my tears which had been assuaged were rekindled in such wise that my eyes seemed two things which desired only to weep; and often it happened that through the long continuance of weeping there came a purple color around them, such as is wont to appear after any torment that one may endure; whence it seems that they were worthily rewarded for their vanity, so that from that time forward they could not gaze at any one who might so look at them as to have power to draw them to a like intention. Wherefore I, wishing that this wicked desire and vain temptation should be seen to be destroyed, so that the rhymed words which I had before written should give rise to no question, resolved to make a sonnet in which I would include the purport of this account. And I said then, *Alas! by force.*

I said *Alas!* inasmuch as I was ashamed that my eyes had so gone astray after vanity. I do not divide this sonnet, for its meaning is sufficiently clear.

> Alas! by force of sighs that oft return,
>   Springing from thoughts which are within my heart,
>   Mine eyes are conquered, and have lost the art

> To look at one whose gaze on them may turn.
> And they are such, they two desires appear,
>   Only to weep, and sorrow to display;
>   And ofttimes they lament in such a way
>   That Love gives them the martyr's crown to wear.
> These thoughts and sighs that issue with my breath,
>   Become within my heart so full of pain
>   That Love, subdued by woe, falls senseless there;
> For on themselves these grieving ones do bear
>   That sweet name of my Lady written plain,
>   And many words relating to her death.

Chapter XL

After this tribulation it came to pass, at that time when many people were going to see the blessed image which Jesus Christ left to us as the likeness of his most beautiful countenance, which my lady in glory now beholds, that certain pilgrims were passing through a street which is near the middle of that city where the most gentle lady was born, lived, and died; and they were going along, as it seemed to me, very pensive. Wherefore I, thinking on them, said within myself: "These seem to me pilgrims from some far-off region, and I do not believe that they have even heard speak of this lady, and they know nothing of her; nay, their thoughts are rather of other things than of these here; for perchance they are thinking of their distant friends, whom we do not know." Then I said within me: "I know that, if these were from a neighboring land, they would show some sign of trouble as they pass through the midst of the grieving city." Then again I said within me: "If I could hold them awhile, I would indeed make them weep before they should go out from this city; since I would say words which should make whoever might hear them weep."

Wherefore, they having passed out of my sight, I resolved to make a sonnet in which I would set forth that which I had said to myself; and in order that it might appear more piteous, I resolved to say it as if I had spoken to them, and I devised this sonnet which begins, *O pilgrims.*

I said *pilgrims* in the wide sense of the word: for pilgrims may be understood in two senses, in one wide and in one narrow. In the wide, forasmuch as every one is a pilgrim who is away from his native land; in the narrow sense, by pilgrim is meant only he who goes to or returns from the House of St. James. And further it is to be known that the folk who journey on the service of the Most High are distinguished by three terms. Those who go beyond the sea, whence they bring back the palm, are called *palmers*; those who go to the House of Galicia are called *pilgrims*, because the burial-place of St. James was more distant from his country than that of any other of the Apostles; and those are called *romers*, who go to Rome, where these whom I call *pilgrims* were going.

This sonnet is not divided, because it sufficiently declares its own meaning.

O pilgrims, who in pensive mood move slow,
    Thinking perchance of those who absent are,
    Say, do ye come from folk away so far
    As your appearance seems to us to show?
For ye weep not the while ye forward go
    Along the middle of the mourning town;
    Seeming as persons who have nothing known
    Concerning the sad burden of her woe.
If, through your will to hear, awhile ye stay,
    Truly my heart with sighs declares to me
    That ye shall afterward depart in tears.
Alas! her Beatrice now lost hath she;
    And all the words that one of her may say
    Have virtue to make weep whoever hears.

Chapter XLI

After this, two gentle ladies sent to ask me to send to them some of these rhymed words of mine; wherefore I, thinking on their nobleness, resolved to send to them, and to make a new thing which I would send to them with these, in order that I might fulfill their prayers with the more honor. And I devised then a sonnet which relates my condition, and I sent it to them accompanied by the preceding sonnet, and by another which begins, *To hearken now.* The sonnet which I made then is, *Beyond the sphere*, etc.

This sonnet has five parts. In the first, I say whither my thought goes, naming it by the name of one of its effects. In the second, I say wherefore it goes on high, namely, who makes it thus to go. In the third, I say what it sees, namely, a lady in honor. And I call it then a *pilgrim spirit*; since spiritually it goes on high, and as a pilgrim who is out of his own country. In the fourth, I say how he sees her such, namely, of such quality, that I cannot understand it; that is to say, that my thought rises into the quality of her to a degree that my understanding cannot comprehend it; since our understanding is in regard to those blessed souls as weak as our eye is before the sun; and this the Philosopher says in the second book of his *Metaphysics*. In the fifth, I say that, although I cannot understand there where my thought transports me, namely, to her marvellous quality, at least I understand this, namely, that this my thought is wholly of my lady, for I often hear her name in my thought. And at the end of this fifth part I say, *Ladies dear*, to indicate that it is to ladies that I speak. The second part begins: *A new Intelligence*; the third, *When at*; the fourth, *He sees her such*; the fifth, *But at that gentle one*. It might be divided still more subtly, and its meaning be more fully set forth, but it can pass with this division, and therefore I do not concern myself to divide it further.

> Beyond the sphere that widest orbit hath
>> Passeth the sigh which issues from my heart:
>> A new Intelligence doth Love impart
>> In tears to him, which leads him on his path.
> When at the wished-for place his flight he stays,
>> A lady he beholds in honor dight,
>> Who so doth shine that through her splendid light
>> The pilgrim spirit upon her doth gaze.
> He sees her such that his reporting words
>> To me are dark, his speech so subtle is
>> Unto the grieving heart which makes him tell.
> But of that gentle one he speaks, I wis,
>> Since of the Beatrice's name records;
>> Thus, ladies dear, I understand him well.

Chapter XLII

After this sonnet, a wonderful vision appeared to me, in which I saw things which made me resolve to speak no more of this blessed one, until I could more worthily treat of her. And to attain to this, I study to the utmost of my power, as she truly knows. So that, if it shall please Him through whom all things live, that my life be prolonged for some years, I hope to say of her what was never said of any woman.

And then may it please Him who is the lord of Grace, that my soul may go to behold the glory of its lady, namely, of that blessed Beatrice, who in glory looks upon the face of Him *qui est per omnia sæcula benedictus* [who is through all ages blessed].

THE CONVIVIO

(THE BANQUET)

translated by Philip H. Wicksteed

INTRODUCTION

On the whole, the *Convivio* (the Italian word for *banquet*) defies precise identification. It is most commonly thought of as a treatise of philosophical inquiry delving into the nature of wisdom, truth, knowledge, meaning, cosmological structures, education, civil government, love, and nobility, written specifically for those who did not have the privilege of philosophical instruction. But it is also a work of literary criticism, commentary, spiritual and bibliographic autobiography, poetic analysis, personal vindication, and pedagogy. In other words, Dante does not present a monochromatic work, easily categorized within a single literary form. He himself describes the *Convivio* as a commentary, though his exact language is *quasi comento*—"a kind of commentary,"[1] or *almost* commentary. This particular style offered Dante the flexibility to shift genres at will, allowing him the freedom to discuss what he wanted to and in the manner he thought best.

Like the *Vita nuova*, the *Convivio* is written as a prosimetrum, a mixture of prose and poetry. In many ways, this latter work can be read as a counterpart to the earlier one; here he discusses and explains three of the lyric canzoni written during his younger days before he was exiled from Florence, including "Ladies, who have intelligence of Love (see *Vita nuova* XIX). One of the central differences between the two is tone. Dante draws attention to the relationship and explains this difference in the first chapter of the *Convivio*:

> And if in the present work (which is entitled, and which I wish
> to be, the *Banquet* [*Convivio*]) the handling be more virile than
> in the *New Life* [*Vita nuova*], I do not intend thereby to throw

---

1   *Conv.* I.iii.2.

> a slight in any respect upon the latter, but rather to strengthen
> that by this; seeing that it conforms to reason that that should
> be fervid and impassioned, this temperate and virile. For a dif-
> ferent thing is comely to say and to do at one age than at anoth-
> er; wherefore certain ways are suitable and laudable at one age
> which are foul and blameworthy at another...[2]

To put it bluntly, Dante has grown up. Exile has tempered him,
setting him at some distance from his "fervid and impassioned"
youth. He is no longer interested in limiting himself to a particular
theme or style, such as the courtly love poems of the *Vita nuova*.
Rather, he is filled with the more manly ("virile" [Ital: *virilmente*]
from the Latin *vir* for man) desire to explore the furthest reaches
of philosophy. It is as if exile has motivated him to understand,
with both depth and breadth, the kind of cosmos in which he lives,
with all its allusiveness to and interconnectedness with the realms
beyond. Had he finished the *Convivio*, it would have been a rare
and significant achievement in the history of philosophical and
theological inquiry, especially as it would have been the first of its
kind in Italian, unlike all works of real academic significance which
were written in Latin.

Why write the *Convivio* in Italian and not Latin? As noted
above, the word *convivio* means *banquet*; here it refers to a philosophic feast, or banquet, of knowledge. The "viands" of this feast
were gleaned from the crumbs that had fallen from the table of the
trained intellectuals, which many lay persons have had neither the
ability nor the opportunity to receive. Dante opens the *Convivio*
with the first line of Aristotle's *Metaphysics*, aligning his intentions
for the whole work with the authority of "the Philosopher." The
fact that "all men naturally desire to know" is the foundation of
his entire argument. Knowledge, he explains, is the ultimate perfection of man's soul and is, therefore, our ultimate happiness. Un-
fortunately, many are deprived of this most noble perfection and
for a variety of reasons. The banquet Dante is spreading before the
reader constitutes his attempt to fix that problem. Having escaped
the "pasture of the common herd,"[3] he was able to collect the bits

---

2   *Conv.* I.i.16–17.

3   *Conv.* I.i.10.

and crumbs that fell from the table of those "blessed few" who eat the "bread of angels."[4] It is these "gathered" pieces, these bits of wisdom and understanding, Dante wishes to share with those who have great need of their nutritional value. But where did Dante himself gain such wisdom? He tells us:

> And as it is wont to chance that a man goeth in search of silver and beyond his purpose findeth gold, the which some hidden cause presents, not, I take it, without divine command; so I, who was seeking to console myself, found not only a cure for my tears, but words of authors, and of sciences, and of books, pondering upon which I judged that Philosophy, who was the lady of these authors, of these sciences, and of these books, was a thing supreme; and I conceived her after the fashion of a gentle lady, and I might not conceive her in any attitude save that of compassion; wherefore the sense for truth so loved to gaze upon her that I could scarce turn it away from her; and impelled by this imagination of her, I began to go where she was in very truth revealed, to wit, to the schools of the religious orders, and to the disputations of the philosophers; so that in a short time, I suppose some thirty months, I began to feel so much of her sweetness that the love of her expelled and destroyed every other thought.[5]

The *Convivio*, therefore, is a sharing of the (considerable) philosophical and theological knowledge Dante gained through his studies at the Franciscan, Dominican, and Augustinian schools of Florence. There, as he states, he studied under the headmistress "Philosophy," who was the "gentle lady" of those "authors... sciences... and books" that filled him with great wonder and consolation following the death of Beatrice. Philosophy for Dante was more than simply a science or art. Philosophy was a lady, "the daughter of God, queen of all things, most noble, and most beauteous..."[6] Using the symbol of a lady, Dante was able to highlight the role of love in the pursuit of wisdom, that philosophy was in fact the love (*philo*) of wisdom (*sophia*). For Dante, to love wisdom is to love the

---

4   *Conv.* I.i.7.

5   *Conv.* II.xii.5–7.

6   *Conv.* II.xii.9.

fundamental principle of all things, that which was there at the beginning of everything. This meant at least two things: 1) to rightly know and understand anything about the cosmos you must first love wisdom (with all of its "fear of the Lord is the beginning of"[7] connotations), and 2) to love wisdom is to love her fruit, that is, the whole of the cosmos. Thus, no subject ought to be neglected in the pursuit of wisdom, for every subject can be a path to knowing Christ better.[8] This is the trajectory of the *Convivio*, which again, if finished, would have been an impressive feat.

Thus, Dante proposes to share the bits and crumbs he has gathered from the table of wisdom in all its fullness with those who are without access to philosophic inquiry. The main dish of each course (fourteen were intended, but only three were completed) is one of Dante's previously published canzoni, followed by commentary in which he explains the literal and allegorical meaning of each poem (save the third canzone in Book IV, where he purposefully discusses only the literal). The whole work is prefaced by the first book which acts as an introduction or prologue, beginning with a defense of the democratization of knowledge. In chapters i–iv, Dante explains what he is doing in this work and how he is going about it (i); the danger and difficulty of speaking about oneself in print (ii); the complications of being a public figure (iii); and how he will counter any prejudice with a "loftier style" (iv).

In chapters v–xiii, Dante gives a detailed defense of his use of the vernacular in this work. Because it is primarily a commentary on pre-existing canzoni, and because those canzoni are written in Italian, Latin would have been inappropriate, for Latin is inherently superior to Italian (v). The servant (the commentary) must actually serve the master (the canzone) (vi); thus, a Latin commentary could not "obey" the vernacular canzone (vii). However, there are more and better reasons for using the vernacular than simply the inappropriateness of Latin in this circumstance (viii), not least of which is the greater number of people who will benefit from the vernacular (ix). Dante goes on to explain why he loves the vernacular (x), and to condemn those who would deny the usefulness and validity of the vernacular (xi). Finally, he demonstrates how his

---

7   Job 28:28.

8   See *Par.* X.1–12.

love for the vernacular was engendered (xii), and how it continues to be strengthened (xiii).

Book II opens with the first canzone to be analyzed: *Voi che 'ntendendo il terzo ciel movete* ("Ye who by understanding move the third heaven"). He prefaces his commentary by explicating the standard (for the medieval world) fourfold method of interpretation, by which one reads a text for its literal, allegorical, moral, and anagogical meanings (i), before moving into an examination of the canzone's structure (ii). Given the celestial nature of the poem (*il terzo ciel*), Dante presents us with a detailed explanation of his cosmology (iii), the nature of celestial beings, also known as "intelligences" (iv), their order in the heavens (v), and the influence specifically of the third heaven, Venus (vi). He begins his actual explication of the canzone with its literal interpretation (vii), but immediately interrupts this with a discussion of the nature and immortality of the soul (viii). He concludes the literal explication (ix–xi), and proceeds to an allegorical interpretation (xii), interrupting this as well to establish a relationship between the ten spheres (Moon, Mercury, Venus, Sun, Mars, Jupiter, Saturn, Fixed Stars, *Primum Mobile*, Empyrean) and the sciences (grammar, logic, rhetoric, arithmetic, music, geometry, astrology, physics and metaphysics, moral philosophy, and theology), associating each science with a particular sphere (xiii–xiv). With these correspondences articulated, Dante closes the second book by asserting the subject of his canzone is none other than Lady Philosophy herself (xv).

Book III opens with the second canzone, *Amor che nella mente mi ragiona* ("Love, that discourses to me in my mind "). Dante begins his exposition by rehearsing his love for Lady Philosophy, and explaining why this canzone was written for her (i). He continues with another discussion of the soul and the mind (ii), the ineffability of his theme (iii), and, therefore, the deficiency of its treatment due to the limited nature of man's finite intellect (iv). He continues with a description of the heavens, centered on the circuit of the sun (v), before returning to an exposition of the canzone, in which he praises the virtues of Lady Philosophy (vi). This is followed by more specific praise of her soul (vii) and her body, specifically her face/eyes, in which Dante sees "the pleasures of Paradise" (viii). His explication next leads him into a discussion of sight and the eye (ix), after which he concludes his commentary on the literal meaning of the poem (x). The last third of Book III lays out Dante's allegorical interpretation. He begins with a summary of the nature of philosophy, specifically as the "love of wisdom" (xi), and how human philosophy is to be distinguished from divine philosophy (xii). He then turns to the nature of philosophy within the celestial intelligences and how the "infernal Intelligences are deprived of the countenance of this most beautiful lady" (xiii). Dante then praises love, "which is part of philosophy" and foundational to its right practice (xiv). Finally, he praises wisdom itself, closing the book with the following exhortation:

> Oh worse than dead, who flee from her friendship! Open your eyes and see that, before ye were, she loved you, preparing and ordering your progress; and, after ye were made, to direct you aright, she came to you in your own likeness. And if ye may not all come to look upon her herself, do honour to her in her friends and follow their commandments, as who proclaim to you the will of this eternal empress. Close not your ears to Solomon who bids you thereto when he says that "the way of the righteous is a shining light that goes on and increases until the day of blessedness," following after them, gazing upon their doings, which should be a light to you on the path of this most brief life.[9]

Book IV opens with the third canzone: *Le dolci rime d'amor* ("The sweet rhymes of love"). Dante begins his analysis by stating the reason for the canzone, which was to correct a common error regarding nobility (i). What follows is a description of the prefatory stanza in which he promises to discuss truth (ii); an outline of the argument to be made (iii); a short digression on the necessity of world empire (iv) and the divine establishment of the Roman Empire (v); and a discussion of authority, with a brief overview of the development of philosophy (vi). He then returns to the error concerning the origins of nobility, whether they are given or inherited (vii), desiring to show reverence to both Aristotle and the Emperor (who say nobility is inherited), but above all to truth

---

9   *Conv.* III.xv.17–18.

(viii). He demonstrates the limitations of both the civil authority and human reason (ix), and that the Emperor was wrong to say money and titles confer nobility (x). Indeed, riches are base (xi), deceptively dangerous to the soul (xii), and imperfect in that they can never ultimately satisfy (xiii). Therefore, ancestry is irrelevant to true nobility (xiv), and Dante goes on to prove arguments to the contrary are fallacious (xv). What, then, does the word "nobility" actually mean? It is the "perfection of the nature proper to each thing" (xvi). This leads to a discussion of the eleven moral virtues named by Aristotle in the *Nicomachean Ethics* (xvii), and how true nobleness comprehends every virtue (xviii). Nobility is the sky in which virtue shines, though nobility comprehends more than the moral virtues; it also houses beauty, strength, health, and the intellectual virtues as well (xix). Therefore, it is something only God can bestow (xx). Dante next discusses how nobility is given to men (xxi) and gives an explication of man's chief end: the moral and intellectual virtues leading to the beatific vision (xxii). The tokens by which we can recognize nobility in men are examined (xxiii), which necessitates a discussion of the four ages of man (xxiv). First the nature of youth (xxv), then of maturity (xxvi), of old age (xxvii), and finally of senility (xxviii) is discussed in greater detail. After a few final words on the reality of lineage and ancestry (xxix), Dante concludes the fourth book with a recap of the whole canzone, calling nobility a true friend of Lady Philosophy, for

> so much doth the one love the other that nobleness ever demands her, and philosophy turns not her most sweet regards in any other direction. Oh how great and beauteous adornment is this which at the end of this ode is given to her, calling her the friend of her whose true abode is in the most secret place of the divine mind![10]

In conclusion, the unfinished *Convivio* provides a fascinating look into a mind richly endowed with knowledge, understanding, and great wisdom. Dante was a brilliant student of both the ancients (especially Aristotle and Cicero) and the early Medievals (such as Augustine and Boethius), but more than both he was a student of

---

10   *Conv.* IV.xxx.6.

Scripture itself. Despite being described as a work of philosophy, the *Convivio* is a work firmly rooted in the Word of God. For Dante, there could be no answers to the questions philosophy raises (who are we?, how do we know?, and what do we do?) without reference to a theological understanding of the Triune God of Scripture and the world He made to reflect His own glory. Though abandoned in favor of the *Comedy*, the *Convivio* remains a valuable resource to understand many of the philosophical and theological truths that are enfleshed in the narrative of Dante's great poem.

For Further Reading:

Gilson, Étienne. *Dante the Philosopher.* Translated by David Moore. New York: Sheed and Ward, 1949.

Scott, John A. "The Unfinished 'Convivio' as a Pathway to the 'Comedy.'" Dante Studies, no. 113 (1995): 31–56.

Took, J. F. *Dante: Lyric Poet and Philosopher.* Oxford: Clarendon Press, 1990.

THE CONVIVIO

(1302–1304, 1307–1308)

BOOK I

Chapter I

1 As saith the Philosopher[1] in the beginning of the First Philosophy, "All men by nature desire to know";[2] the reason whereof may be that each thing, impelled by its own natural foresight, inclines to its own perfection; wherefore, inasmuch as knowledge is the distinguishing perfection of our soul, wherein consists our distinguishing blessedness, all of us are naturally subject to the longing for it.

2 Yet of this most noble perfection many are bereft, for diverse causes; which, inside of the man and outside of him, keep him from acquiring the habit of knowledge.

3 Inside of the man there may be two defects and impediments, the one from the side of the body, the other from the side of the soul. From the side of the body is it when the parts are unduly disposed, so that it can receive nought, as with the deaf and the dumb, and their likes. From the side of the soul is it when vice hath such supremacy in her that she giveth herself to pursuing vicious delights, wherein she is deluded to such a point that for their sake she holds all things cheap.

4 Outside of the man, likewise, two causes may be detected, one of which brings about compulsion, the other indolence. The former is that family and civic care which rightly engages to itself the greater number of men, so that they may not abide in leisure of speculation. The latter is the defect of the place where the person

---

1   Here and throughout Dante's works, "the Philosopher" is Aristotle.

2   *Metaphysics* I.1.

is born and nurtured, which may chance to be not only void of all provision for study, but remote from studious folk.

5 The two first of these causes, to wit, the first from the inner side and the first from the outer side, are not to be blamed but to be excused, and deserve to be pardoned. The two others (though one of them more than the other) deserve to be blamed and abominated.

6 Manifestly then may he perceive who rightly considers that few be left who may reach to that habit which is desired by all, and well-nigh beyond number are they which be hindered and which live all their lives famished for this universal food.

7 Oh, blessed those few who sit at the table where the bread of angels is consumed, and wretched they who share the food of sheep![3]

8 But inasmuch as every man is naturally friendly to every man, and every friend is grieved by the defect of his friend, they who are fed at so lofty a table are not without compassion towards those whom they see browsing round on grass and acorns in the pasture of brutes.

9 And inasmuch as compassion is the mother of benefaction, they who know ever proffer freely of their good wealth to those poor indeed, and are as a living spring at whose waters the natural thirst above-spoken of is refreshed.[4]

10 And I, therefore, who sit not at the blessed table, but, having fled the pasture of the common herd, gather, at the feet of them who sit at meat, of that which falls from them; and who, by reason of the sweetness which I experience in that which little by little I gather, recognize the wretched life of those whom I have left behind me; moved to compassion, though not forgetting myself, have reserved somewhat for the wretched; which somewhat, already some time agone, I have displayed to their eyes, and thereby have made them the more eager.

---

3   *Par.* II.10–15.

4   *Purg.* XXI.1–3.

11 Wherefore, desiring now to make provision for them, I purpose to make a general banquet of that which I have already displayed to them and of the bread which is needful for suchlike viand, without which they might not eat it at this banquet; such bread, to wit, as is worthy of the viand which I well understand to have been offered them in vain.

12 And therefore I would not have any take his seat who is ill-disposed as to his organs, inasmuch as he has neither tooth nor tongue nor palate; nor any addicted to vice, inasmuch as his stomach is full of poisonous and contrary humors, so that it would not retain my viands.

13 But let come whosoever, because of family and civil care, hath been kept in human hunger, and let him seat himself at the same table with others impeded in like manner. And at their feet let all place themselves who have been excluded by their sloth, for they are not worthy to sit more high. And let these and those take my viand, together with the bread which will enable them both to taste and to digest it.

14 The viands of this banquet will be served in fourteen fashions, that is to say fourteen odes, treating as well of love as of virtue, which without the present bread had the shadow of a certain obscurity, so that to many their beauty was more in favour than their excellence.

15 But this bread, to wit, the present exposition, will be the light which shall make apparent every hue of their significance.

16 And if in the present work (which is entitled, and which I wish to be, the *Banquet*) the handling be more virile than in the *New Life*,[5] I do not intend thereby to throw a slight in any respect upon the latter, but rather to strengthen that by this, seeing that it conforms to reason that that should be fervid and impassioned, this temperate and virile.

---

5   The *Vita nuova.*

17 For a different thing is comely to say and to do at one age than at another; wherefore certain ways are suitable and laudable at one age which are foul and blameworthy at another, as will be shown on its own account further on, in the fourth treatise of this book. And in that I spoke before entrance on the prime of manhood, and in this when I had already passed the same.

18–19 And inasmuch as my true purport was other than the aforesaid odes outwardly display, I intend to set them forth by allegorical exposition after having discussed the literal story. So that the one account and the other will supply a relish to those who are invited to this feast; whom I pray, one and all, that if the banquet be not so magnificent as consorts with the proclamation thereof, they shall impute every defect not to my will but to my power, because what my will herein aims at is a full and hearty liberality.

Chapter II

1 At the beginning of every well-ordered banquet, the servants are wont to take the bread that is set out and cleanse it from every blemish. Wherefore I, who in this present writing am taking their place, purpose at the outset to cleanse this exposition, which counts for the bread in my repast, from two blemishes.

2 The one is that for any one to speak of himself seems unjustifiable, and the other that for an expounder himself to discourse too profoundly seems unreasonable. And this appearance of what is unjustifiable and unreasonable the knife of my judgment cleanses away in the fashion that follows.

3 Rhetoricians forbid a man to speak of himself except on needful occasion, and from this a man is prohibited, because it is impossible to speak of any without the speaker either praising or blaming him of whom he speaks. And there is a want of urbanity in either of these kinds of discourse finding a place on a man's own proper lips.

4 And to solve a doubt which rises here, I say that it is worse to blame than to praise, though neither the one nor the other should be done. The reason is that what is directly blameworthy is fouler than what is incidentally so.

5 To dispraise oneself is directly blameworthy, because a man should tell his friend of a fault in secret, and there is no closer friend to a man than himself. Wherefore it is in the chamber of his own thoughts that he should take himself to task and bewail his faults, not openly.

6 Again, for lacking the power or the knowledge to conduct himself rightly a man for the most part is not blamed, but for lacking the will he always is, for it is by willing and not willing that our badness and goodness is judged. And so he who blames himself, by showing that he knows his fault, exposes his lack of goodness, and therefore a man must refrain, on his own account, from speaking in blame of himself.

7 Self-praise is to be avoided as evil by implication, inasmuch as such praise cannot be given without its turning to yet greater blame. It is praise on the surface of the words, it is blame if we search into their entrails, for words are produced to demonstrate what is not known. Wherefore, whosoever praises himself shows that he does not believe himself to be well thought of, which will not happen unless he has an evil conscience, which in his self-praise is revealed, and when revealed is blamed.

8 And further, self-praise and self-blame are to be shunned for one common reason, as the bearing of false witness; for there is no man who is a true and just measurer of himself, so does our kindness to ourselves deceive us.

9 Whence it happens that everyone hath in his judgment the measures of the unjust trader who sells with one and buys with another; and each one takes stock of his evil doing with a large measure and takes stock of his good with a little one, so that the number and quantity and weight of the good seems to him greater than if it were assayed with a just measure, and that of the evil less.

10 Wherefore, when speaking of himself in praise or the contrary, either he speaks falsely with respect to the thing of which he speaks, or he speaks falsely with respect to his own belief; and the one and the other is falsity.

11 And this is why (inasmuch as assenting to an opinion is a way of professing it) he is guilty of discourtesy who praises or blames another to his face; because he who is thus estimated can neither assent nor protest without falling into the error of praising or blaming himself. Save, be it understood, in the way of due rebuke, which cannot be without blame of the fault which is to be corrected; and save in the way of due honouring and magnifying, which cannot come about without mention made of the virtuous deeds or of the dignities acquired.

12 But, returning to the main purport, I say, as indicated above, that speaking of himself is permitted on needful occasions, and amongst other needful occasions two are most manifest.

13 The one is when it is impossible without speaking of himself to quash great infamy and peril; and then it is allowed by reason that taking the least evil path of two is in a way taking a good one. And this necessity moved Boethius to speak of himself, so that under cover of consolation he might ward off the perpetual infamy of his exile, showing that it was unjust, since no other arose to ward it off.

14 The other is when by a man discoursing of himself the highest advantage, in the way of instruction, follows therefrom to others, and this reason moved Augustine in the *Confessions* to speak of himself.[6] For by the progress of his life, which was from bad to good, and from good to better, and from better to best, he gave example and instruction which could not have been received otherwise on such sure testimony.

15 Wherefore, if the one and the other of these occasions excuses me, the bread of my leavening is purged from its first blemishes. I am moved by the fear of infamy, and I am moved by the desire to give instruction which, in very truth, no other can give.

---

6   See especially *Confessions* X.3–4.

16 I fear the infamy of having pursued so great a passion as he who reads the above-named odes conceives to have had dominion over me, which infamy is entirely quenched by this present discourse concerning myself, which shows that not passion but virtue was the moving cause.

17 I purpose also to reveal the true meaning of the said odes, which none may perceive unless I relate it, because it is hidden under figure of allegory, and this will not only give fair delight to hear, but subtle instruction, both in discoursing after this fashion, and in understanding after this fashion the writings of others.

Chapter III

1 Worthy of much blame is the thing which, being appointed to remove some special defect, itself induces that same. As if one should be appointed to part a strife, and before he had parted it, set another on foot.

2 And now that my bread has been purged on one side, it behoves me to purge it on the other, that I may escape this latter blame. For my present writing, which may be called a kind of commentary, while commissioned to remove the defect of the aforesaid odes, may, perhaps, in certain places, be a little difficult itself, which difficulty is here designed to avoid a greater defect, and not in ignorance.

3 Oh, that it had pleased the disposer of the universe that the occasion of my excuse had never been! For then neither would others have sinned against me, nor should I have unjustly suffered penalty—the penalty, I mean, of exile and of poverty.

4 Since it was the pleasure of the citizens of the most beauteous and the most famous daughter of Rome, Florence, to cast me forth from her most sweet bosom (wherein I was born, and nurtured until the culmination of my life, wherein with their good leave, I long with all my heart to repose my wearied mind and end the time which is granted me), through well-nigh all the regions whereto

this tongue extends, a wanderer, almost a beggar, have I paced, revealing against my will the wound of fortune, which is often wont to be unjustly imputed to him who is wounded.

5 Verily have I been a ship without sail and without helm, drifted upon diverse ports and straits and shores by the dry wind that grievous poverty exhales. And I have seemed cheap in the eyes of many who perchance had conceived of me in other guise by some certain fame; in the sight of whom not only has my person been cheapened, but every work of mine, already accomplished or yet to do, has become of lower price.

6 The reason why this comes to pass (not only in me but in all) it is my pleasure here briefly to touch upon. And first, why a man's reputation dilates things more than truth demands. And then, why, more than truth demands, his presence makes them shrink.

7 Good report, begotten at the beginning in the mind of a friend by a good action, is first brought to birth by this mind, for the mind of an enemy, even though it receives the seed, does not conceive.

8 This mind which first gives it birth, further to adorn its present and also for love of the friend who receives it, does not restrain itself within the limits of the truth but passes beyond them. And when it passes beyond them in order to adorn its utterances, it speaks against conscience. When it is the illusion of love that makes it pass beyond them, it does not speak against it.

9 The second mind, which receives it thus, is not contented to abide by the dilating of the first mind, but sets about to adorn its own report (as being its own proper effect in the matter), and so both for the sake of so adorning it, and also by means of the illusion which it receives from the love begotten in it, it makes the dilation more ample than it was when it came to it; and this in concord and in discord with conscience, as before. And the like doth the third receiving mind, and the fourth, and so to infinity it dilates.

10 And in like manner, reversing the aforesaid causes, we may see the reason why infamy is magnified in like fashion. Wherefore Vergil saith in the fourth of the *Aeneid*, "that fame lives by moving and grows by going."[7]

11 Clearly, then, may who so will perceive that the image begotten by fame alone is ever more ample, whatsoever it may be, than the imagined thing in its true state.

Chapter IV

1 The reason having now been shown why fame dilates the good and the evil beyond their true magnitude, it remains in this chapter to show the reasons which reveal to us why a man's presence contracts them in the other direction. And when these have been shown, we shall easily advance to our main purpose, which concerns the above-mentioned excuse.

2 I say, then, that for three causes presence makes a person count for less than his real worth, the first of which is childishness. I do not mean of age, but of mind. The second is envy, and these two exist in the judge. The third is the alloy of humanity, and this is in the person judged.

3 The first can be briefly discoursed of thus. The greater part of men live after sense, and not after reason, like children, and such know not things save only on their outer surface, and their excellence, which has reference to their due end, they do not see, because they have the eyes of their reason shut, which penetrate to the perception of that end. Whence they quickly perceive everything that they can perceive at all, and judge according to their vision.

4 And because they form a certain opinion on the strength of a man's fame, by hearsay, wherefrom in the man's presence the imperfect judgment, which judges not after reason but after sense alone, is at variance, they hold all that they have heard before to be a lie, and despise the person whom before they prized.

---

7   *Aeneid* IV.175.

5 Wherefore, with such as these (and almost every one is such) a man's presence makes the one and the other quality shrink. Such as these are quickly set a-longing and are quickly satisfied. They are often rejoiced and often saddened with brief delights and glooms, and they quickly become friends and quickly enemies. They do all things like children, without use of reason.

6 The second may be understood by these considerations. Likeness, in the vicious, is the cause of envy, and envy is the cause of hostile judgment, because it suffers not reason to plead on behalf of the object of envy. And the power of judgment is then like to the judge who listens only to one side.

7 Wherefore, when such as these see the famous person, they are straightway envious, because they look upon his members and upon his faculties, which are like their own, and they fear, because of the excellence of such a one, to be the less prized.

8 And these not only pass a hostile judgment under the influence of passion, but, by defaming, cause others also to pass a hostile judgment. Wherefore, with them presence makes the good and the ill in everyone presented to them shrink. And I say "the ill" because many, taking delight in ill deeds, envy ill-doers.

9 The third is the alloy of humanity, which has its source in him who is judged, and works not save by some familiarity and intercourse. To make which clear, be it known that man is blemished in many directions, and, as Augustine says, "no man is without blemish."[8]

10 One while the man is blemished by some passion, which, may be, he cannot resist, another while he is blemished by some distorted member, and another by some stroke of fortune, or he is blemished by the infamy of his parents or of someone nigh of kin to him. Which things are not borne by fame, but by the man's presence, and by his intercourse he reveals them.

11 And these blemishes throw some shadow over the brightness of his excellence, so as to make it seem less clear and less worthy.

---

8   *Confessions* I.vii.11.

And this is why every prophet is less honoured in his own country. This is why a man of excellence should grant his presence to few and his intimacy to fewer, that his name may have acceptance and not be despised.

12 And this third cause may operate in the case of evil as well as good if each element in the argument concerning it be turned the opposite way. Wherefore, it is clearly seen that, because of the alloy from which no man is free, presence contracts the good and the ill in every man further than truth wills.

13 Wherefore, because, as said above, I have exposed myself to nearly all the Italians, and therefore have perchance cheapened myself more than the truth wills, not only to them whom my reputation has reached but to others also, whereby all that I have done has doubtless been more lightly esteemed together with myself, it behoves me to give something of weight to the present work by a loftier style, that it may seem a thing of more authority. And let this excuse for the severity of my comment suffice.

Chapter V

1 Now that this bread has been cleansed of the accidental blemishes, it remains to apologize for a substantial one, to wit, that it is vernacular and not Latin, which by similitude may be called oaten instead of wheaten.

2 And in brief the apology consists in three considerations which moved me to choose this rather than the other. The first springs forth from the desire to avoid undue inversion of order, the second from zealous liberality, the third from natural love of one's own speech.

3 And these reasons, and the grounds on which they rest, that I may satisfy the objections that might be urged on the aforesaid ground, I purpose duly to discuss in fashion as follows.

4 That which most adorns and commends the doings of man, and which most directly leads them to a prosperous end, is the habit of those dispositions which are ordained to the end in view, as, for instance, courage of mind and strength of body are ordained to the end of chivalry.

5 And so he who is appointed to the service of another should have those dispositions which are ordained to that end, to wit, subjection, knowledge, and obedience, without which a man is not duly disposed for service. For if he be not subject in all his conditions he ever goeth irksomely and heavily in his service, and seldom continueth therein. And if he be not obedient he serveth not safe at his own discretion and will, which is rather the service of a friend than of a servant.

6 Wherefore, to avoid this inversion of order, it behoves this comment, which is made to be servant of the oaths hereinafter written, to be subject to them in its whole ordainment. And it should have acquaintance with the affairs of its lord, and should be obedient to him.

7 All which dispositions would be lacking to it were it Latin and not vernacular, seeing that the oaths are vernacular. For firstly, if it were Latin it would not be subject but sovereign, both by reason of nobility and of virtue and of beauty. Of nobility, because Latin is stable and uncorruptible and the vernacular is unstable and corruptible.

8 Wherefore, we see in the ancient writings of the Latin comedies and tragedies, which cannot be changed, that same speech that we have to-day, and this is not the case with the vernacular, which takes fashion at our will, and changes.

9 Whence we see in the cities of Italy, if we choose to look closely, that within fifty years from now many words have been quenched and borne and changed, and if a short time makes so much change, far more change does greater time effect. So that I assert that if they who parted from this life a thousand years agone were to re-

turn to their cities, they would believe them to be inhabited by a strange folk, because of the tongue discordant from their own.

10 Of this I shall discourse more at large elsewhere, in a book which I intend to make, God granting, concerning Eloquence in the Vernacular.[9]

11 Further, Latin were sovereign rather than subject by reason of its virtue. Everything hath virtue of nature which accomplishes that for which it was ordained, and the better it doth it, the more virtue it hath. Whence we call the man virtuous who lives in the life of contemplation or action to which he is naturally ordained; we speak of the equine virtue of pacing swift and far, whereto the horse is ordained; we speak of the virtue of a sword which smartly cuts things hard, whereto it is ordained.

12 Thus speech, which is ordained to manifest human conceptions, hath virtue when it doth this thing, and that speech hath the most virtue which doth it most. Wherefore, since Latin revealeth many things conceived in the mind which the vernacular may not reveal (as they know who hath the habit of the one speech and the other), its virtue is more than that of the vernacular.

13 Again, it were sovereign rather than subject by reason of its beauty. Men call that thing beautiful the parts whereof duly correspond, because from their harmony pleasure results. Wherefore, we think a man beautiful when his members duly correspond to each other. And we call singing beautiful when the voices correspond mutually according to the requirements of the art.

14–15 Therefore that speech is the more beautiful wherein the words correspond more duly, and they correspond more duly in Latin than in the vernacular, because the vernacular followeth use and the Latin art. Wherefore, it is admitted to be of more beauty, of more virtue, and of more nobility, and hereby the chief contention of this discourse is established, to wit, that a Latin comment would not have been the subject of the odes but their sovereign.

---

9   See *De vulgari eloquentia* in *Writing in Exile: The Prose Works of Dante Alighieri, Volume II: The Latin Works* published by Roman Roads Press.

Chapter VI

1 Having shown how the present comment would not have been subject to the odes, had it been in Latin, it remains to show that it would not have been familiar with them nor obedient to them. And then the conclusion will follow, that to avoid undue inversion of order it was needful to speak in the vernacular.

2 I say that Latin would not have been familiar with its vernacular master for this reason. The servant's familiarity with his master is chiefly needed in order to give him perfect understanding of two things.

3 The first is the nature of his master, for there be masters of such asinine nature that they order the contrary of what they desire; and others who desire to be served and understood without giving orders at all; and others who will not have the servant go about to do any needful thing except they command it.

4 And why there be such varieties amongst men I do not purpose at present to expound (for it would make the discretion too multiplex) save so far as to say generically that such are little other than beasts, who have small good of their reason. Wherefore, if the servant does not understand his master's nature, it is manifest that he cannot perfectly serve him.

5 The second thing is that the servant must needs be acquainted with his master's friends, for otherwise he would neither honour nor serve them, and so would not perfectly serve his own master. For friends are, as it were, parts of a single whole, that whole being unity in willing and in not willing.

6 Now the Latin comment would not have had knowledge of these things, whereas the vernacular itself has. That Latin hath no familiarity with the vernacular and its friends is thus proved. To know a thing generically is not to know it perfectly, just as he who perceives an animal afar off has no perfect understanding of it, not knowing whether it be dog or wolf or goat.

7 Latin has cognizance of vernacular speech generically, but not in its distinctions, for if it recognized its distinctions, it would recognize all the vernaculars, since there is no reason why it should recognize one more than another. And therefore if any man had acquired complete command of Latin, he would enjoy discriminating familiarity with vernacular speech.

8 But this is not so, for he who has perfect command of Latin, if he be of Italy, does not recognize the vernacular of the German, nor if a German, the Italian or the Provençal. Whence it is manifest that Latin is not familiar with vernacular speech.

9 Again, it is not familiar with its friends, because it is impossible to know the friends having no knowledge of the principle. Wherefore, if Latin is not acquainted with the vernacular (and it has been shown above that it is not), it is impossible for it to be acquainted with its friends.

10 Again, without intercourse and familiarity it is impossible to be acquainted with men, and Latin hath not intercourse with so many in any tongue as the vernacular of that tongue hath, to which they all are friends. And consequently it cannot know the friends of the vernacular.

11 And this is not contradicted by what might be urged, namely, that Latin does converse with certain of the friends of the vernacular, for it is not therefore familiar with them all, and so it is not completely acquainted with the said friends. And it is complete and not defective knowledge that is needed.

Chapter VII

1 Having shown that the Latin comment would not have served with understanding, I will tell how it would not have been obedient.

2 He is obedient who possesses that excellent disposition which is called obedience. True obedience must needs have three things, without which it may not be. It must be sweet, not bitter, and completely under command, not self-moved, and measured, not out of measure.

3 The which three things it were impossible for the Latin comment to have, and therefore it were impossible for it to be obedient. That it would have been impossible for the Latin to be obedient is manifested by the argument that follows.

4 Whatsoever proceeds in inverted order is irksome, and therefore bitter and not sweet. Like sleeping by day and watching by night, or going backwards and not forwards. For the subject to command the sovereign is proceeding in inverted order. For the right order is for the sovereign to command the subject, wherefore it is bitter and not sweet. And since it is impossible sweetly to obey a bitter command, it is impossible when the subject commands for the obedience of the sovereign to be sweet.

5 Wherefore if the Latin is sovereign of the vernacular, as has been shown above by many arguments, and the odes which take the place of commanders are vernacular, it is impossible that their relation should be sweet.

6 Further, obedience is wholly commanded and in no part self-moved when he who does a thing in obedience would not, unless commanded, have done it of his own motion, either in whole or in part.

7 Wherefore, if I were ordered to bear two cloaks on my back, and should have borne one without orders, I say that my obedience is not wholly under command, but is in part self-moved. And such would have been the obedience of the Latin comment, and consequently it would not have been an obedience wholly under command.

8 That it would have been such appears hereby, that Latin without the command of this master would have expounded many parts of his meaning (and actually expounds it, if any one closely inspect writings that are written in Latin) which the vernacular does not in any degree.

9 Again, obedience is measured and not out of measure when it goes to the edge of the command and not beyond it. Just as particular nature is obedient to universal nature when it gives a man thirty-two teeth, neither more nor less, and when it gives five fingers to the hand, neither more nor less. And man is obedient to justice when he does what she commands to the evildoer.

10 Now this the Latin would not have done, but would have sinned not only in defect and not only in excess, but in both. And thus its obedience would not have been measured but out of measure, and consequently it would not have been obedient.

11 That Latin would not have filled out its master's command, and that it would also have exceeded it may easily be shown. This master, to wit, these odes, to which this comment is ordained as servant, command and will that they be expounded to all such to whom their meaning can so come, that when they speak they shall be understood. And no one doubts that if they could utter their commands in words, this is what they would order.

12 Now, Latin would only have expounded them to the lettered, for others would not have understood it. Wherefore, inasmuch as there are far more unlettered than lettered who desire to understand them, it follows that Latin would not have fully accomplished their order, as does the vernacular, which is understood alike by the lettered and the unlettered.

13 Moreover, Latin would have expounded them to folk of another tongue, such as Germans and English and others. And here it would have exceeded their command, for, speaking at large, I declare that it would have been against their will that their meaning should be expounded where they themselves could not carry it together with their beauty.

14 And therefore let every one know that nothing which hath the harmony of musical connection can be transferred from its own tongue into another without shattering all its sweetness and harmony.

15 And this is the reason why Homer is not translated from Greek into Latin, as are the other writings that we have of theirs. And this is the reason why the verses of the Psalter are without the sweetness of music and harmony, for they were translated from Hebrew into Greek, and from Greek into Latin, and in the first translation all their sweetness perished.

16 And thus is the conclusion reached which was promised at the beginning of the chapter immediately before this.

Chapter VIII

1 Now that it has been shown by sufficient reasons how, to avoid undue inversion of order, the aforesaid odes must needs have a vernacular and not a Latin comment to reveal and expound them, I purpose to show how zealous liberality likewise made me choose the one and drop the other.

2 Zealous liberality, then, is marked by three things which cleave to this vernacular and would not have cleft to the Latin. The first is giving to many, the second is giving things useful, the third is giving the gift without its being asked.

3 For to give to and to help one is good, but to give to and to help many is zealous goodness, inasmuch as it taketh its likeness from the benefactions of God, who is the most universal benefactor.

4 And, moreover, it is impossible to give to many without giving to one, inasmuch as one is included in many. But it is entirely possible to give to one without giving to many. Wherefore, he who helps many doth the one good deed and the other. He who helps one doth the one good deed only. Whence we see the makers of the laws keeping their eyes chiefly fixed on the general good in making them.

5 Again, to give things that are of no use to him who receives them is indeed good, insofar as he who gives shows at least his friendship. But it is not perfectly good and so is not zealous giving. As if a knight should give a shield to a doctor, and the doctor should give a copy of the *Aphorisms* of Hippocrates or the *Art* of Galen to the knight, wherefore, the wise say that the face of the gift ought to resemble that of the receiver, that is to say should be suitable to him, and should be useful. And herein is the liberality deemed zealous of the man who is thus discerning in his gifts.

6 But inasmuch as moral counselings are wont to create a desire to investigate their origin, in this chapter I purpose to briefly expound four reasons why a gift must needs be useful to him who receives it in order that there may be zealous liberality therein.

7 Firstly, because virtue should be cheerful, and not gloomy in its every act. Wherefore, if the gift be not cheerful in the giving and in the receiving, there is not perfect nor zealous virtue in it. This cheerfulness nought else can secure save utility, which abides in the giver by the giving and which comes to the receiver by the receiving.

8 The giver, then, must show foresight in so doing, that on his side remains the utility of the comeliness which is above all utility. And in so doing, that to the receiver shall go over the utility of the use of the thing given. And thus the one and the other will be cheerful, and consequently there will be more zealous liberality.

9 Secondly, because virtue should always move things for the better. Thus, as it would be blameworthy action to make a spade out of a beautiful sword, or to make a beautiful goblet out of a beautiful lyre, so it is blameworthy to move a thing from a place where it is useful and bear it to a place where it will be less useful.

10 And, because futile action is blameworthy, it is blameworthy not only to put a thing where it will be less useful but also to put it where it will be equally useful.

11 Wherefore, in order that the changing of things may be praiseworthy, it must ever be for the better, because it should aim at being praiseworthy in the highest degree. And the gift cannot affect this except it become more dear by the change, nor can it become more dear except it become more useful for the receiver to use than the giver. Whence the conclusion follows, that the gift must

be useful to him who receives it, in order that there may be zealous liberality in the giving.

12 Thirdly, because the operation of virtue ought in itself to acquire friends, since our life has need of such, and the end of virtue is that our life should be satisfied. Wherefore, in order that the gift may make the receiver friendly, it should be useful to him, because utility stamps the memory with the image of the gift, which same is the food of friendship. And it stamps the more strongly in measure as the utility is greater.

13 Wherefore, Martin is wont to say, "I shall not forget the present which John made me." So that, in order for its proper virtue to reside in the gift, to wit, liberality, and for it to be zealous, the gift must be useful to him who receives it.

14 Finally, because virtue should be free and not constrained in its actions. Action is free when a person goes spontaneously in any direction, and it is shown by his turning his face that way. Action is constrained when a man goes against his will, and it is shown in his not looking in the direction in which he is going.

15 Now the gift looks that way when it is directed to the need of him who receives it. And since it cannot be directed thereto unless it is useful, in order that the virtue may be free in its action, the gift must have free course in the direction in which it travels together with the receiver, and consequently the utility of the receiver must be comprised in the gift in order that there may be zealous liberality in it.

16 The third thing wherein zealous liberality may be noted is giving without being asked. Because when a thing is asked for, then the transaction is, on one side, not a matter of virtue but of commerce, inasmuch as he who receives buys, though he who gives sells not. Wherefore Seneca saith, "that nothing is bought more dear than that on which prayers are spent."[10]

---

10   *De beneficiis* II.i.3–4.

[17] Wherefore, in order that there may be zealous liberality in the gift, and that it may be noted therein, it behoves that it be clear of every feature of merchandise, and so the gift must be unasked.

[18] Why the thing begged for costs so dear I do not propose to discourse of here, because it will be sufficiently discoursed of in the last treatise of this book.

Chapter IX

[1] Now from all the three above-named conditions, which must unite in order that zealous liberality may reside in a benefaction, the Latin commentary would have been remote, whereas the vernacular is accompanied by them, as may be manifestly demonstrated thus.

[2] The Latin would not have served many. For (if we call to mind what was said above) lettered men who have not the Italian tongue could not have enjoyed this service. And as for those who have this tongue (should we choose to examine closely who they are), we shall find that they would have been served by it perhaps in the proportion of one to a thousand, for the rest would not have received it, so zealous are they towards avarice, which parts them from all nobility of mind, which is the chief cause for desiring this food.

[3] And in reproof of them I say that they ought not to be called lettered, because they do not acquire literature for its own use, but just insofar as they may gain money or office by it; just as we ought not to call him a harper who hath a harp in his house to hire out for a price, and not to use it to play upon.

[4] Returning, then, to the main proposition, I say that it is clear enough how the Latin would have conferred its benefit upon few, whereas verily the vernacular will be of service to many.

[5] For goodness of mind, which awaits this service, is to be found in them who, by the grievous disuse of the world, have abandoned literature to such as have made her a harlot instead of a lady; which

noble ones are princes, barons, and knights, and many other noble folk, not only men, but women, of which men and women alike there are many of this tongue who command the vernacular but are not lettered.

6 Further, Latin would not have been the giver of a useful gift which the vernacular will be, because nothing is useful save insofar as it is used, nor does its excellence consist in potentiality which is not perfected existence, as in the case of gold, gems, and other treasures which be buried—albeit those which are in the hand of a miser are in a baser place than is the earth wherein the treasure is hidden.

7 Now what this comment gives verily is the meaning of the odes, for which purpose it is made. The principle design whereof is to lead men to knowledge and virtue, as will be seen in the progress of the treatment of them.

8 Of this meaning none can avail themselves save such in whom true nobility is sown, after the fashion which will be related in the fourth treatise. And almost all of these command the vernacular only, even as those noble ones named above in this chapter.

9 And this is not contradicted by a lettered man here and there being one of them. For as saith my master Aristotle in the first of the *Ethics*, "one swallow does not make spring."[11] It is plain, then, that the vernacular will give a useful thing, whereas the Latin would not have given it.

10 Further, the vernacular will give a gift unasked, which the Latin would not have done. For it will give itself as a commentary, which was never yet asked by any one. And this cannot be said of the Latin, for it has been demanded ere now as commentary and gloss to many writings, as may be seen clearly at the head of many of the same.

11 And thus it is manifest that zealous liberality moved me to the vernacular rather than to the Latin.

---

11   *Nicomachean Ethics* I.7. Hereafter simply *Ethics*.

Chapter X

1 Great must be the excuse when at a banquet so noble in its viands and so distinguished in its guests, oaten and not wheaten bread is presented. And evident must be the reason which shall make a man depart from that which hath long been observed by others, to wit, commenting in Latin.

2 And therefore the reason must be made manifest, for the issue of new things is uncertain, because there hath never been experience thereof, by which things of usage and tradition are regulated both in their progress and in their end.

3 And this is why Reason was moved to command that men should have careful respect of entering on a new path, saying that "in ordaining new things the reason must be evident which shall make us depart from that which hath long been of use."

4 Let none marvel, then, if the digression of my apology be long, but let him patiently endure its length as necessary.

5 And following it out I declare that (inasmuch as it hath been shown how I was moved to the vernacular, and forsook the Latin commentary to prevent undue inversion of order and in zeal of liberality) the order of the whole apology will have me show how I was moved thereto by the natural love of my own tongue, which is the third and last reason which moved me to it.

6 Hereto, I say, that natural love chiefly moves the lover to three things. The first is to magnify the loved object, the next to be jealous for it, the third is to defend it, as every one may see continually happening. And these three things made me adopt it, to wit, the vernacular, for both naturally and incidentally I love it and have loved.

7 I was moved in the first place to magnify it, and that herein I do magnify it may be seen by this reason. Albeit things can be magnified, that is, made great, by many conditions of greatness, none

of them makes so great as the greatness of their own proper excellence, which is the mother and preserver of the other greatnesses.

8 Wherefore, a man can have no greatness more than that of the virtuous operation which is his own proper excellence, whereby the greatness of true dignities and of true honors, of true power, of true riches, of true friends, of true and clear fame, are both acquired and preserved.

9 And this greatness do I give to this friend, inasmuch as the excellence which it had in potentiality and in secret, I make it have in actuality and publicity, in its own proper operation, which is to make manifest the thought conceived.

10 I was moved in the second place by jealousy for it. Jealousy for a friend makes a man take anxious thought for his distant future. Wherefore, reflecting that the desire to understand these odes would have induced some unlettered man to have the Latin commentary translated into the vernacular, and fearing lest the vernacular should be set down by one who should make it appear hideous, as did he who translated the Latin of the *Ethics*, I was careful myself to set it down, trusting rather in myself than in another.

11 I was further moved to defend it from its many detractors who dispraise it and commend the others, especially the Langue d'Oc,[12] saying that this is more beauteous and better than that, departing herein from the truth.

12 For by this comment the great excellence of the vernacular of *Sì*[13] will be perceived, to wit, how by it the most lofty and most novel conceptions are expressed, well-nigh as aptly, as adequately, and as gracefully as in Latin itself; for in rhymed compositions, because of the incidental adornments which are inwoven therein, to wit, rhyme and rhythm and regulated number, its own excellence cannot be made manifest; no more than the beauty of a woman can when the adornment of decking and of garments brings her more admiration than she brings herself.

---

12 Spanish; see *De vulgari eloquentia* I.viii.6.

13 Italian.

13 Wherefore, let him who would rightly judge of a woman look on her when only her natural beauty accompanies her, severed from all incidental adornment; even as this comment will be wherein shall be perceived the smoothness of its syllables, the propriety of its rules, and the sweet discourses that are made of it, all which he who shall rightly consider it will perceive to be full of sweetest and most attractive beauty.

14 But since it is a most effective part of invention to demonstrate the viciousness and malice of the accuser, I will tell, to the confusion of those who accuse the Italian speech, what it is that moves them thereto. And of this I will presently make a separate chapter, that their infamy may be the more conspicuous.

Chapter XI

1 To the perpetual infamy and suppression of the evil men of Italy who prize the vernacular of another and disprize their own, I declare that their impulse arises from five detestable causes:

2 The first, blindness in discernment; the second, disingenuous excusing; the third, desire of vainglory; the fourth, the prompting of envy; the fifth and last, abjectness of mind or pusillanimity. And each one of these guilty tendencies has so great a following that there be few exempt from them.

3 Of the first, one may thus discourse. Like as the sensitive part of the mind hath its eyes whereby it apprehendeth the difference of things, insofar as they are colored externally, even so hath the rational part its eye whereby it apprehendeth the difference of things, insofar as they be ordained to some certain end. And this same eye is discernment.

4 And like as he who is blind with the eyes of sense must ever judge of evil or good according to others, so he who is blind of the light of discernment must ever follow in his judgment, after mere report, true or false. And so, whensoever the leader is blind, he himself, and also the one, blind likewise, who leaneth upon him, must

needs come to an evil end. Wherefore it is written that "the blind shall lead the blind, and so shall they both fall into the ditch."[14]

5 Now this same report hath long been counter to our vernacular, for reasons which shall be discoursed of below. Following the which, the blind ones spoken of above, who are almost without number, with their hands upon the shoulders of these liars, have fallen into the ditch of the false opinion from which they know not how to escape.

6 To the habit of this light of discernment the populace are specially blinded, because they are occupied from the beginning of their lives with some trade, and so direct their minds to it, by force of necessity, that they give heed to nought else.

7 And because the habit of a virtue, whether moral or intellectual, may not be had of a sudden, but must needs be acquired by practice, and they devote their practice to some art, and are not careful to discern other things, it is impossible for them to have discernment.

8 Wherefore it comes to pass that they often cry "long live their death," and "death to their life," if only some one raise the cry. And this is the most perilous defect involved in their blindness. Wherefore Boethius considers popular glory an empty thing, because he sees that it has no discernment.[15]

9 Such are to be regarded as sheep and not men. For if one sheep were to fling itself over a precipice of a thousand paces, all the others would go after it. And if one sheep leap for any reason as it passes a street, all the others leap, although they see nothing to leap over.

10 And ere now I myself have seen one after another leap into a well because one leapt into it (thinking, I suppose, that it was leaping over a wall) although the shepherd, wailing and shouting, set himself with arms and breast before them.

---

14   Matthew 15:14.
15   *Consolation* III, pr. vi.6.

11 The second sect who oppose our vernacular is made up by disingenuous excusings. There are many who love to be thought masters rather than to be such, and to avoid the opposite, to wit, not being thought such, they ever find fault with the material of their art that is furnished them, or else the instrument. For example, a bad smith finds fault with the iron furnished him, and a bad harper finds fault with the harp, thinking to throw the blame of the bad knife or the bad music upon the iron and upon the harp, and to remove it from himself.

12 And in like manner there be some, and they are not few, who would have men think them poets, and to excuse themselves for not poetizing, or for poetizing badly, they accuse and blame the material, to wit, their own vernacular, and praise that of others, which they are not required to forge.

13 And if any one would see how far this iron is really to be blamed, let him look upon the works which the good artificers make from it, and he will recognize the disingenuousness of those who by blaming it think to excuse themselves.

14 Against such as these Tully cries out in the beginning of a book of his, which is called the book *Concerning the Goal of Good*, because in his time they found fault with the Latin of the Romans, and commended the grammar of the Greeks, for the like reasons for which these others now make the Italian speech cheap, and that of Provence precious.

15 The third sect against our vernacular is made up by desire of vain glory. There are many who by handling things composed in some tongue, not their own, and by commending the said tongue, look to be more admired than by handling things in their own tongue. And doubtless it is a matter of some praise of intellect, rightly, to apprehend a foreign tongue. But it is blameworthy to commend it beyond the truth, in order to vaunt oneself for such acquirement.

16 The fourth is made up by the prompting of envy. As was said above, there is envy wherever there is similarity. Amongst men of one tongue there is similarity in vernacular, and because one cannot handle it as another can, envy springs up.

17 So the envious man goes subtly to work, and doth not find with him who poetizes the fault of not knowing how to write, but finds fault with that which is the material of his work, so that by sliding the work on that side he may deprive the poet of honor and of fame; as one should find fault with the steel of a sword for the sake of discrediting not the steel, but the whole work of the master.

18 The fifth and last sect is impelled by abjectness of mind. The large-souled man ever exalts himself in his heart, and so counterwise the small-souled man ever holds himself less than he really is.

19 And because magnifying and minifying always have regard to something in comparison to which the large-souled man makes himself great, and the small-souled man makes himself little, it comes to pass that the large-souled man always makes others of less account than they are, and the small-souled man of more.

20 And because with the same measure wherewith a man measures himself he measures the things that are his, which are, as it were, a part of himself, it comes to pass that the large-souled man's things always seem to him better than they are, and the things of others worse, and the small-souled man always thinks of his things of little worth, and the things of others of much.

21 Wherefore many, by reason of this abjectness, depreciate their own vernacular, and praise that of others. And all these together make up the detestable wretches of Italy who hold cheap that costly vernacular, if which be vile in aught it is only insofar as it sounds upon the prostitute lips of these adulterers, by whose guidance the blind men go of whom I made mention under the head of the first cause.

Chapter XII

1 If the flame of fire were issuing plain to see from the windows of a house, and one should ask whether there was a fire therein, and another should answer him yay, I could not well judge which of the two were most to be derided. And of no other fashion were his question and my answer should one ask me, after the reasons set forth above, whether love of my own tongue is in me and should I answer him yay.

2 But none the less I have yet to show that not only love but most perfect love of it, abides in me, and I have yet further to denounce its adversaries. And in demonstrating this to whoso shall rightly understand, I will tell how I became its friend, and then how the friendship was confirmed.

3 I say, then (as Tully may be seen to write in that of *Friendship*, not departing therein from the teaching of the Philosopher set forth in the eighth and ninth of the *Ethics*) that nearness and excellence are the natural causes which generate love, and benefaction, community of study, and comradeship are the causes which foster love, and all these causes have been at work begetting and strengthening the love which I bear to my vernacular, as I will briefly show.

4 A thing is near in proportion as of all the things of its kind it is most closely united to a man. Wherefore a son is nearest to his father, and of all arts medicine is nearest to the doctor, and music to the musician, because they are more closely united to them than are the rest. Of all lands that is nearest to a man wherein he maintains himself, because it is more closely united to him.

5 And thus a man's proper vernacular is nearest to him, inasmuch as it is most closely united to him. For it is singly and alone in his mind before any other. And not only is it united to him essentially, in itself, but also, incidentally, inasmuch as it is conjoined with the persons closest to him, as his relatives, his fellow-citizens, and his own people.

6 Such, then, is a man's own vernacular, which we will not call near, but most nearest to him. Wherefore, if nearness be the seed of friendship, as was said above, it is clear that it is amongst the causes of the love which I bear to my tongue, which is most near to me above the others.

7 It was the above-said cause, namely, that that is most closely united which at first has sole possession of the mind, that gave rise to the custom which makes first-born sons succeed alone as the closer, and because closer, more loved.

8 Again, its excellence makes me its friend. And here you are to know that every excellence proper to a thing is to be loved in that thing, as in masculinity to be well bearded, and in femininity to be well smooth of beard over all the face, as in a setter good scent, and in a boar-hound good speed.

9 And the more proper is the excellence, the better is it to be loved. Wherefore, though every virtue is to be loved in man, that is most to be loved in him which is most human, and that is justice which abides only in the rational or intellectual part that is in the will.

10–11 This is so much to be loved that, as the Philosopher says in the fifth of the *Ethics*, they who are its foes, as are robbers and plunderers, love it; and therefore we see that its contrary, to wit, injustice, is most hated, as treachery, ingratitude, forgery, theft, rapine, cheating, and their likes, which be such inhuman sins that, to shield himself from the infamy thereof, long usage alloweth that man may speak of himself, as was said above, and that he have leave to declare himself faithful and loyal.

12 Of this virtue I shall hereafter speak more at length in the fourteenth treatise, and here leaving it I return to the matter in hand. That has been shown, then, to be the most proper excellence of a thing which is most loved and praised in it, and we must see in each case what that excellence is.

13 Now we see that in all matters of speech rightly to manifest the conception is the most loved and commended. This, then, is its prime excellence, and inasmuch as this excellence abideth in our vernacular, as hath been shown above, in another chapter, it is clear that it is of the causes of the love which I bear to the said vernacular, because, as already said, excellence is a cause that generates love.

Chapter XIII

1 Having told how these two things exist in my own tongue, whereby I was made its friend—to wit, its nearness to myself and its own excellence—I will tell how, by benefaction and harmony of study, and the good will of long comradeship, the friendship has been confirmed and fostered.

2 I say first that I in myself have received the greatest of benefactions from it, and therefore be it known that amongst all benefactions that is greatest which is most precious to him who receives it; and nothing is so precious as that for the sake of which all the others are desired, and all other things are desired for the perfection of him who desires them.

3 Wherefore, since a man hath two perfections, the first and the second (the first gives him being, and the second gives him well-being), if my proper tongue hath been the cause both of the one and of the other, I have received the very greatest benefaction from it. And that it hath been the cause of my existence, if my being here at all did not establish it, may be briefly shown.

4 May not there be many efficient causes with respect to one thing, though one of them be so in a higher degree than the others? For the fire and the hammer are efficient causes of the knife, though the smith is so in chiefest place. Now this my vernacular it was that brought together them who begat me, for by it they spoke, even as the fire disposes the iron for the smith who is making the knife. Wherefore it is manifest that it took part in my begetting, and so was a certain cause of my being.

5 Moreover, this my vernacular led me into the way of knowledge, which is our specific perfection, inasmuch as by it I entered upon Latin which was explained to me in it, which Latin was then my path to further advance. Wherefore it is plain and is acknowledged by me that it hath been my benefactor in the highest degree.

6 Also it hath been of one same purpose with me which I can thus prove. Everything naturally studies its own preservation. Wherefore if the vernacular could in itself pursue any purpose, it would study this preservation, and this would be adapting itself to greater stability, and greater stability it could not have save by binding itself in numbers and in rhymes.

7 And this same study hath been mine, as is so manifest as to need no witness. Wherefore one same study hath been common to it and to me. Whence by this harmony our friendship hath been confirmed and fostered.

8 Further, ours is the good will of comradeship. For from the beginning of my life I have abode in good will and communion with it, and have used it in pondering, in explaining, and in questioning.

9 Wherefore if friendship grows by comradeship, as is plain to the sense, it is manifest that it hath grown in me to the highest, since I have passed all my time in company with this same vernacular.

10 Wherefore it appears that all the causes which can generate and foster friendship have combined for this friendship. Whence the conclusion that not only love but most perfect love for it, is that which I ought to have, and which I have.

11 So, turning back our eyes, and gathering up the reasons already noted, it may be seen that this bread with which the viands of the odes written below must be eaten is sufficiently purged from its blemishes, and from being made of oats. Wherefore it is time to set about serving the viands.

12 This shall be that oaten bread whereby thousands shall be sated, and my baskets shall be left full for me. This shall be the new light, the new Sun, which shall rise when the wanted Sun shall set, and shall give light to them who are in darkness and in shadow as to the wanted Sun which shines not for them.

Book II

Voi che intendendo il terzo ciel movete

I

Ye who by understanding move the third heaven,
hearken to the discourse which is in my heart,
for I may not tell it to any other, so strange it seemeth me.
Tis the heaven which followeth your worth, gentle creatures,
that ye be, that draweth me into the state wherein I find me.
Wherefore the discourse of the life which I endure
meseems were worthily directed unto you.
Therefore I pray that ye give me heed anent[16] it.
I will tell the wondrous story of my heart,
how the sad soul waileth in it,
and how a spirit discourseth counter to her
that cometh upon the rays of your star.

II

Is wont to be the life of my grieving heart,
a sweet thought that would take its way
many a time to the feet of your Sire,
Where it beheld a lady in glory,
of whom it discoursed to me so sweetly,
that my soul said ever, 'Fain would I go thither.'
Now one appears who puts him to flight,
and lords it over me with such might,
that my heart so trembles thereat as to reveal it in outward semblance.
He makes me gaze upon a lady,
and saith, 'Who would behold salvation,
heedfully let him look upon this lady's eyes,
if he fear not the anguish of sighings.'

III

Findeth such an adversary as destroyeth him,
the humble thought that is wont to discourse to me
of an angel who is crowned in heaven.
The soul wails, so doth she still grieve thereat,

---

16   About, concerning.

and saith, 'O wretched me! how fleeth
that tender one who hath consoled me!'
Of my eyes this afflicted one exclaimeth,
'What hour was that wherein such lady looked upon them!
and wherefore did they not believe me concerning her?
I ever said, *Verily in her eyes
must he needs stand who slays my peers.*
And my perceiving it availed me nought
against their gazing upon such an one that I am slain thereby.'

IV

'Thou art not slain, only thou art dismayed,
O soul of ours who dost so lament thee,'
saith a little spirit of gentle love.
'For this fair lady, whom thou perceivest,
hath so transformed thy life,
that thou art terrified, so cowardly hast thou become.
See how tender she is, and humble,
sage and courteous in her greatness,
and think henceforth to call her lady.
For if thou deceive not thyself, thou shalt see
adornment of such lofty miracles
that thou shalt say, *Love, very lord,
behold thy handmaid, do as pleaseth thee.*'

TORNATA

Ode! I believe that they shall be but rare
who shall rightly understand thy meaning,
so intricate and knotty is thy utterance of it.
Wherefore, if perchance it come about,
that thou take thy way into the presence of folk
who seem not rightly to perceive it,
then I pray thee to take heart again,
and say to them, O my beloved lastling,
'Give heed at least how beautiful I am.'

Chapter I

[1] Now that, by way of introductory discourse, my bread has been sufficiently prepared by my ministration in the preceding treatise, time calls and requires that my ship should issue from the port. Wherefore, adjusting the sail of reason to the breeze of my longing, I enter upon the open sea, with the hope of a fair journey, and of a wholesome port and praiseworthy, at the close of this my feast. But that this my food be the more profitable, ere the first viands are served I would show how it must be eaten.

[2] I say that, as was told in the first chapter, this exposition must be both literal and allegorical, and that this may be understood, it should be known that writings may be taken and should be expounded chiefly in four senses.

[3] The first is called the literal, and it is the one that extends no further than the letter as it stands. The second is called the allegorical, and it is the one that hides itself under the mantle of these tales, and is a truth hidden under beauteous fiction. As when Ovid says that Orpheus with his lyre made wild beasts tame and made trees and rocks approach him, which would say that the wise man with the instrument of his voice maketh cruel hearts tender and humble, and moveth to his will such as have not the life of science and of art. For they that have not the rational life are as good as stones.

[4] And why this way of hiding was devised by the sages will be shown in the last treatise but one. It is true that the theologians take this sense otherwise than the poets do, but since it is my purpose here to follow the method of the poets, I shall take the allegorical sense after the use of the poets.

[5] The third sense is called the moral, and this is the one that lecturers should go intently noting throughout the scriptures for their own behoof and that of their disciples. Thus we may note in the gospel, when Christ ascended the mountain for the transfiguration, that of the twelve apostles he took with him but three, wherein the moral may be understood that in the most secret things we should have but few companions.

6 The fourth sense is called the anagogical, that is to say, "above the sense," and this is when a scripture is spiritually expounded which even in the literal sense, by the very things it signifies, signifies again some portion of the supernal things of eternal glory, as may be seen in that song of the prophet which saith that when the people of Israel came out of Egypt, Judea was made whole and free.

7 Which, although it be manifestly true according to the letter, is nonetheless true in its spiritual intention; to wit, that when the soul goeth forth out of sin it is made holy and free in its power.

8 And in thus expounding, the literal sense should always come first as the one in the meaning whereof the others are included, and without which it were impossible and irrational to attend to the others, and especially to the allegorical.

9 It is impossible because in everything that has an inside and an outside it is impossible to come at the inside save we first come at the outside. Wherefore, inasmuch as in the scriptures the literal sense is ever outside, it is impossible to come at the others without first coming at the literal.

10 Again, it is impossible because in every natural and artificial thing it is impossible to proceed to the form without first duly disposing the subject on which the form must be impressed. Just as it is impossible for the form of gold to accrue if the material, to wit, its subject, be not first digested and prepared, or for the form of a chest to come if the material, to wit, the wood, be not first disposed and prepared.

11 Wherefore, inasmuch as the literal meaning is always the subject and material of the others, especially the allegorical, it is impossible to come at the knowledge of the others before coming at the knowledge of it.

12 Further, it is impossible because in every natural or artificial thing it is impossible to proceed unless the foundation be first made, as in a house, and as in study. Wherefore, since the demonstration is the building up of knowledge, and the literal demonstra-

tion is the foundation of the others, especially the allegorical, it is impossible to come at the others before coming at this.

13 Again, suppose it were possible, it would be irrational, that is to say, out of order, and would therefore be carried on with much irksomeness and with much error. Wherefore, saith the Philosopher in the first of the *Physics*, nature wills that we should proceed in due order in our learning, to wit, by proceeding from that which we know better to that which we know not so well.[17] I say that nature wills it, inasmuch as this way of learning is naturally born in us.

14 And therefore, if the other senses are less known than the literal (which it is manifestly apparent that they are) it would be irrational to proceed to demonstrate them if the literal had not been demonstrated first.

15 Therefore, for these reasons, I shall always first discourse concerning each ode as to the literal sense of the same, and after that I shall discourse of its allegory, that is, its hidden truth, and from time to time I shall touch upon the other senses incidentally, as shall suit place and time.

Chapter II

1 To begin with, then, I say that the star of Venus had twice already revolved in that circle of hers which makes her appear at even or at morn, according to the two diverse periods, since the passing away of that blessed Beatrice who liveth in heaven with the angels and on earth with my soul, when that gentle lady, of whom I made mention in the end of the *New Life*, first appeared to my eyes accompanied with love, and took some place in my mind.[18]

2 And, as is told by me in the aforesaid book, more of her gentleness than of my choice it came to pass that I consented to be hers, for she showed herself to be impassioned by so great pity for my widowed life that the spirits of my eyes became in supreme degree her

---

17   *Physics* I.1.

18   See *Vita nuova* XXXIV.

friends. And when thus affected, they so wrought within me that my pleasure was content to put itself at the disposal of this image.

3 But because love cometh not to birth and growth and perfect state in a moment, but needeth some certain time and nourishment of thoughts, especially where there be counter-thoughts that impede it, it was necessary ere this new love became perfect that there should be much strife between the thought which nourished it and that which was counter to it, and which still held the citadel of my mind on behalf of that glorified Beatrice.

4 Wherefore, the one was constantly reinforced from before and the other by memory from behind. And the reinforcement from before increased day by day (which the other might not) as hindering me, in a certain sense, from turning my face backwards. Wherefore, it seemed to me so strange and also so hard to endure that I might not sustain it.

5 And with a kind of cry (to excuse myself for the change wherein, methought, I showed lack of firmness) I directed my voice to that quarter whence came the victory of the new thought (and the same, being a celestial virtue, was most victorious), and I began to say, *Ye who by understanding move the third heaven.*

6 Rightly to grasp the meaning of the ode it is necessary first to understand its divisions, so that it may thereafter be easy to perceive its meaning. And that there may be no need of setting these same words in front of the expositions of the other odes, I say that this same order, which will be observed in this treatise, it is my intention to follow in all the others.

7 I say, then, that the ode before us is composed of three chief parts. The first is the first verse of it, wherein are introduced, that they may hearken to that which I intend to say, certain Intelligences, or, to name them after the more customary use, certain Angels, which are set over the revolution of the heaven of Venus, as its movers.

8 The second is the three verses which follow after the first, wherein is shown that which was heard in the spirit within as between the diverse thoughts.

9 The third is the fifth and last verse, wherein a man is wont to address the work itself, as though to hearten it. And all these three parts in order are to be expounded after the fashion above expressed.

Chapter III

1 The more clearly I discern the literal sense (which is our present concern) of the first part, according to the above division, we must know who and how many are they who are summoned to hear me; and what is this third heaven which I declare that they move. And first I will speak of the heaven, and then I will speak of those to whom I address myself.

2 And albeit these things, in proportion to the reality, may be but little known, yet what little human reason sees of them hath more delight than the much and the certain concerning things whereof we judge more fully according to the opinion of the Philosopher in that *Of the Animals*.[19]

3 I say, then, that concerning the number of the heavens and their position, diverse opinions have been held by many, although the truth hath at last been found. Aristotle, following only the ancient grossness of the astrologers, believed that there were no more than eight heavens, the extremest of which, containing all the sum of things, was that whereon the stars are fixed, to wit, the eighth sphere, and that outside of that there was no other.

4 Moreover, he believed that the heaven of the Sun came next after that of the Moon, that is that it was the second from us. And this so erroneous opinion of his, whoso wills may see in the second *Of Heaven and the World*, which is in the second of the *Books Of Nature*. But truly he shows his excuse for this in the twelfth of the *Metaphysics*, where he lets us clearly see that he was just following the opinion of others where he had to speak of Astrology.[20]

---

19   *De partibus animalium* I.5.

20   *Metaphysics* XII.8.

5 Thereafter Ptolemy, perceiving that the eighth sphere had more than one movement, since he saw that its circle departed from the direct circle, which turns the whole from east to west, constrained by the principles of philosophy (which of necessity will have a *Primum Mobile* of perfect simplicity) laid down the existence of another heaven, outside that of the stars, which should make that revolution from east to west. And I say that it is completed in about four and twenty hours, that is, in twenty hours and three hours and fourteen out of fifteen parts of another, roughly reckoning.

6 So that, according to him and according to the tenets of astrology and philosophy (after the observation of these motions) the moving heavens are nine; and their relative position is manifested and determined according as, by the arts of perspective, arithmetic, and geometry, it is perceived by sense and reason; and by further observation of the senses, as in the eclipse of the Sun, it appears sensibly that the Moon is beneath the Sun, and by the testimony of Aristotle, who saw with his own eyes (as he tells us in the second *Of Heaven and the World* [21]) the Moon, being at the half, pass below Mars with her darkened side, and Mars remain hidden, till he reappeared from the other shining side of the Moon which was facing the west.

7 And the order of their position is this. The first in the enumeration is that wherein is the Moon. The second is that wherein is Mercury. The third is that wherein is Venus. The fourth is that wherein is the Sun. The fifth is that wherein is Mars. The sixth is that wherein is Jupiter. The seventh is that wherein is Saturn. The eighth is that of the fixed stars. The ninth is that which is not perceived by the senses, save by that movement which was spoken of above. And it is called by many the crystalline heaven, that is, the diaphanous, or all-transparent.

8 But beyond all these the Catholics assert the Empyrean heaven, which is as much as to say, the heaven of flame, or the luminous heaven, and they assert it to be immovable, because it hath in itself with respect to every part that which its manner demandeth.

---

21   *De coelo* II.12.

9 And this is the cause of the *Primum Mobile* having the swiftest motion, because by reason of the most fervid appetite wherewith every part of this ninth heaven, which is the next below it, longeth to be conjoined with every part of this divinest and tranquil heaven, it revolves therein with so great yearning, that its swiftness is scarce to be comprehended.[22]

10 But still and tranquil is the place of that supreme deity which alone completely perceiveth itself. This is the place of the blessed spirits, according as holy Church, which may not lie, will have it. And Aristotle likewise seemeth to agree hereto (to whoso rightly understandeth) in the first *Of Heaven and the World*.[23]

11–12 This is the sovereign edifice of the world wherein all the world is included, and outside of which there is not. And it is not itself in space but was formed only in the Primal Mind, which the Greeks call *Protonoë*. This is that "magnificence" whereof the psalmist spoke, when he saith to God, "Thy magnificence is exalted above the heavens."[24] And thus, gathering up what hath been discoursed, it appears that there are ten heavens, of which that of Venus is the third, whereof mention is made in that passage which I am intent on expounding.[25]

13 And be it known that every heaven beneath the Crystalline has two poles fixed with respect to itself, and the ninth has them firm and fixed, and immutable in every respect; and each one, the ninth as well as the rest, has a circle which may be called the equator of its proper heaven, which is equally distant in every part of its revolution from either pole, as he may see by the senses who revolves an apple, or other circular thing. And this circle in each heaven hath greater swiftness of motion than any other part in that heaven, as may be seen by whoso rightly considereth.

14 And each part in proportion as it is nearer thereto moveth more rapidly, and in proportion as it is remote therefrom and nearer to

---

22 *Par.* I.76–78, 121–123, XXIII.112–114, XXVII.97–99.

23 *De coelo* I.3.

24 Psalm 8:2.

25 *Par.* XXVII.109–111.

the pole more slowly, because its revolution is smaller and must of necessity take place in the same time as the greater.

15 I say, further, that in proportion as the heaven is nearer to the equatorial circle, it is more noble in comparison to its poles, because it hath more movement, and more actuality, and more life, and more form, and it touches more of the one which is above, and by consequence hath more virtue. And so the stars of the starry heaven are fuller of virtue, as between themselves, the nearer they are to this circle.

16 And upon the hump of this circle in the heaven of Venus, of which we are at present treating, is a spherule which revolves on its own account in that heaven, the circle of which the astrologers call an "epicycle." And even as the great sphere revolves on two poles, so does this little one, and so has this little one its equatorial circle. And so is it more noble in proportion as it is nearer thereto, and upon the arc or hump of this circle is fixed the most shining star of Venus.

17 And although it be said that there are ten heavens, yet according to very truth this number doth not embrace them all; for this of which mention hath been made, to wit, the epicycle whereon the star is fixed, is a heaven or sphere of itself; and it hath not one same essence with that which beareth it, though it be more co-natural to it than to the others, and is spoken of as one heaven with it, and the one and the other is called the heaven of the star.

18 How the other heavens and the other stars be, we are not at present to treat; let that suffice which hath been said of the truth of the third heaven, with which I am at present concerned and as to which all that is needful for us for the present purpose has been completely expounded.

Chapter IV

[1] Now that it has been demonstrated in the preceding chapter what this third heaven is, and how it is disposed in itself, it remains to expound who they be who move it.

[2] Be it known, therefore, firstly, that the movers thereof are substances sejunct[26] from matter, to wit, Intelligences, which are vulgarly called Angels. And of these creatures, as of the heavens, diverse have held diverse opinions albeit the truth has been now found.[27]

[3] There were certain philosophers, of whom Aristotle appears to be in his *Metaphysics*[28] (although in the first *Of Heaven and the World* he incidentally appears to think otherwise[29]), who believed that there were only so many of them as there were circulating in the heavens, and no more, saying that the rest would have been eternally in vain without operation, which, they held, was impossible, inasmuch as their being consists in their operation.

[4] Others were there such as Plato, a man of supreme excellence, who laid down not only as many Intelligences as there are movements of heaven but just as many as there are kinds of things. As all men one kind, and all gold another kind, and all riches another, and so throughout the whole.

[5] And they would have it that as the Intelligences of the heavens are the generators of the same, each of his own, so those others were the generators of the other things, and the exemplars each one of its own kind. And Plato calls them Ideas, which is as much as to say Forms and Universals.

[6] The Gentiles called them gods and goddesses, though they did not conceive them so philosophically as did Plato; and they adored images of them, and made most magnificent temples for them; for

---

26   Separated.

27   *Par.* II.133–138, IV.61–63, XXVIII.70–78.

28   *Metaphysics* XI.8.

29   *De coelo* I.3.

Juno, for example, whom they called the goddess of power; for Vulcan, whom they called god of fire; for Pallas or Minerva, whom they called goddess of wisdom; and for Ceres, whom they called goddess of corn.

7 The which opinion is manifested by the testimony of the poets, who from time to time outline the fashion of the Gentiles both in their sacrifices and in their faith; and it is also manifested in many ancient names, which survive either as names or as surnames of places and of ancient buildings, as whoso will may easily discover.

8 And although the above-mentioned opinions were furnished by human reason and by no small observation, the truth was not yet perceived, and this both by defect of reason and by defect of instruction. For even reason may perceive that the above-said creatures are in far greater number than are the effects which men are able to note.

9 And one reason is this. No one—neither philosopher nor Gentile nor Jew nor Christian nor any sect—doubts that either all of them, or the greater part, are full of all blessedness, or doubts that these blessed ones are in the most perfect state.

10 And as, inasmuch as human nature, as it here exists, hath not only one blessedness but two, to wit, that of the civil life and that of the contemplative life, it were irrational did we perceive those others to have the blessedness of the active that is the civil life, in guiding the world, and not that of the contemplative life, which is more excellent and more divine.

11 And inasmuch as the one that hath the blessedness of guiding may not have the other, because their intellect is one and continuous, there must needs be others exempt from this ministry whose life consists only in speculation.

12 And because this life is the more divine, and because in proportion as the thing is more divine it is more like to God, it is manifest that this life is more loved by God. And if it be more loved, its share of blessedness hath been more ample. And if it be more ample, he hath assigned more living beings to it than to the other.

Wherefore, we conclude that the number of these creatures is very far in excess of what the effects reveal.

13 And this is not counter to what Aristotle seems to say in the tenth of the *Ethics*, to wit, that the speculative life alone fits with the sejunct substances.[30] For if we allow that the speculative life alone fits with them, yet upon the speculation of certain of these followeth the circulation of the heavens, which is the guiding of the world, which world is a kind of ordered civility perceived in the speculation of its movers.

14 The second reason is that no effect is greater than its cause, for the cause cannot give what itself hath not. Wherefore, since the divine intellect is the cause of everything, especially of the human intellect, it follows that the human intellect transcendeth not the divine, but it is out of all proportion transcended by it.

15 So that if we, for the reason above given and for many others, understand that God could have made almost innumerable spiritual creatures, it is manifest that he hath indeed made this greater number. Many other reasons may be perceived, but let these suffice for the present.

16 Nor let any marvel if these and other reasons which we may have for this belief are not brought to complete demonstration. Because for that very reason we should wonder at the excellence of these beings, which transcends the eyes of the human mind (as saith the Philosopher in the second of the *Metaphysics*), and should affirm their existence.

17 For, albeit we have no perception of them by sense, wherefrom our knowledge hath its rise, yet is there in our intellect a kind of reflected glow of the light of their most vivid existence, insofar as we perceive the above-said reasons and many others. Just as a man whose eyes are closed may affirm that the air is luminous because of some certain glow, or as a ray that passes through the pupils of the bat. For even so are the eyes of our intellect closed, so long as the mind is bound and imprisoned by the organs of our body.

---

30   *Ethics* X.8.

Chapter V

1 It hath been said that by defect of instruction the ancients perceived not the truth concerning the spiritual creatures, albeit the people of Israel were in part instructed by their prophets, through whom, after many manners of speech and by many modes, God spoke to them,[31] even as saith the Apostle.

2 But as for us, we have been taught about this by him who came from him, by him who made them, by him who preserves them, to wit, the emperor of the universe, who is Christ, son of the sovereign God, and son of the Virgin Mary (very woman and daughter of Joachim and Anna), very man who was slain by us, whereby he brought us life.

3 And he was the light which lightens us in the darkness,[32] as saith John the Evangelist; and he told us the truth of these things, which we might not know without him, nor see them as they are in truth.

4 The first thing and the first secret which he showed us thereanent was one of the aforesaid creatures themselves; which was that great ambassador of his who came to Mary, a young damsel of thirteen years, on the part of the holy king celestial. This our Saviour said with his own mouth, that the Father could give him many legions of angels. When it was said to him that the Father had given commandment to his angels to minister unto him and serve him, he denied it not.

5 Wherefore, it is manifest to us that these creatures exist in most extended number. Because his spouse and secretary, Holy Church (of whom Solomon saith, "Who is this that cometh up from the wilderness, full of those things that give delight, leaning upon her friend?"[33]) affirms, believes, and preaches that these most noble creatures are, as it were, innumerable, and she divides them into three hierarchies, which is to say, three holy or divine principali-

---

31   Hebrews 1:1.

32   John 1:5.

33   Song of Solomon 8:5.

ties. And each hierarchy has three orders, so that the church holds and affirms nine orders of spiritual creatures.[34]

6 The first is that of the Angels, the second of the Archangels, the third of the Thrones; and these three orders make the first hierarchy, not first in the order of nobility, nor in order of creation (for the others are more noble, and all were created at once), but first in the order of our ascent to their loftiness. Next come the Dominations, afterwards the Virtues, then the Principalities; and these make the second hierarchy. Above these are the Powers, and the Cherubim, and above all are the Seraphim; and these make the third hierarchy.

7 And the number of the hierarchies, and that of the orders, constitutes a most potent system of their speculation. For inasmuch as the Divine Majesty is in three persons which have one substance, they may be contemplated in threefold manner.

8 For the supreme power of the Father may be contemplated; and this it is that the first hierarchy, to wit, first in nobility and last in our enumeration, gazes upon. And the supreme wisdom of the Son may be contemplated; and this it is that the second hierarchy gazes upon. And the supreme and most burning love of the Holy Spirit may be contemplated; and this it is that the third hierarchy gazes upon; the which being nearest unto us gives us of the gifts which it receiveth.[35]

9 And inasmuch as each person of the divine Trinity may be considered in threefold manner, there are in each hierarchy three orders diversely contemplating.

10 The Father may be considered without respect to aught save himself; and this contemplation the Seraphim do use, who see more of the first cause than any other angelic nature. The Father may be considered according as he hath relation to the Son, to wit, how he is parted from him and how united with him; and this do the Cherubim contemplate. The Father may further be considered

---

34   *Par.* XIII.58–60, XXVIII.91–93, 115–120.
35   *Inf.* III.4–6.

according as from him proceedeth the Holy Spirit, and how he is parted from him and how united with him; and this contemplation the Powers do use.

11 And in like fashion there may be speculation of the Son and of the Holy Spirit. Wherefore, it behoves that there be nine manners of contemplating spirits to gaze upon the light which alone seeth itself completely.

12 And here is a word which may not be passed in silence. I say that out of all these orders some certain were lost so soon as they were created, I take it to the number of a tenth part, for the restoration of which human nature was afterward created.[36] The revolving heavens, which are nine, declare the numbers, the orders, and the hierarchies. And the tenth proclaimeth the very oneness and stability of God. And therefore, saith the Psalmist, "the heavens declare the glory of God, and the firmament proclaimeth the works of his hands."[37]

13 Wherefore, it is rational to believe that the movers of the Moon be of the order of Angels, and those of Mercury be Archangels, and those of Venus be Thrones. The which, taking their nature from the love of the Holy Spirit, make their work conatural thereto, to wit, the movement of that heaven which is full of love. Whence the form of the said heaven conceiveth an ardour of virtue to kindle souls down here to love, according to their disposition.

14 And because the ancients perceived that this heaven was the cause of love down here, they said that Love was the son of Venus. Even as Vergil testifieth in the first of the *Aeneid*, where Venus saith to Love, "My son my power, son of the supreme father, who heedest not the darts of Typhoeus."[38] And Ovid in the fifth of the *Metamorphoses*, when he tells how Venus said to Love, "My son my arms, my might."[39]

---

36   *Par.* XXV.124–126.

37   Psalm 19:1.

38   *Aeneid* I.664.

39   *Metamorphoses* V.365; *Purg.* I.19, *Par.* VIII.1–9.

15 And it is these Thrones that be appointed for the guidance of this heaven, in no great number. But the philosophers and the astrologers have diversely estimated it, according as they diversely estimated the circulation of the heavens, although all be at one in this that they be so many as the movements which the heaven makes.

16 Which movements are (according as we find the best demonstration of the astrologers summarized in the book of the *Collection of the Stars*) three. One according to which the star moves in its epicycle. The second according as the epicycle moves together with its whole heaven, equally with that of the Sun. The third according as that same whole heaven moves, following the movement of the starry sphere, from west to east one degree in a hundred years. So that for these three movements there are three movers.

17 Further, the whole of this heaven is moved and revolves together with the epicycle, from east to west, once every natural day. Whether which movement be of some intellect, or whether it be of the swaying of the *Primum Mobile*, God knoweth. For to me it seemeth presumptuous to judge.

18 It is by understanding solely that these movers produce the circulation in that proper subject which each moveth. The most noble form of heaven, which hath in itself the principle of this passive nature, revolves at the touch of the moving virtue which understandeth it. And I mean by "touch" not bodily touch but virtue which directeth itself thereto. And these movers be they to whom my speech is addressed, and to whom I make my demand.[40]

Chapter VI

1 According as was said above in the third chapter of this treatise, rightly to understand the first part of the ode before us it was needful to discourse of those heavens and of their movers. And discoursed it hath been in the three preceding chapters. I say then to those whom I have shown to be the movers of the heaven of Venus,

---

40   *Par.* II.127–138.

ye who by understanding (to wit, with the intellect alone, as said above) *move the third heaven, hearken to the discourse*, and I say not "hearken" as though they hear any sound, for they have not sense, but I say "hearken," to wit, with that hearing which they have, which is understanding by the intellect.

² I say, *hearken to the discourse which is in my heart*, to wit, inside of me, for it hath not yet appeared without. Be it known that in all this ode, according to one sense and the other, the heart is to be taken as the secret recess within and not as any other special part of the soul or of the body.

³ When I have called them to hearken to that which I would say, I assign two reasons why I should fitly speak to them. The one is the strangeness of my state, which since it hath not been experienced by other men might not be so well understood by them as by those beings who understand their own effects in their operation. And this reason I hint at when I say, *for I may not tell it to any other, so strange it seemeth me*.

⁴ The other reason is, that when a man receiveth a benefit or a hurt he should rehearse it to him who doth it to him, if he may, ere he rehearse it to another. So that if it be a benefit, he who receiveth it may show himself grateful towards the benefactor, and if it be a hurt, he may lead the doer by his gentle words to salutary compassion.

⁵ And this reason I hint at when I say, *tis the heaven which followeth your worth, gentle creatures that ye be, that draweth me into the state wherein I find me*. That is to say "your operation," to wit, "your circulation," is it that has drawn me into my present state. Wherefore, I conclude and say, that my speech ought to be to them, as was declared above, and this I say here, *wherefore the discourse of the life which I endure meseems, were worthily directed unto you*. And after assigning these reasons I pray them to give heed when I say, *therefore I pray that ye give me heed anent it*.

⁶ But inasmuch as in every manner of discourse the speaker should be chiefly intent on persuasion—to wit, on the propitiating those

who hear him, which is the beginning of all other persuasions, as the rhetoricians know—and since the most potent persuasion to render the hearer attentive is the promise to tell novel and imposing things, I add this persuasion, or propitiation, to the prayers which I have made for a hearing, announcing to them my intention, which is to relate strange things to them, to wit, the strife which there is in my mind, and great things, to wit, the worth of their star. And this I say in these last words of the first part, *I will tell the wondrous story of my heart, how the sad soul waileth in it; and how a spirit discourseth counter to her, that cometh upon the rays of your star.*

7 And for the full understanding of these words I say that this spirit is nought else than a frequent thinking upon and commending and propitiating of this new lady; and this "soul" is nought else than another thought, accompanied by assent, which, repelling the former, commends and propitiates the memory of Beatrice in glory.

8 But inasmuch as the final verdict of the mind, that is, its assent, was still retained by that thought which supported the memory, I call it the "soul" and the other a "spirit." Just as when we speak of "the city" we are wont to mean those who are in possession of it, not those who are attacking it, albeit the one and the other be citizens.

9 I say, then, that this spirit comes upon the "rays of the star," because you are to know that the rays of each heaven are the path whereby their virtue descends upon things that are here below. And inasmuch as rays are no other than the shining which cometh from the source of the light through the air even to the thing enlightened, and the light is only in that part where the star is, because the rest of the heaven is diaphanous (that is transparent), I say not that this "spirit," to wit, this thought, cometh from their heaven in its totality but from their star.

10 Which star, by reason of the nobility in them who move it, is of so great virtue that it has extreme power upon our souls and upon other affairs of ours, notwithstanding that it be distant, when nighest to us, 167 times as far as it is to the middle of the earth, which is

a space of 3250 miles. And this is the literal exposition of the first part of the ode.

CHAPTER VII

1 A sufficient understanding may be had, by the above words, of the literal meaning of the first part, wherefore, attention is to be turned to the second, wherein is declared what I experienced within in the matter of this conflict.

2 And this part hath two divisions, for in the first, to wit, in the first verse, I tell the quality of these conflicting thoughts according to their root, which was within me. Then I tell that which was urged by the one and the other conflicting thought, and so first that which the losing side urged. And this is in the verse which is the second of this part and the third of the ode.

3 To make evident, then, the meaning of the first division, be it known that things should be named from the distinguishing nobility of their form, as man from reason and not from sense, nor from aught else that is less noble. Hence when we say that a man is living, it should be understood that the man hath the use of his reason, which is his special life, and is the actualising of his most noble part.

4 And therefore he who severs himself from reason, and hath only use of his sensitive part, doth not live as a man, but liveth as a beast, as saith that most excellent Boethius, "he liveth as an ass"[41]—rightly, as I maintain, because thought is the proper act of the reason, since beasts think not, because they have not reason. And I affirm this not only of the lesser beasts but of those who have the semblance of man and the spirit of sheep, or some other detestable beast.[42]

5 I say, then, that "the life of my heart" (that is, my inner life) "was wont to be a sweet thought" ("sweet" is the same as "suasive," that

---

41   *Consolation* IV.iii.

42   *Inf.* V.37–39; *Purg.* XXVI.82–84.

is "ingratiated," "dulcet," "pleasing," "delightsome") namely, that thought which often went to the "Sire" of them to whom I speak, which is God; that is to say that I, in thought, contemplated the kingdom of the blessed.

6 And straightway I declare the final cause why I rose up there in my thought, when I say, where it beheld a lady in glory, to give to understand that I was certain (as I am, by her gracious revelation) that she was in heaven. Wherefore, many a time, pondering on her as deeply as I might, I went thither as though rapt.

7 Then following on I tell the effect of this thought, to give to understand its sweetness, which was so great that it made me long for death, to go thither where it went; and this I say here, of whom it discursed to me so sweetly, that my soul said ever, 'Fain would I go thither.' And this is the root of one of the conflicting sides in me.

8 And you are to know that I call it a "thought," and not the "soul" which rose to look upon this one in bliss, because it was the special thought addressed to this act. "Soul," as was said in the preceding chapter, means "thought in general, with assent."

9 Then when I say, Now one appears who putteth him to flight, I tell of the root of the other conflicting side, saying that even as this thought, spoken of above, was wont to be my life, so another appeareth which maketh it cease. I say "putteth him to flight" to show that this is an adversary, for naturally one adversary flees the other, and the one that flees shows that it is by defect of valour that it flees.

10 And I say that this thought, which newly appears, has power to lay hold of me, and to conquer the whole soul, saying that it so lords it that "the heart," that is my inward self, "trembles," and it is revealed "without," by a certain changed semblance.

11 Following on, I show the power of this new thought by its effect, saying that it maketh me gaze upon "a lady" and saith flattering words to me, that is discourseth before the eyes of my intellectual affection the better to draw me over, promising me that the sight of her eyes is its weal.

[12] And the better to gain this credence with the experienced soul, it says that the eyes of this lady are not to be looked upon by any who fears "anguish of sighs." And this is a fine figure of rhetoric, when there is the outward appearance of depreciating a thing, and the inward reality of embellishing it. This new thought of love could not better draw my mind to consent than by so deeply discoursing of the virtue of that lady's eyes.

Chapter VIII

[1] Now that it has been shown how and why love was born, and the conflict which distracted me, it is meet that we proceed to unveil the meaning of that part wherein diverse thoughts fight within me.

[2] I say that it is meet first to speak on the side of the soul, that is to say the ancient thought, and then of the other. For this reason, that that upon which the speaker doth purpose to lay chiefest stress should ever be reserved for the last, because that which is last said doth most abide in the mind of the hearer.

[3] Wherefore, since it is my purpose to speak and to discourse more fully of that which the work of those beings whom I address makes than of that which it unmakes, it was reasonable first to speak and discourse of the condition of that side which was being destroyed, and then of that side which was being produced.

[4] But here arises a difficulty which is not to be passed over without explanation. Since love is the effect of these Intelligences whom I am addressing, and the former thought was love as much as the latter, someone may ask why their power destroys the one and produces the other, whereas it should rather preserve than destroy the former, for the reason that every cause loves its effect, and loving it preserves it.

[5-6] To this question the answer may easily be given; to wit, that their effect is indeed love, as hath been said, and inasmuch as they cannot preserve it save in those objects which are subject to their circulation, they change it from that region which is outside their

power to that which is within it; that is to say, from the soul which has departed from this life to the soul which is yet in it, just as human nature transfers its preservation of the human form from father to son because it may not perpetually preserve its effect in the father himself. I say "its effect" inasmuch as the soul united with the body is in truth its effect, for the soul which is parted endureth perpetually in a nature more than human. And so is the problem solved.

7 But inasmuch as the immortality of the soul has here been touched upon, I will make a digression, discoursing thereof, for in such discourse will be a fair ending of my speech concerning that living Beatrice, in bliss, of whom I propose to speak no further in this book.

8 And by way of preface I say that of all stupidities that is the most foolish, the basest, and the most pernicious, which believes that after this life there is no other. For if we turn over all the scriptures both of the philosophers and of the other sage writers, all agree in this that within us there is a certain part that endures.[43]

9 And this we see in the earnest contention of Aristotle, in that *Of the Soul*, this the earnest contention of all the Stoics, this the contention of Tully, especially in that booklet *Of Old Age*. This we see is the contention of every poet who has spoken according to the faith of the Gentiles, this the contention of every religion, Jews, Saracens, and Tartars, and all others who live according to any law.

10 So that if all of them were deceived there would follow an impossibility which it would be horrible even to handle. Everyone is assured that human nature is the most perfect of all other natures here below, and this is denied of none. And Aristotle averreth it when he saith in the twelfth *Of the Animals* that man is the most perfect of all the animals.

11 Whence, inasmuch as many living creatures are entirely mortal, as are the brute beasts, and are all, so long as they live, without this hope, to wit, of another life, if our hope were vain the flaw in

---

43   *Inf.* X.10–15.

us would be greater than in any other animal; because there have been many ere now who have surrendered this life for the sake of that, and so it would follow that the most perfect animal, to wit, man, was the most imperfect, which is impossible; and that part, to wit, the reason, which is his chief perfection, would be the cause to him of having this greater flaw, which seemeth a strange thing indeed to aver.

12 Further, it would follow that nature had set this hope in the human mind in opposition to herself, since we have said that many have hastened to the death of the body for to live in the other life, and this is also impossible.

13 Further, we witness unbroken experience of our immortality in the divinations of our dreams, which might not be if there were not some immortal part in us, inasmuch as the reveller, whether corporeal or incorporeal, must needs be immortal if we think it out subtly[44] (and I say, "whether corporeal or incorporeal" because of the diversity of opinion which I find in this matter); and that which is set in motion, or informed, by an immediate informer must stand in some ratio to the informer, and between the mortal and the immortal there is no ratio.

14 And further, we are assured of it by the most truthful teaching of Christ, which is the way, the truth, and the light. The way, because in it we advance unimpeded to the blessedness of this very immortality; the truth, because it suffereth no error; the light, because it lighteth us in the darkness of earthly ignorance.

15 This teaching, I say, assureth us above all other reasons, because he hath given it to us who seeth and measureth our immortality, the which we ourselves may not perfectly see so long as our immortal part is mingled with our mortal part. But by faith we see it perfectly, and by reason we see it with a shadow of obscurity, which cometh about because of the mingling of the mortal with the immortal.

---

44   *Purg.* IX.13–18.

16 And this should be the most potent argument that both the two exist in us; and so I believe, so aver, and so am assured of the passage after this life to another better life, where this lady liveth in glory, of whom my soul was enamoured when I strove in such fashion as shall be told in the following chapter.

Chapter IX

1 Returning to the subject, I say that in this verse which begins, *Findeth such an adversary as destroyeth him*, I intend to reveal what my soul discoursed within me, that is to say, the discourse of the ancient thought in opposition to the new. And first I briefly reveal the cause of her woeful speech when I say, *Findeth such an adversary as destroyeth him, the humble thought that is wont to discourse to me of an angel who is crowned in heaven.* This is that special thought of which it is said above that it was wont to be the life of the grieving heart.

2 Then, when I say, *The soul wails, so doth she still grieve thereat*, I show that my soul is still on its side, and speaks with sadness; and I say that she speaks words of lamentation, as though amazed at the sudden change, saying, *O wretched me! how fleeth that tender one who hath consoled me.* She may rightly say "consoled," for in her great loss this thought, which would ascend to heaven, had given her great consolation.

3 Then afterwards, in her excuse, I say that all my thought, to wit, my "soul," of whom I use the phrase, "this afflicted one," turns upon the eyes and denounces them; and this is manifested here, *Of my eyes this afflicted one exclaimeth.* And I tell how she says three things of them, and against them.

4 The first is that she curses the hour when this lady looked upon them. And here be it known that though many things may pass into the eye at the same time, yet the one which comes along the straight line into the centre of the pupil is the only one that is really and truly seen, and that stamps itself upon the imagination.

5 And this is because the nerve along which the visual spirit runs faces in this direction, and therefore one eye cannot really look upon another without being seen by it. For just as the one which looks receives the form in the pupil along the straight line, so along that same straight line its form proceeds into the one whereon it is looking. And many times it is in thus directing the straight line that his bow is discharged against whom all arms are light. Wherefore, when I say that, *Such lady looked upon them*, it is as much as to say that her eyes and mine looked upon one another.

6 The second thing that she saith is that she rebukes their disobedience when she saith, *And wherefore did they not believe me concerning her?* Then she proceeds to the third thing, and says that the reproach is not hers, as though she had not foreseen, but theirs in that they did not obey. Wherefore, she says that from time to time, discoursing of this lady, she said, "In her eyes must needs reside a power over me, were the path of access open to it"; and this she saith here, *I ever said, "Verily in her eyes must he needs stand who slays my peers."*

7 And in truth we are to believe that my soul recognized its own disposition, prone to receive the efficacy of this lady, and therefore feared her; for the efficacy of the agent is apprehended in the duly disposed patient, as saith the Philosopher in the second *Of the Soul*. And therefore, if wax had the spirit of fear, it would more greatly dread coming into the ray of Sun than would a stone, because its disposition receiveth it in more potent operation.

8 Finally, the soul makes manifest in her discourse that their presumption was perilous when she saith, *And my perceiving it availed me nought against their gazing upon such a one, that I am slain thereby.* She means, from looking there upon him of whom she has before said, that he "slays my peers"; and so she ends her words, to which the new thought answers as shall be set forth in the following chapter.

Chapter X

1 The meaning has been expounded of that part wherein the soul speaks, to wit, the ancient thought which was being destroyed. And now, in sequence, the meaning should be explained of the part wherein the new and adverse thought speaks. And this part is all contained in the verse which begins, *Thou art not slain*.

2–3 Which part, that it may be rightly understood, is to be divided into two, for in the first part which begins, *Thou art not slain*, and the rest, he proceeds to say (attaching himself to her two final words), "It is not true that thou art slain, but the reason that it seemeth thee that thou art slain is a certain dismay wherein thou art basely fallen, because of the lady who hath appeared to thee." And here be it noted that, as Boethius saith in his *Consolation*, "No sudden change of things cometh to pass without some certain running asunder of the mind."[45] And this is the meaning of the reproof made by that thought.

4 And he is called a "little spirit of love" to give to understand that my assent was swaying towards him. And thus what follows may be better understood and his victory recognized, since he says already, *O soul of ours*, making himself her familiar.

5 Then, as was said, he gives command as to what this soul that he reproves is to do to come to this lady, and he thus discourses to her, *See how tender she is, and humble*. Now these are two things which are the proper remedy for fear, whereby the soul was seen to be impassioned, and, especially when united, they beget good hope concerning a person, and chiefly piety,[46] which maketh every other excellence glow with its light. Wherefore, Vergil, speaking of Aeneas, calls him pious as his greatest praise.[47]

6 And piety is not what the common herds suppose it to be, namely, grieving at another's woe, which is rather a special effect of it which is called pity, and is an emotion. But piety is not an emotion,

---

45   *Consolation* II, pr. i.6.

46   Wicksteed translates the Italian (*pietoso*) as tenderness. I have changed it to piety to draw out the linguistic connection he is making to Vergil's *pietas*, alluded to in the next sentence and defined in the next paragraph.

47   *Aeneid* I.305ff.

but rather a noble disposition of mind ready to receive love, pity, and other charitous emotions.[48]

7 Then he saith, see also how *sage and courteous in her greatness she is.* Here he mentions three things, which, amongst things which we have the power to acquire, most chiefly make a person pleasing. He says "sage." Now, what is more beautiful in woman than to be wise? He says "courteous." Nothing is more becoming in woman than courtesy. And let not the wretched vulgar be deceived as to this word also, thinking that courtesy is no other than open-handedness, for open-handedness is a special form of courtesy, and not courtesy in general.

8 Courtesy and honour are all one, and because in courts of old time virtuous and fair manners were in use (as now the contrary), this word was derived from courts, and "courtesy" was as much as to say "after the usage of courts." Which word, if it were now taken from courts, especially of Italy, would mean nought else than baseness.

9 He says "in her greatness." Temporal greatness, which is here intended, is then most comely when accompanied by the two aforesaid excellencies, because it is the light which brings out with clearness the good in a person and its opposite. And how much wisdom and how much virtuous disposition remains concealed by not having this light, and how great madness and how great vices are exposed to view by having this light!

10 Better were it for the wretched magnates, mad, foolish, and vicious, to be in base estate, for so neither in the world nor after their lives' end would they be infamous. Truly it is for them that Solomon saith in Ecclesiastes, "Another most grievous infirmity have I seen beneath the Sun, to wit, riches kept to the hurt of their master."[49]

---

48 Piety and pity (compassion, tenderness) are the same word in the Italian, "pietà"; see *Inf.* XX.28–30.

49 Ecclesiastes 5:13.

11 Then in sequence he lays it upon her (to wit, upon my soul) that she is henceforth to call her her lady, promising her that therefrom she will have much solace when she shall be aware of her graces. And this he saith here, *For if thou deceive not thyself, thou shalt see.* Nor does he speak of aught else even to the end of this verse. And here endeth the literal meaning of all that I say in this ode addressing these celestial Intelligences.

Chapter XI

1 Finally (as the text of this comment said above, when dividing out the chief parts of this ode), I turn me with the face of my discourse to the ode itself, and speak to it.

2 And in order that this part may be the more fully understood, I say that generally, in every ode, it is called the *tornata*, because the poets who were first used to make it, did so in order that when the ode had been sung they should return to it again with a certain part of the air.

3 But I seldom made it with this intention; and that folk might perceive this, I seldom composed it after the arrangement of the ode, in point of numbers, which is essential to the music. But I made it when there was need to say something for the adornment of the ode outside of its own purport, as may be seen in this and in the others.

4 And therefore I say, for the present turn, that the excellence and the beauty of every discourse are separate and diverse the one from the other, for its excellence lies in its meaning, and its beauty in the adornment of the words, and both the one and the other give delight, although the excellence is most delightsome.

5 And so, since the excellence of this ode was difficult to perceive, because of the diverse persons who are introduced as speaking, wherein many divisions are needful, and since the beauty was easy to perceive, meseemed it was for the behoof of the ode that folk should pay more heed to its beauty than to its excellence. And this it is that I declare in this part.

6 But inasmuch as it often comes to pass that admonishment seems presumptuous under certain conditions, the rhetorician is wont to speak indirectly to a man, addressing his words not to him on whose account he is speaking, but to another. And this method is in fact observed in this instance, for the words are addressed to the ode and their purport to men.

7 I say, then, *Ode, I believe that they shall be but rare*, that is to say, few, who "rightly understand" thee, and I tell the reason, which is two-fold. First, because thy speech is "intricate" (I call it "intricate" for the reason that has been said), and secondly, because thy speech is "knotty" (I call it "knotty" with reference to the strangeness of the meaning).

8 Now afterwards I admonish it, and say, *If perchance it come about*, "that thou go" where are "folk" who seem to thee to be perplexed by thy discourse, be not thou dismayed, but say to them, "Since ye perceive not my excellence, give heed at least to my beauty."

9 For herein I aim at saying nought else (as declared above) save: "O men who cannot perceive the meaning of this ode, do not therefore reject it, but give heed to its beauty which is great, both in virtue of syntax, which pertains to grammarians, and in virtue of the ordering of the discourse, which pertains to rhetoricians, and by virtue of numbers in its parts, which pertains to musicians. Which thing may be seen to be beautiful in it by him who giveth good heed."

10 And this is all the literal meaning of the first ode, which is signified by the first-served dish spoken of above.

Chapter XII

1 Now that the literal meaning has been adequately explained, we are to proceed to the allegorical and true exposition. And, therefore, beginning again from the beginning, I say that when I lost the first delight of my soul, whereof mention is made above, I was pierced by so great sorrow that no comfort availed me.

2 Yet after a certain time, my mind, which was casting about to heal itself, made proof (since neither my own consolation nor that of others availed) to fall back upon the manner which a certain disconsolate one had erst followed to console himself. And I set myself to read that book of Boethius,[50] not known to many, wherein, a captive and an exile, he had consoled himself.

3 And hearing further that Tully had written another book wherein, treating *Of Friendship*, he had touched upon words of the consolation of Lelius, a man of highest excellence, on the death of Scipio his friend, I set myself to reading it.

4 And although it was at first difficult for me to enter into their meaning, finally I entered as deeply into it as my command of Latin, and what little wit I had, enabled me to do; by which wit I already began to perceive many things as in a dream, as may be seen in the *New Life*.

5 And as it is wont to chance that a man goeth in search of silver and beyond his purpose findeth gold, the which some hidden cause presents, not, I take it, without divine command, so I, who was seeking to console myself, found not only a cure for my tears but words of authors, and of sciences, and of books, pondering upon which I judged that Philosophy, who was the lady of these authors, of these sciences, and of these books, was a thing supreme.

6 And I conceived her after the fashion of a gentle lady, and I might not conceive her in any attitude save that of compassion, wherefore the sense for truth so loved to gaze upon her, that I could scarce turn it away from her.

7 And impelled by this imagination of her, I began to go where she was in very truth revealed, to wit, to the schools of the religious orders, and to the disputations of the philosophers, so that in a short time, I suppose some thirty months, I began to feel so much

---

50   *The Consolation of Philosophy.*

of her sweetness that the love of her expelled and destroyed every other thought.

8 Wherefore, feeling myself raised from the thought of that first love even to the virtue of this, as though in amazement I opened my mouth in the utterance of the ode before us, expressing my state under the figure of other things, because rhyme in any vernacular was unworthy to speak in open terms of the lady of whom I was enamoured, nor were the hearers so well prepared as to have easily apprehended straightforward words, nor would they have given credence to the true meaning, as they did to the fictitious, and, accordingly, folk did in fact altogether believe that I had been disposed to this love, which they did not believe of the other.

9 I began therefore to say, *Ye who by understanding move the third heaven*, and since, as has been said, this lady was daughter of God, queen of all, most noble and most beauteous Philosophy, we are to consider who were these movers, and this third heaven, and first of the third heaven, according to the order already observed.

10 And there is no need here to proceed dividing and expounding text by text, for by turning fictitious words from their sound to their import the exposition that has already been made will adequately explain this present meaning.

Chapter XIII

1 To see what is meant by the third heaven we must first consider what I mean by the word "heaven" taken by itself, and then it will be clear how and why this third heaven was to our purpose.

2 I say that by heaven I mean sincere, and by the heavens the sciences, because of three points of similarity which the heavens have with the sciences, especially in connection with their order and their number, wherein they seem to agree, as will be seen when we treat of the word "third."

3 The first point of similarity is that the one and the other revolves round a something that it does not move. For each moving heaven

revolves upon its own centre, which is not moved by the motion of that heaven, and in like manner each science moves round its own subject, but does not move it, because no science demonstrates its own subjects but presupposes it.

4 The second point of similarity is the illuminating power of the one and of the other. For each heaven illuminates visible things, and in like manner each science illuminates intelligible things.

5 And the third point of similarity is that they infuse perfection into things that are duly disposed. Of which infusion, so far as the first perfection, to wit, substantial generation, is concerned, all philosophers agree that the heavens are the cause; although they lay it down in different ways, some attributing it to the movers, as Plato, Avicenna, and Algazel; some to the stars themselves (especially in the case of human souls) as Socrates and Plato and Dionysius the Academician; and some to celestial virtue, which is in the natural heat of the seed, as Aristotle and the other Peripatetics.

6 And in like manner the sciences are the cause in us of the infusion of the second perfection, by the habit of which we can speculate concerning the truth, which is our distinguishing perfection, as saith the Philosopher in the sixth of the *Ethics*, when he says that truth is the good of the intellect.[51] Because of these, together with many other points of similarity, science may be called heaven.

7 We are now to examine why the third heaven is mentioned, whereto we must needs consider a comparison that holds between the order of the heavens and that of the sciences. As was narrated above, then, the seven heavens that are first with respect to us are those of the planets; next come two moving heavens above them; and one above them all, which is quiet.

8 To the seven first correspond the seven sciences of the Trivium and of the Quadrivium, to wit, Grammar, Dialect, Rhetoric, Arithmetic, Music, Geometry, and Astrology. To the eighth, to wit, the Starry Sphere, answers natural science which is called Physics, and first science which is called Metaphysics. To the ninth sphere

---

51   *Ethics* VI.2; see also *Inf.* III.16–18.

answers moral science; and to the quiet heaven answers divine science, which is called Theology. And the reason that all this is so must be briefly inspected.

9 I say that the heaven of the Moon is like Grammar, as being comparable to it. For if the Moon be rightly examined, two special things are perceived in her which are not perceived in the other stars. The one is the shadow upon her which is nought else than the rarity of her substance, whereon the rays of the Sun may not be stayed and thrown back, as from her other parts. The other is the variation of her luminosity, which now shines from the one side and now from the other, according as the Sun looks upon her.

10 And these two properties Grammar possesses, for because of its infinity the rays of reason cannot be arrested, especially in the direction of words, and it shines now on this side, now on that, insofar as certain words, certain declensions, certain constructions are now in use which were not of old, and many once were, which shall be again; as Horace says in the beginning of his *Poesy*, when he says, "Many words shall be born again which have now fallen," and the rest.[52]

11 And the heaven of Mercury may be compared to Dialectic in virtue of two special properties; for Mercury is the smallest star of heaven, for the magnitude of his diameter is not more than 232 miles, as Alfregenus states it, saying that it is 1/28th part of the diameter of the earth which is 6500 miles. The other special property is that its orbit is more veiled by the rays of the Sun than that of any other star.

12 And these two properties belong to Dialectic, for Dialectic is smaller in its body than any other science, for it is completely constructed and terminated in so much of text as is contained in the

---

52   *Ars Poetica*, lines 70–71.

Old Art and in the *New*,[53] and its orbit is more veiled than that of any other science, inasmuch as it proceeds with more sophisticated arguments and more disputable than any other.

13 And the heaven of Venus may be compared to Rhetoric because of two special properties. The one is the brightness of her aspect, which is sweeter to look upon than any other star. The other is her appearing now at morn and now at even.

14 And these two properties characterize Rhetoric, for Rhetoric is the sweetest of all the other sciences, since this is what it chiefly aims at. It appears at morn when the rhetorician speaks before the face of his hearer, it appears at even, that is from behind, when the rhetorician discourses through writing, from the distant side.

15 And the heaven of the Sun may be compared to Arithmetic because of two special properties. The one is that all the other stars are informed by his light. The other that the eye may not look on him.

16 And these two properties are seen in Arithmetic, for by its light all the sciences are lightened. For all their subjects are considered under some numerical aspect, and in the consideration of them there is always a numerical process.

17–18 As in natural science, mobile matter is the subject, which mobile matter has in itself the principle of continuity, and this has in itself the principle of infinite number. And as for the speculations of natural science, they are chiefly concerned with the principles of natural things, which are three, to wit, material, privation, and form; in which we see that there is not only number collectively but there is also number in each one severally, if we consider subtly. Wherefore Pythagoras, as Aristotle says in the first of the *Physics*,

---

53   The *Ars Vetus* (Old Art) refers to a small selection of Aristotle's works translated into Latin by Boethius. The *Ars Nova* (New Art) refers to a larger selection of Aristotle's works translated from the Arabic in the latter part of the twelfth century. "The analogy with Mercury, writes D(ante), is that dialectic is 'smaller in its body' because it is contained in the text of the [*Ars Nova*], the Old Art and the New" (Frisardi, notes on II.xiii.12).

laid down "even" and "odd" as the principles of natural things, considering all things to be number.[54]

19 The second property of the Sun is also seen in number, with which arithmetic is concerned, for the eye of the intellect may not look upon it, because number (considered in itself) is infinite, and such we may not understand.

20 And the heaven of Mars may be compared to Music by two properties. The one is the special beauty of its relation to the others. For if we count the revolving heavens, whether we begin from the lowest or the highest, this same heaven of Mars is the fifth. And so it is half-way between every pair, that is to say, the two first, the two second, the two third, the two fourth.

21 The second is that this same Mars drieth and burneth things, because his heat is like to the heat of fire; and this is why he appeareth enkindled in colour, sometimes more and sometimes less, according to the thickness and rarity of the vapours which follow him, which vapours often blaze up of themselves, as is established in the first of the *Meteorics*.

22 And therefore Albumassar says that the kindling of these vapours signifies the death of kings and transmutation of kingdoms, because they are effects of the lordship of Mars. And therefore Seneca says that at the death of the emperor Augustus he saw aloft a globe of fire. And in Florence, at the beginning of its ruin, was seen in the air, in the figure of a cross, a great quantity of these vapours that follow the star of Mars.

23 And these two properties are found in Music, which all consists in relations, as we perceive in harmonized words and in tunes; wherefrom the resulting harmony is the sweeter in proportion as the relation is more beauteous. Which relation is the chiefest beauty in that science, because this is what it chiefly aims at.

24 Moreover, Music so draweth to itself the spirits of men (which are, in principle, as though vapours of the heart) that they well-

---

54   *Physics* I.5 (see also Aquinas' commentary on this text).

nigh cease from all operation, so united is the soul when it hears it, and so does the virtue of all of them, as it were, run to the spirit of sense which receiveth the sound.

25 And the heaven of Jove may be compared to Geometry for two special properties. The one is that it moveth between two heavens repugnant to its own fair temperance, to wit, that of Mars and that of Saturn. Wherefore Ptolemy saith, in the book I have cited, that Jove is a star of temperate composition betwixt the cold of Saturn and the heat of Mars. The other is that he shows white among the stars, as though of silver.

26 These things characterize the science of Geometry. Geometry moves between two things repugnant to itself, to wit, the point and the circle (and I use "circle" in the larger sense of everything round, whether body or surface). For according to Euclid the point is its beginning, and according to what he says the circle is its most perfect figure, which must therefore needs have the nature of an end.

27 So that Geometry moves between the point and the circle as between its beginning and its end. And these two are repugnant to its certainty, for the point, because of its indivisibility, cannot be measured, and the circle, because of its curve, is impossible to square perfectly, and therefore is impossible to measure exactly. And, moreover, Geometry is supremely white, insofar as it is without taint of error, and is most certain both in itself and in its handmaid which is called perspective.[55]

28 And the heaven of Saturn has two properties by which it may be compared to Astrology. The one is the slowness of its movement through the 12 signs, for its orbit needs the time of 29 years and more, according to the writings of astrologers. The other is that it is exalted above all the other planets.

29 These two properties characterize Astrology, for in completing its circle, that is to say in learning it, a most long space of time revolves, both because of its demonstrations, which are more than

---

55   *Par.* XXXIII.133–138.

those of any other of the above-named sciences, and because of the observation which is needed rightly to judge it.

30 And further, it is more exalted than all the rest, because, as Aristotle says in the beginning *Of the Soul*, a science is exalted in nobility by the nobleness of its subject matter and by its certainty.[56] And this, more than any of the above-mentioned, is noble and exalted by the nobility and exaltation of its subject matter, which concerns the movement of heaven. And it is exalted and ennobled by its certainty, which is without any flaw, being that it cometh from the most perfect and regular principle. And if any suppose that there be a flaw in it, it is not on its side, but, as Ptolemy says, it is because of our negligence, and thereto should it be imputed.[57]

Chapter XIV

1 After the comparisons made concerning the seven first heavens, we are to proceed (as more than once declared) to the others, which are three. I say that the starry heaven may be compared to Physics because of three properties, and to Metaphysics because of three others; for it displays to us two visible objects, to wit, the multitude of stars and the Milky Way, which is that white circle which the vulgar call Saint Jacob's way; and it reveals one of its poles to us and conceals the other from us; and it reveals one only motion to us, from east to west, and the other which it makes from west to east, it well-nigh conceals from us. Wherefore, in due order, we are to consider first its comparison with Physics and then with *Metaphysics*.

2 I say that the starry heaven reveals a multitude of stars to us, for, according to the observation of the sages of Egypt they reckon, inclusive of the extremist star which appears to them in the south, a thousand and twenty-two separate stars, and it is of them that I am speaking. And herein it hath the greatest resemblance to Physics,

---

56   *De anima* I.1.
57   *Quadripartitus* I.ii.12.

if we subtly consider these three numbers, to wit, two, twenty, and a thousand.

3 For by two we understand local movement, which is of necessity from one point to another. And by twenty is signified movement by modification, for since, after ten, we can only proceed by modifying ten itself, by means of the other nine and of itself (the most elegant modification it receives being its own modification by itself), and since the first which it receives is twenty, it is fitting that the said movement should be signified by this number.

4 And by a thousand is signified the movement of growth; for this "thousand" is the highest number that has a name of its own, and there can be no further growth save by multiplying it. And physics manifests these three movements only, as is proved in the fifth of the fundamental treatise about it.

5 And because of the Milky Way this heaven hath great likeness to Metaphysics. Wherefore, we are to know that concerning this milky way philosophers have held diverse opinions. For the Pythagorean said that once upon a time the Sun strayed in his course, and passing through other portions not suited to his heat scorched the place among which he passed; and this appearance of scorching was left there. And I believe that they were moved thereto by the fable of Phaëton, which Ovid tells in the beginning of the second of the *Metamorphoses*.[58]

6 Others (of whom were Anaxagoras and Democritus) said that it was caused by the light of the Sun reflected in this part. And these opinions they support by arguments to prove them. What Aristotle may have said on this point cannot be rightly known, because his opinion does not appear the same in one translation as in the other.

7 And I suppose there must have been a mistake made by the translators, for in the New he seems to say that it is a congregation of vapours beneath the stars of that region which ever draw them up, and this doth not seem to set forth a true cause. In the Old he says that the Milky Way is nought else than a multitude of fixed

---

58 *Metamorphoses* II.35ff.

stars, in that region, so small that from here below we may not distinguish them, though they produce the appearance of that glow which we call the Milky Way; and it may be that the heaven in that region is denser, and therefore arrests and throws back the light; and this opinion seems to be shared with Aristotle by Avicenna and Ptolemy.

8 Wherefore, inasmuch as the Milky Way is an effect of those stars which we may not see save that we are aware of these things by their effect, and metaphysics treats of the primal existences, which in like manner we may not understand save by their effects, it is manifest that the starry heaven hath great similitude to Metaphysics.

9 Further, the pole that we see signifies the things of sense, of which, taken in their full compass, Physics treats; and the pole that we see not signifies things that are immaterial and are not sensible, whereof Metaphysics treats; and therefore the said heaven hath great similitude to the one science and to the other.

10 Further, by its two movements it signifies these two sciences; for by the movement wherewith it revolveth day by day, and maketh a fresh return from point to point, it signifieth the corruptible things of nature, which day by day complete their course, and their material changeth from form to form; and of these Physics treats.

11 And by the almost insensible movement which it makes from east to west, at the rate of a degree in a hundred years, it signifieth the incorruptible things which had of God a created beginning and shall have no end; and of these Metaphysics treats.

12 And this is why I say that this movement signifieth them, because the circulation in question had a beginning and shall have no end; for the end of a circulation is returning to one identical point, and this heaven shall never return to such with reference to this movement.

13 For since the beginning of the world it has revolved little more than one-sixth part; and we are already in the final age of the world, and are verily awaiting the consummation of the celestial

movement. And so it is manifest that the starry heaven, because of many properties, may be compared to Physics and to Metaphysics.

14 The crystalline heaven, which has been counted above as the *Primum Mobile*, has very manifest comparison with Moral Philosophy, because, as Thomas, on the second of the *Ethics* says, it disposes us rightly for other sciences.

15 For, as says the Philosopher in the fifth of the *Ethics*, legal justice regulates the sciences with a view to learning, and commands them to be learnt and taught that they be not forsaken; and so doth the said heaven regulate with its movement the daily revolution of all the others, whereby every day they all receive from above the virtue of all their parts.

16 For if the revolution of this heaven did not thus regulate the same, little of their virtue would come down here, and little sight of them.[59] Wherefore, suppose it were possible for this ninth heaven not to move, in any given place on earth a third part of the starry heaven would never yet have been seen, and Saturn would be 14 years and a half concealed from any given place on the earth, and Jove would be concealed for 6 years, and Mars about a year, and the Sun 182 days and 14 hours (I say "days" to signify the length of time which so many days measure), and Venus and Mercury would be concealed and revealed about 150 like the Sun, and the Moon for 14 days and a half would be hidden from all folk.

17 Of a truth there would be no generation here below, nor life of animal nor plant; night would not be, nor day, nor week, nor month, nor year; but all the universe would be disordered, and the movement of the other heavens would be in vain.

18 And, not otherwise, were Moral Philosophy to cease, the other sciences would be hidden a certain space, and there would be no generation, nor life, nor felicity; and in vain would the other sciences have been written down and discovered of old. Whereby it is right clear that this heaven may be compared to Moral Philosophy.

---

59   *Par.* II.12–114.

19 Further, the Empyrean heaven in virtue of its peace is like the divine science, which is full of all peace, which suffereth not any strife of opinions or of sophistical arguments, because of the most excellent certainty of its subject matter, which is God. And of it saith he himself unto his disciples, "My peace I give unto you, my peace I leave with you,"[60] giving and leaving them his teaching, which is this science whereof I speak.

20 Of her saith Solomon, "Sixty are the queens and eighty are the concubines, and of the young maidens there is no number; one is my dove and my perfect one."[61] All the sciences he calls queens and paramours and handmaidens, and this he calls dove because it is without taint of strife, and this he calls perfect because it makes us see the truth perfectly, wherein our soul is quieted.[62]

21 And so, this comparison of the heavens and the sciences being expounded, we may perceive that by the third heaven I mean Rhetoric, which resembles the third heaven as appears above.

Chapter XV

1 In virtue of the similitudes now expounded, it may be seen who are those movers whom I address which move this heaven, such as Boethius and Tully, who with the sweetness of their discourse set me upon the way of love, as related above (that is to say, devotion to this most gentle lady Philosophy), with the rays of their star, which is the scripture that concerns her. For in every science scripture is a star, full charged with light, which showeth forth that science.

2 And when this is understood we may see the true meaning of the first verse of the ode before us by means of the fictitious and literal exposition. And by means of this same exposition we may adequately understand the second verse up to the place where it says, *He makes me gaze upon a lady.*

---

60   John 14:27.

61   Song of Solomon 6:6–7.

62   *Purg.* XXXI.106–108.

3 Where you are to know that this lady is Philosophy, who in truth is a lady full of sweetness, adorned with honour, wondrous in wisdom, glorious in freedom, as in the third treatise, where her nobleness will be dealt with, shall be made manifest.

4 And in the place where it says, *Who would behold salvation heedfully, let him look upon this lady's eyes*, the eyes of this lady are her demonstrations, the which, when turned upon the eyes of the intellect, enamour that soul which is free in its conditions. Oh most sweet and unutterable looks, of a sudden ravishing the human mind, which appear in the demonstrations in the eyes of Philosophy when she discourses to her lovers! Verily in you is the salvation whereby whoso looketh on you is blessed, and saved from the death of ignorance and of vice.

5 Where it says, *If he fear not the anguish of sighings*, there must be understood, if he fear not the toil of study, and the strife of perplexities which rise in manifold fashion from the beginning of the glances of this lady, and then as her light continueth fall away like morning clouds from the face of the Sun; and the intellect that hath become her familiar remains free and full of certainty, even as is the air purged and lightened by the midday rays.

6 The third verse, likewise, may be understood by the literal exposition up to where it says, *The soul wails*. Here we must give good heed to a certain moral which may be noted in these words; namely, that a man ought not, because of a greater friend, to forget the services received from the lesser, but if it really behoves him to follow the one and leave the other, when he follows the better the other is not to be abandoned without some fitting lamentation, wherein he giveth cause to the one he followeth of all the greater love.

7 Then when it saith "of my eyes" it means nought else save that mighty was the hour when the first demonstration of this lady entered into the eyes of my intellect, which was the most immediate cause of this enamourment.

8 And where it saith "my peers," souls are meant that are free from wretched and vile delights, and from the ways of the vulgar, endowed with intellect and memory. And then it saith "slays," and then saith "am slain," which seems counter to what was said above of this lady's saving power.

9 And therefore be it known that here one of the sides is speaking, and there the other, which two contend diversely, according as was expounded above. Wherefore, it is no marvel if the one says yea, and the other nay, if it be rightly noted which is declining and which ascending.

10 Then in the fourth verse, where it says "a little spirit of love," it means a thought which springs from my study. Wherefore, be it known that by love in this allegory is always meant that very study which is the application of the mind enamoured of a thing to that thing itself.

11 Then when it saith, *Thou shalt see adornment of such lofty miracles*, it declares that through her shall be perceived the adornments of the miracles; and it says true, for the adornment of marvels is the perception of the causes of them, which is what she demonstrates, as the Philosopher appears to feel in the beginning of the *Metaphysics*, when he says that by perceiving these adornments men begin to be enamoured of this lady. And of this word, to wit, marvel, there will be fuller discourse in the following treatise.

12 All the rest of this ode which follows is adequately explained by the other exposition. And so, at the close of this second treatise, I declare and affirm that the lady of whom I was enamoured after my first love was the most fair and noble daughter of the Emperor of the universe, to whom Pythagoras gave the name of Philosophy. And here ends the second treatise, which is served as the first course.

Book III

Amor, che nella mente mi ragiona

I

Love, that discourses to me in my mind
yearningly of my lady,
moveth many a time such things with me anent her,
that my intellect loses its way concerning them.
His discourse soundeth so sweetly,
that the soul that heareth him and feeleth,
crieth, 'Oh me, that I have not power
to tell that which I hear about my lady.'
And verily it behoveth me first to drop,
Would I treat of that which I hear of her,
all that my intellect apprehendeth not,
and of that which it understandeth
great part, because I should not know to tell it.
Wherefore, if defect shall mark my rhymes,
which shall enter upon her praises,
for this let our feeble intellect be blamed,
and our speech which hath not power
to tell again all that love speaketh.

II

The Sun seeth not, who circleth all the world,
a thing so gentle as in that hour
when he shineth on the place, where sojourneth
the lady of whom love constraineth me to speak.
Every supernal intellect gazes upon her,
and such folk as are here enamoured
still find her in their thoughts,
when love maketh them feel of his peace.
Her being is to him who gives it her so pleasing,
that he ever poureth his power into her,
beyond what our nature asketh.
Her pure soul, which receiveth from him this salvation,
maketh it show forth in that which she doth guide,
for her beauties are things clear to view,
and the eyes of those in whom she shineth

send messages thereof to the heart, filled with longings,
which gather air and turn to sighs.

III

On her descendeth the divine power,
as it doth upon an angel who beholdeth it,
and whatsoever gentle lady not believeth this,
let her go with her, and mark well her gestures.
Where she speaks, there cometh down
a spirit from heaven, who gives us faith
that the lofty worth which she possesses
transcends all that consorts with our nature.
The sweet gestures which she shows to others
go calling upon love, each vying with the other
in that voice which maketh him to hear.
Of her it may be said,
Gentle is that in lady which in her is found,
and beauteous is so much only as is like to her.
And affirm we may that to look on her gives help
to accept that which seems a miracle, whereby our faith is aided.
Therefore from eternity such was she ordained.

IV

Things are revealed in her aspect
which show us of the joys of Paradise,
I mean in her eyes and in her sweet smile,
which love assigneth there as to their proper place.
They transcend our intellect,
as the Sun's rays the feeble vision,
and because I may not gaze fixedly upon them,
needs must I content me with scant speech of them.
Her beauty rains down flamelets of fire,
made living by a gentle spirit,
which is the creator of every good thought,
and they shatter like thunder
the inborn vices that make folk vile.
Wherefore whatsoever lady heareth her beauty
blamed for not seeming tranquil and humble,
let her gaze on her who is the pattern of humility.
It is she who humbleth each perverse one
Of her was he thinking who set the universe in motion.

TORNATA

Ode! It seemeth that thy speech is counter
to the utterance of a little sister whom thou hast.
For this lady, whom thou makest to be humble,
she calleth cruel and disdainful.
Thou knowest that the heaven is ever shining and clear,
and, as concerns itself, is disturbed never,
but our eyes, for many a cause,
call the star clouded time and time again.
So when she calleth her orgulous,
she considereth her not according to the truth,
but only according as to her she appeared.
For the soul was in terror,
aye, and is in such terror yet,
that it seemeth to me a dire thing
whensoever I look where she perceiveth me.
Thus plead thy excuse if thou have need,
and when thou canst, present thyself to her,
and say, 'My lady, if it be acceptable to thee,
I will discourse of thee on every side.'

Chapter I

1 As hath been told in the preceding treatise, my second love took its beginning from the compassionate semblance of a lady. Which love afterward, finding my life disposed for its ardour, kindled, after the fashion of fire, from a little flame to a great; so that, not only when I woke but when I slept, into my head was light from her guided.

2 And how great was the yearning which love gave me to see her could neither be uttered nor comprehended! And not only of her was I thus desirous but of all those persons who were in any way connected with her, whether by intimacy or by any tie of kinship.

3 Oh, how many nights there were wherein the eyes of others were resting, closed in sleep, and mine were fixedly gazing on the abiding place of my love! And since the redoubled conflagration must needs reveal itself outwardly (because it cannot possibly remain concealed) a wish came upon me to speak of love, which I was utterly unable to restrain.

4 And though I might have but little command over my own counsel, yet I so far approached it from time to time, either by the will of love or by my own eagerness, that I comprehended and perceived that, in speaking of love, there was no more fair nor profitable discourse than that which commended the loved person.

5 And this deliberation was inspired by three reasons; of which the first was the proper love of myself, which is the beginning of all the rest, even as every one perceives that there is no more legitimate nor more gracious method of a man doing honour to himself than by honouring his friend. For, inasmuch as friendship may not be between unlikes, wheresoever friendship is perceived likeness is understood to be; and wheresoever likeness is understood to be praise and blame run common.

6 And from this argument two great lessons may be learnt. The one is, not to be willing that any vicious one should show himself to be our friend, because therein an evil opinion of him to whom he shows himself friendly is conceived. And the other is that no one should blame his friend publicly, because—if the preceding reason be rightly considered—he is thereby thrusting a finger into his own eye.

7–8 The second reason was the desire to perpetuate this friendship. Wherefore, you are to know that, as saith the Philosopher in the ninth of the *Ethics*,[63] in the friendship of folk of unlike condition there must be, in order to preserve it, a certain proportion between them, which shall in a way reduce the unlikeness to likeness; as in the case of a master and servant. For although the servant cannot render a like benefit to his master when he receives a benefit from him, he must nevertheless render such as he best can with so much zeal and openness that that which is unlike in itself shall be made like by the manifestation of good-will, which reveals and confirms and preserves the friendship.

---

63   *Ethics* IX.1.

9 Wherefore I, reflecting upon my inferiority to this lady, and seeing myself benefited by her, resolved to commend her according to my power. If the which be not like in itself to hers, at least my zealous will shows that, if I could do more, more would I do; and so it likens itself to that of this gentle lady.

10 The third reason was a motive prompted by forethought. For, as says Boethius, "it doth not suffice to look only upon that which is before the eyes, to wit, the present; and therefore forethought is given to us, which looks beyond, even to that which may come to pass."[64]

11 I mean that I reflected that by many who come after me I might perchance be reproved for likeness of mind when they heard that I had changed from my first love. Wherefore, to remove this blame, there was no better means than to tell of the quality of the lady who had changed me.

12 For by the manifestation of her excellence, consideration of her power might accrue; and when her supreme power was understood, it might be thought that no stability of mind could resist being changed by her; and so I might not be deemed light or unstable.

13 I undertook, therefore, to speak this lady's praise, and, if not in fashion as were fitting, at least so far forth as I might; and I began to say, *Love, that discourses to me in my mind.* This ode has three chief parts. The first is all the first verse, wherein the discourse is by way of proem. The second is all the three following verses, wherein is treated that which it is the purport of the ode to utter, to wit, the praise of this gentle one. And the first of these begins, *The Sun seeth not, who circleth all the world.* The third part is the fifth and last verse, wherein, directing my words to the ode, I purge her of a certain difficulty. And of these three parts we are to discourse in order.

---

64   *Consolation* II, pr.i.15.

Chapter II

1 Addressing myself then to the first part, which was ordained as proem of this ode, I say that we must divide it into three parts. For first, the ineffable quality of the theme is touched upon. Secondly, my insufficiency to deal perfectly with it is set forth; and this second part begins, *And verily it behoveth me first to drop*. Finally, I excuse myself for my insufficiency, for which no fault should be found with me; and this I begin when I say, *Wherefore, if defect shall mark my rhymes*.

2 I say then, *Love that discourses to me in my mind*, where, in the first place, we are to consider who this is who discourses, and what that place is wherein I assert that he makes discourse.

3 Love, truly taken and subtly considered, is nought else than a spiritual union of the soul and of the loved thing; to which union the soul, in virtue of its own nature, runs swift or slow according as it is free or impeded.

4 And the reason of this natural property may be that every substantial form proceeds from its own first cause, which is God, as is written in the *Book of Causes*; and they derive their diversities not from it, for it is most simple, but from the secondary causes or from the material upon which it descends. Wherefore, in that same book, in treating of the infusion of the divine goodness it is written, "And make the excellences and the gifts diverse, in virtue of the cooperation of the thing which receives."[65]

5 Wherefore, inasmuch as every effect retains something of the nature of its cause (as Alpetragius says when he affirms that what is caused by a circular body has, in a certain fashion, a circular existence), every form possesses, in a fashion, the existence of the divine nature; not that the divine nature is divided and communicated to them, but it is participated by them, something after the mode wherein the Sun is by participation in the other stars.

---

65   *Book of Causes* XVII (XVIII).148.

6 And the more noble the form is, the more does it retain of this nature. Wherefore, the human soul, which is the noblest form of all those that are generated beneath the heaven, receives more of the divine nature than any other.

7 And since it is most germane to the nature of God to will to be (because, as we read in the aforesaid book, "being comes first of all, and before that there is nought"[66]), the human soul naturally desires, with the whole force of its longing, to be. And because its being depends on God, and by him is preserved, it naturally desires and wills to be united to God, in order to fortify its own being.

8 And because it is in the excellences of nature that the divine principle reveals itself, it comes to pass that the human soul naturally unites herself with them in spiritual fashion, the more swiftly and the more mightily in proportion as they appear more perfect. And they so appear in proportion as the soul's power of recognition is clear or obstructed.

9 And this union it is which we call love, whereby the inner quality of the soul may be recognized by examining outwardly the things which it loves. This love, to wit, the union of my soul with this gentle lady, in whom full much of the divine light was revealed to me, is he who discourses, and of whom I speak; because from him unbroken thoughts had birth, by gazing and pondering upon the worth of this lady, who was spiritually made one thing with my soul.

10 The place wherein I say that he discoursed is the mind, but to say that it is the mind gives us no more understanding of it than before; and therefore we are to examine what this word mind properly signifies.

11 I say then that the Philosopher in the second *Of the Soul*, when analysing its powers, says that the soul has in the main three powers, to wit, life, sense, and reason; and he also mentions motion, but this may be united with sense, for every soul that has sense (either

---

66 *Book of Causes* IV.37–39.

with all the senses or some one of them only), has motion also; so that motion is a power inseparable from sense.

12 And, as he says, it is quite plain that these powers are so related to each other that one is the foundation of the other. And that which is the foundation may exist by itself apart; but the other which is founded upon it may not exist apart from it. Wherefore, the vegetative power, whereby things live, is the foundation upon which rests the sensitive life, to wit, sight, hearing, taste, smell, and touch; and this vegetative power may constitute a soul in itself, as we see in all the plants.

13 The sensitive power cannot exist without this; there is nothing that feels, without being alive. And this sensitive power is the foundation of the intellectual power, to wit, the reason; and therefore, amongst mortal things that have life, the rational power without the sensitive is not to be found, but the sensitive power is to be found without the other, as we see in the beasts and in the birds and in the fishes and in every brute animal.

14 And that soul which embraces all these powers is the most perfect of all the rest. And the human soul, which is associated with the nobility of the highest power, to wit, reason, participates in the divine nature after the fashion of an eternal intelligence, because the soul is so ennobled and stripped of material in this sovereign power that the divine light shines in it as an angel; and therefore man has been called by the philosophers the "divine animal."[67]

15 In this most noble part of the soul exist many faculties, as says the Philosopher, especially in the sixth of the *Ethics*, where he says that there is a capacity in it which is called the scientific, and another which is called the ratiocinative, or counselling; and together with this are certain faculties, as Aristotle says in that same place, such as the inventive faculty and the judicial.[68]

16 And all these most noble faculties, and the rest that abide in this excellent power, are called collectively by this name, as to the

---

67   *Purg.* XXV.52–57, 67–75.

68   *Ethics* VI.10.

meaning of which we are inquiring, to wit, "mind." Whereby it is manifest that by mind we understand this highest and most noble part of the soul.

17 And that this is the meaning is seen from the fact that it is only of man and of the divine substances that this "mind" is predicated; as may be plainly seen from Boethius, who first predicates it of men, when he says to Philosophy, "Thou, and God who placeth thee in the minds of men";[69] and afterwards predicates it of God, when he says to God, "Thou dost produce all things after supernal pattern, oh thou most beauteous, bearing the beauteous world in thy mind."[70]

18 Nor ever was it predicated of a brute animal; nay, rather there are many men who seem lacking in this most perfect part, of whom it seems that we neither should nor can predicate it; and therefore such are called in grammar *amenti* and *dementi*, that is, "without mind."

19 So now we can see what is that mind, which is the culmination and the most precious part of the soul, which is Deity. And this is the place wherein I declare that love discourseth to me of my lady.

Chapter III

1 Not without cause do I say that this love plies his operation "in my mind"; but this is said with reason, to give to understand what manner of love this is, by telling of the place wherein it operates.

2 Wherefore, be it known that everything, as said above, and for the reason above set forth, hath its specific love, as, for example, the simple bodies have a love which has an innate affinity to their proper place; and that is why earth ever drops to the centre; but the love of fire is for the upper circumference, under the heaven of the Moon, and therefore it ever riseth thereto.[71]

---

69   *Consolation* I, pr. iv.8.

70   *Consolation* III, met. ix.6–8.

71   *Par.* I.109–117.

3 Primary compound bodies, like the minerals, have a love for the place where their generation is ordained, and therein they grow, and thence draw vigour and power. Whence we see the magnet ever receive power from the direction of its generation.

4 Plants, which are the primary living things, have a more manifest love for certain places, according as their composition requires; and therefore we see certain plants almost always gather along water-courses, and certain on the ridges of mountains, and certain on slopes and at the foot of hills, the which, if we transplant them, either die altogether or live as if in gloom, like things parted from the place dear to them.

5 As for the brute animals, not only have they a more manifest love for their place, but we see that they love one another. Men have their proper love for perfect and comely things. And because man (though his whole form be one sole substance) has in himself, by his nobility, something of the nature of each of these things, he may have all these loves, and has them all indeed.

6 For in virtue of the nature of the simple body, which predominates in the subject, he naturally loves to descend; and therefore when he moves his body upward it is more toilsome. By the second nature, of a complex body, he loves the place and further the time of his generation, and therefore every one is naturally of more efficient body at the place where he was generated, and at the time of his generation, than at any other.

7 Wherefore we read in the stories of Hercules, and in Great Ovid, and in Lucan,[72] and in other poets, that, when he was fighting with the giant called Antaeus, whenever the giant failed and his body was stretched upon the earth, whether of his own will or by the might of Hercules, force and vigour rose up again in him, renovated by the earth, wherein and wherefrom he had been generated.

8 Perceiving which, Hercules, at the last, grasping him and lifting him from the earth, held him so long, and suffered him not to re-unite himself with the earth, that with overmastery he conquered

---

72   *Metamorphoses* IX.183–184 and *Pharsalia* IV.593–653, respectively.

and slew him. And this battle was in Africa, according to the testimony of the scriptures.

9 And by the third nature, to wit, that of plants, man hath love for certain food, not insofar as it affects the sense but insofar as it is nutritious; and such food maketh the working of this nature most perfect, and other food does not so, but makes it imperfect. And therefore we see that some certain food shall make men fair of face and stout of limb and of a lively colour, and certain other shall work the contrary of this.

10 And in virtue of the fourth nature, that of animals, to wit, the sensitive, man hath another love whereby he loveth according to sensible appearance, like to a beast; and this is the love in man which most needeth a ruler, because of its overmastering operation, especially in the delight of taste and touch.

11 And by the fifth and last nature, that is to say the truly human or, rather say, the angelic, to wit, the rational, man hath love to truth and to virtue; and from this love springeth the true and perfect friendship, drawn from nobility, whereof the Philosopher speaks in the eighth of the *Ethics*, when he treats of friendship.[73]

12 Wherefore, inasmuch as this nature is called mind, as shown above, I declared that love discoursed "in my mind" to give to understand that this love was that which is native to this most noble nature, to wit, the love of truth and of virtue, and to exclude every false opinion concerning me, whereby my love might have been suspected to be love for delight of sense.

13 And then I say "yearningly" to give to understand its continuity and its fervour. And I say that he often moveth things which make my intellect lose its way; and I speak truth, because my thoughts, when discoursing of her, often strove to bring things to an issue about her which I might not comprehend; and I was all astray, so that outwardly I appeared as though distraught, like to a man who looks with his sight along a straight line, and first clearly sees the things nighest to him, then, as he goes on, sees them less clearly,

---

73   *Ethics* VIII.3.

then further on is at a loss concerning them, then going on even to the furthest of all, his sight is unfocused and he sees nought.

14 And this is the one source of the unutterableness of that which I have taken as my theme. And then, in sequence, I tell of the other, when I say, "His discourse" and the rest. And I say that my thoughts (which are the discourse of love) have such sweet sound that my soul (that is, my affection) burns to be able to relate this with the tongue. And because I may not tell it, I say that the soul laments thereat, saying, *Oh me! that I have not power.*

15 And this is the other source of unutterableness, namely that the tongue cannot completely follow that which the intellect perceives. And I say, *the soul that heareth him and feeleth*, "heareth" as touching the words, and "feeleth" as touching the sweetness of sound.

Chapter IV

1 Having discoursed of the twofold unutterableness of this subject matter, it is fitting to proceed to tell of my own insufficiency. I say, then, that my insufficiency hath a twofold origin even as the loftiness of that lady hath a twofold transcendency, after the fashion expounded.

2 For, through poverty of intellect, needs must I drop much of that which is true concerning her, and which rays in some sort into my mind, which, like a transparent body, receives without arresting it. And this I say in this following clause, *And verily it behoveth me, first to drop.*

3 Then when I say, *And of that which it understandeth*, I assert that not only am I insufficient for that which my intellect cannot support but even for that which I understand, because my tongue hath not such eloquence as to be able to utter the discourse which is held of her in my thought. Whereby it is to be seen that, in proportion to the truth, that which I shall say will be but little, and the outcome of this is greatly to her praise if rightly considered, and that is the main purpose. And that discourse, which at every point has its hand on the main purpose, may well be said to come from the workshop of the rhetorician.

4 Then where it says, *Wherefore if defect shall mark my rhymes,* I excuse myself for my fault, for which, when folk see that my words are beneath her dignity, I ought not to be blamed. And I say that if there be defect in my rhymes, that is to say, in my words, which are ordained to treat of her, the blame must fall upon the weakness of intellect,and the scant power of our speech, which is vanquished by the thought, so that it may scarce follow it, especially where the thought springs from love, because there the soul exercises herself more profoundly than elsewhere.

5 It might be said, "Thou art excusing and at the same time accusing thyself," for it is a conviction of blame and not a purgation from it, insofar as the blame is thrown upon the intellect and upon speech, which are mine, so that if the same be good, I ought to be praised therefore to the extent of the goodness, and if defective, to be blamed. To this it may be answered briefly, that I do not accuse myself, but do genuinely excuse myself.

6 And hereto be it known that, according to the Philosopher in the third of the *Ethics,* man deserves praise or blame only for those things which it is in his power to do or not to do, but in those things wherein he has no power he deserves neither praise nor blame, inasmuch as both are to be rendered to some other, albeit the things themselves be part of the very man.[74]

7 Wherefore we should not blame a man because of a body deformed from his birth, because it was not in his power to make himself beautiful, but we are to blame the faulty disposition of the material whereof he was made, which was the source of the failure of nature. And in like manner we should not praise a man for any beauty of body which he may have from his birth, for he was not the maker thereof; but we ought to praise the artificer, to wit, human nature, which produces such great beauty in its material when it is not impeded by it.

---

74   *Ethics* III.1.

8 And therefore the priest well answered the Emperor who laughed and scoffed at his deformity of body, "God is the Lord, he made us, and not we ourselves."[75] And these are the words of the prophet in a verse of the Psalter, written as they stand in the priest's answer, without addition or subtraction. And therefore let the ill-conditioned wretches look to it who make it all their study to deck out their person (which should be treated with all dignity), for this is nought else than to ornament the work of another and neglect one's own.

9 Returning then to the purpose, I affirm that our intellect, by defect of that power whence it draws whatsoever it contemplates (which is an organic power, to wit, the fantasy), may not rise to certain things, because the fantasy may not aid it, for it hath not wherewithal. Such are the substances, sejunct from matter, which, even though a certain consideration of them be possible, we may not understand nor comprehend perfectly.[76]

10–11 And for this a man is not to blame, for he was not the maker of this deficiency; nay, rather is it the work of universal nature, that is, of God, who willed that we should lack such light in this life; and why he did this, it were presumptuous to argue. So that if my consideration transported me into a region where fantasy failed the intellect, I am not to blame for not being able to understand. Further, a limit is fixed for our intelligence in each one of its operations, not by us but by universal nature; and therefore be it known that the limits of intelligence are wider in thought than in speech, and wider in speech than in signals.

12 Therefore, if our thought surpasses speech, not only in matters which attain not to perfect understanding but also in those which only just attain to it, we are not to blame for this, because it is not we who make it so.

13 And thus I show that my excuse is a genuine one when I say, *For this let our feeble intellect be blamed and our speech which hath not power to tell again all that love telleth.* For the good will should be right clearly

---

75   Psalm 100:3.
76   *Inf.* XXVIII.4–6; *Par.* XXXIII.142.

seen, and this is what we ought to consider in the matter of human deserts. This then, is how we are to understand the first chief section of this ode which is in hand.

Chapter V

1 Now that the discussion of the first section has revealed its meaning, we are duly to proceed to the second. Whereof, for its better inspection, three divisions should be made according as it is embraced in three verses. For in the first I commend this lady in her entirety and without distinction, alike in soul and in body. In the second I come down to the special praise of the soul, and in the third to the special praise of the body.

2 The first division begins, *The Sun seeth not, who circleth all the world.* The second begins, *On her descendeth the divine power.* The third begins, *Things are revealed in her aspect.* And these divisions are to be discussed in order.

3 I say then, *The Sun seeth not, who circleth all the world*, wherein, for perfect understanding, we must know how the world is circled by the Sun. In the first place, I say that by "the world" I do not here understand the whole body of the universe, but only this region of sea and land, according to the common speech, which uses so to call it. Just as one says, "Such an one has seen all the world," meaning the region of sea and land.

4 Pythagoras and his followers declared that this world was one of the stars, and that there was another, of like fashion, opposite to it; and this they called Antichthon. And he said that they were both on one sphere which turned from east to west, and that it was in virtue of this revolution that the Sun circled round us and was now visible and now invisible.

5 And he said that fire was betwixt these two, laying it down that it was a nobler substance than water and than earth, and laying it down that the centre was the noblest among the places of the four simple bodies. And therefore he said that fire, when it seemed to rise, was really descending to its own centre.

6 Afterwards Plato adopted another opinion, and wrote, in a book of his which is called *Timaeus*, that the earth, with the sea, was really the centre of the whole, but that its whole globe turned round on its centre, following the primal movement of heaven, but very slowly, because of its gross material, and because of its extreme distance from that primal movement.

7 These opinions are refuted as false in the second *Of Heaven and Earth* by that glorious Philosopher to whom nature opened her secrets more than to any other;[77] and by him it is there shown that this world, to wit, the earth, stands for ever stable and fixed in herself. And the proofs which Aristotle enunciates to crush these others and to establish the truth, it is not my purpose here to relate, because it is enough for those whom I am addressing to be assured on his great authority, that this earth is fixed and revolves not, and that it, together with the ocean, is the centre of the heaven.

8 This heaven revolves round this centre, as we perceive, without break; in the revolution of which there must needs be two fixed poles, and a circle, equally distant from them both, which revolves most rapidly. Of these two poles the one, that is to say this northern one, is apparent to almost all the land which is uncovered; the other, to wit, the southern one, is concealed from almost all the uncovered land. The circle which is perceived midway between them is that path of the heaven under which the Sun revolves when he goes in company with the Ram or with the Scales.

9 Wherefore, be it known that if a stone should fall from this our pole, it would fall, away yonder, into the ocean, right upon the hump of the sea, at the spot where, if there were a man, he would always have the star right above his head. And I suppose that from Rome to this spot, measuring straight to the north, there would be a space of some 2600 miles, or a little more or less.

---

77   *De coelo* II.13.

10 Let us imagine, then, for a better understanding, that there be a city on that spot which I have named, and that it be called Maria. I say further, that if a stone should fall from that other pole, that is the southern one, it would fall upon that hump of the Ocean sea which is exactly opposite to Maria on this ball; and I suppose that from Rome to the place where that second stone would fall, measuring straight to the south, would be a space of 6500 miles, a little more or less.

11 And here let us imagine another city and let it be called Lucia, and the space, in whatever direction we draw the cord, would be 10,200 miles between the one and the other, just half the circumference of this ball, so that citizens of Maria would have their feet opposed to the feet of those of Lucia.

12 Let us further imagine a circle upon this ball which at every point should be the same distance from Maria as from Lucia. I suppose that this circle (as I understand by the teachings of the astrologers, and by that of Albert of Germany in his book *Of the Nature of Places and of the Properties of the Elements*, and also by the testimony of Lucan in his ninth book) would divide this uncovered land from the Ocean, down there towards the south, almost along the whole extremity of the first climate, where are, amongst other nations, the Garamanti, who are almost always naked; to whom Cato came with the people of Rome, fleeing the lordship of Caesar.

13 When we have marked these three places upon this ball, it is easy to perceive how "the Sun circleth" it. I say, then, that the heaven of the Sun revolves from west to east, not directly counter to the diurnal movement (that is, the movement of day and night), but obliquely against it. So that its mid-circle, which lies symmetrically between its poles, whereon is the body of the Sun, cuts the circle of the two first poles at two opposite points, to wit, at the beginning of the Ram and at the beginning of the Scales; and it departs from it along two arcs, one toward the north and the other toward the south.

14 And the summits of these arcs depart equally from the first circle, on either side, by 23 degrees and a point more; and one summit is the beginning of the Crab and the other is the beginning of Capricorn. Wherefore, at the beginning of the Ram, when the Sun travels beneath the mid-circle of the first poles, Maria must needs see him circling the world around, down upon the earth, or the ocean, like a millstone, from which not more than half of his body should appear; and she would see him continually rising after the manner of the screw of a press, until he had completed 91 revolutions and a little more.

15 When these revolutions are completed, his elevation at Maria is about as much as it is for us at mid-tierce, when the day and night are equal. And if a man were standing erect in Maria, with his face ever turned to the Sun, he would see it ever moving toward his right hand.

16 Then, following the same path, he seems to descend for another 91 circlings and a little more until he is circling around, down upon the earth or the sea, not displaying his whole bulk; and then he passes out of sight and Lucia begins to see him, and perceives him mounting and descending around her as many circles as Maria does.

17 And if a man were standing erect at Lucia and ever turning his face toward the Sun, he would see him moving toward his left hand. Whereby it may be perceived that these places have one day in the year, six months long, and a night of equal time; and when the one has day, the other night.

18 Again it follows that the circle upon this ball where, as already stated, the Garamanti are, must see the Sun circling right above it, not after the fashion of a millstone but of a wheel, not more than half of which can be seen in any region, when the Sun is travelling under the Ram. And then it perceives him departing from itself and working towards Maria ninety-one days and a little more, and returning towards itself for as many days; and then, when he has come back, he travels beneath the Scales, and again departs and approaches Lucia 91 days and a little more, and returns during as many.

19 And this locality, which girds the whole ball, always has the day equal to the night, whichever side of it the Sun is travelling; and it has twice in the year a most fierce summer of heat, and two little winters.

20 It follows further that the two spaces intermediate between the two imagined cities in the mid-circle must see the Sun in varied fashion according as they are remote or nigh to these places, as may now, by what has been said, be perceived by whosoever hath a noble intellect, to which it is well to leave a little effort.

21 Wherefore it may now be seen that, by divine provision, the world is so ordained that when the sphere of the Sun has revolved and returned to any point, this ball, on which we are placed, has received in its every region an equal time of light and of darkness.

22 Oh, unutterable wisdom that didst thus ordain, how poor is our mind to comprehend thee! And ye for whose behoof and delight I am writing, in what blindness do ye live, not lifting up your eyes to these things but keeping them fixed upon the mire of your folly![78]

Chapter VI

1 In the preceding chapter it has been shown in what way the Sun circles, so that we may now proceed to explain the meaning of the division which we are considering. I say, then, that in this first division I begin to commend this lady by comparing her with other things. And I say that the Sun, circling the world, sees not anything so noble as her; wherefore it follows that she, according to these words, is the most noble of all the things that the Sun shines upon.

2 And I say, *in that hour*, and the rest. Wherefore be it known that "hour" is understood in two ways by the astronomers, one by making 24 hours of the day and night, to wit, 12 of the day and 12 of the night, whether the day be long or short. And these hours are short or long in the day or in the night according as day or night waxes

---

78 *Par.* X.1–12.

or wanes. And these hours the church uses, when she says Primes, Tierce, Sext, and Nones. And these are called the temporal hours.

3 The other is to make day and night 24 hours, of which the day one while has 15 hours and the night 9, and another while the night 16 and the day 8, according as day or night waxes or wanes, and these are called equal hours. And ever at the equinox these, and those which are called temporal, are one and the same thing, because the day being equal to the night it must needs so be.

4 Then when I say, *Every supernal intellect gazes upon her*, I commend her without reference to aught else, and I say that the Intelligences of heaven marvel at her, and that noble folk down here below think of her when they have most of that which is their delight. And here be it known that every supernal intellect, according as it is written in the book *Of Causes*, hath knowledge of that which is above itself, and of that which is below itself.

5 It hath knowledge, then, of God, as its cause; it hath knowledge, then, of that which is beneath it as its effect. And because God is the most universal cause of all things, by having knowledge of him they have knowledge of all things according to the measure of intelligence. Wherefore all the Intelligences have knowledge of the human form insofar as it is regulated by intention in the divine mind. But the motor Intelligences have highest knowledge of it, because they are the most especial causes of it and of every general form. And they know it as perfectly as can possibly be, even as their rule and example.

6 And if the human form itself, when copied and individuated, is not perfect, the defect is not of the example but of the material, which is individual. Wherefore, when I say, *Every supernal intellect gazes upon her*, I would say nought else save that she is made as she is, even as the intentional example of the human essence, which is in the divine mind; and made by that power which exists in highest degree in those angelic minds which, with the heavens, fashion these things here below.

7 And in confirmation of this, I go on and say, *and such folk as are here enamoured* and the rest, where you are to know that each thing most chiefly desires its own perfection, wherein its every longing is stilled, and it is for its sake that any other thing is desired. And it is this longing which always makes every delight seem defective to us; for no delight in this life is so great as to be able to take away the thirst from our soul, so that the longing spoken of shall not remain in our thought.

8 And since this lady is in very truth that perfection, I affirm of the folk that here below receive the greatest delight, that when they are most at peace she still abides in their thoughts. Whereby I assert that she is as perfect as the human essence can supremely be.

9 Then when I say, *her being is to him who gives it to her so pleasing,* I show that not only is this lady the most perfect in the human generation but more than most perfect, insofar as she receives of the divine excellence beyond the due of humanity.

10 Whence we may reasonably believe that as every master loves his best work more than the rest, so God loves the best human person more than all the rest. And since his generosity is not confined by the necessity of any limit, his love hath not regard to the due of him who receiveth it, but surpasses it in the gift and benefaction of power and of grace. Whence I say here that God himself, who gives her being, for love of her perfection, infuses of his excellence into her beyond the limits of the due of our nature.

11 Then when I say, *her pure soul,* I prove what has been said by the testimony of sense, where you are to know that, as saith the Philosopher in the second *Of the Soul,*[79] the soul is the actualizing of the body; and if it is its actualizing, it is its cause, and (because, as is written in the book *Of Causes* already cited,[80] every cause infuses into its effect some of the excellence which it receives from its own cause) it infuses and renders to its body something of the excellence of its cause, which is God.

---

79   *De anima* II.1.

80   *De causis* IV.48.

12 Wherefore, inasmuch as wondrous things are perceived in her under the bodily aspect, so as to make every one who looks on her long to behold them, it is manifest that her form, to wit, her soul, which guides the body as its proper cause, miraculously receives the gracious excellence of God.

13 And so do I prove, by this her appearance, that beyond the due of our nature (which in her is most perfect as has been said above) this lady has been endowed and ennobled by God. And this is all the literal meaning of the first division of the second main section.

Chapter VII

1 After commending this lady generally, with reference both to the soul and to the body, I go on to commend her specially with reference to the soul. And first I commend her according as her excellence is great in itself; then I commend her according as her excellence is great upon others and useful to the world. In this second division begins where I say, *Of her it may be said.*

2 I say then, first, *On her descendeth the divine power.* Where be it known that the divine excellence descends upon all things, and otherwise they could not exist; but although this goodness springs from the most simple principle, it is diversely received, in greater or smaller measure, by the things that receive it. Wherefore it is written in the book *Of Causes,* "The primal excellence makes its excellences flow upon things with one flowing."[81]

3 But each thing receives of this flowing according to the fashion of its power and of its being, and of this we may have an example patent to the senses from the Sun. We see the light of the Sun, which is one, derived from a single source, diversely received by the several bodies; as Albertus says in the book he has made *On the Intellect,* that certain substances, because they have a large measure of the clearness of the transparent mingled in their composition, so soon as the Sun sees them become so luminous that their aspect

---

81   *De causis* XIX (XX).157.

consists in the multiplication of the light in them, and they cast a great splendour from themselves upon other substances, as are gold and certain stones.

4 Certain there are which, because they are altogether diaphanous, not only receive the light but without impeding it render it again, coloured with their colour, to other things. And certain there are so supreme in the purity of their transparency as to become so radiant that they vanquish the temper of the eye, and cannot be looked on without trouble of the sight, as are mirrors. Certain others are so completely without transparency that they receive but little of the light, as is earth.

5 In like manner the excellence of God is received after one fashion by the sejunct substances, to wit, the angels, which are without grossness of material, as though diaphanous, in virtue of the purity of their form; and after another fashion by the human soul, which, although on one side it is free from material, on another side is impeded (like a man who is immersed in the water all except his head, of whom it cannot be said that he is all in the water or all out of it); and after another fashion by animals whose soul is entirely embraced in material, but I speak of it in the measure to which it is ennobled; and after another fashion by the minerals; and by the earth, otherwise than by the other elements, because it is the most material, and therefore the most remote and most out of proportion to the prime, most simple, and most noble power, which alone is intellectual, to wit, God.

6 And though here it is the general degrees that are laid down, nevertheless individual degrees may also be laid down, inasmuch as, of human souls, one receiveth otherwise than another. And because in the intellectual order of the universe the ascent and descent is by almost continuous steps, from the lowest form to the highest and from the highest to the lowest (as we see is the case in the sensible order), and between the angelic nature, which is an intellectual thing, and the human soul there is no intermediate step, but the one is, as it were, continuous with the other in the order of steps; and between the human soul and the most perfect soul of the brute animals there is also no intermediary, and we see many men so vile

and of such base condition as scarce to seem other than beasts; and like manner we are to lay it down and firmly to believe that there be some so noble and of so lofty condition as to be scarce other than angels.

7 Otherwise the human species would not be continued in either direction, which may not be. Such as these Aristotle, in the six of the *Ethics*, calls divine, and such I assert this lady to be, so that the divine virtue descends upon her after the fashion wherein it descends upon an angel.

8 Then when I say, *and whatsoever gentle lady not believeth this*, I prove it by the experience which may be had of her in those doings which are proper to the rational soul, wherein the divine light most freely rays; that is to say, in speech and in expression, which we are wont to call gestures and bearing. Whence you are to know that man alone amongst the animals speaks and has gestures and expression which we call rational, because he alone has reason in him.

9 And if anyone should say in contradiction that certain birds talk, as seems to be the case with some, especially the magpie and the parrot, and that certain beasts have expression or gestures, as the ape and some others seem to have, I answer that it is not true that they speak, nor that they have gestures, because they have no reason, from which these things must needs proceed; nor have they the principle of these things within them, nor do they understand what it is; nor do they purpose to signify anything by them, but they merely reproduce what they see and hear.

10 Wherefore, even as the image of bodies is reproduced by certain shining things (for instance a mirror), and the corporeal image that the mirror displays is not real, so the semblance of reason, namely the expression and the speech which the brute beast reproduces or displays, is not real.

11 I say that, *Whatsoever gentle lady not believeth* what I assert, is to *Go with her and mark well her gestures.* I say not "whatsoever man," because the experience may be gained in more comely fashion by woman than by man. And I tell that which will be perceived con-

cerning her, in her company, by telling the effect of her speech and the effect of her bearing.

12 For her speech, by its loftiness and by its sweetness, begets in the mind of him who hears it a thought of love (which I call a celestial spirit, because its origin is from above, and from above cometh her teaching, as has been told already), from which said thought proceeds the firm belief that she is a miraculous lady of power.

13 And her gestures, by their sweetness and their harmony, make love wake and come to consciousness, wherever his potentiality has been sown by a sound nature. Which natural sowing comes about as is set forth in the following treatise.

14 And when I say, *Of her it may be said,* and the rest, I purpose to narrate how the excellence and power of her soul is good and profitable to others; and first, how it is profitable to other ladies, saying, *Gentle is that in lady which in her is found,* where I render a manifest example to women, gazing upon which they may, by following it, make a gentle semblance.

15 Secondly, I tell how she is profitable to all folk, saying that her aspect aideth our faith, which is profitable more than all other things to the human race, as that whereby we escape from eternal death and acquire eternal life.

16 And it helps our faith because, inasmuch as the chiefest foundation of our faith is the miracles wrought by him who was crucified (which same created our reason and will that it should be inferior to his power), and wrought afterwards in his name by his saints, and inasmuch as many are so stubborn as to doubt of these same miracles, with some certain shade of doubt, who may not believe any miracle unless they have experience of the same; and inasmuch as this lady is a thing visibly miraculous, whereof the eyes of men may take daily experience, and which may assure us of the possibility of the others, it is manifest that this lady, with her wondrous aspect, "aideth our faith."

17 And therefore I finally say that, "from eternity"—that is to say, eternally—she was ordained in the mind of God in testimony of the faith to those who live in these times. And this ends the second division of the second chief section according to its literal meaning.

Chapter VIII

1 Amongst the effects of the divine wisdom, man is the most marvellous, seeing how the divine power has united three natures in one form, and how subtly his body must be harmonized for such a form, having organs for almost all its powers.

2 Wherefore, because of the complex harmony amongst so many organs which is required to make them perfectly answer to one another, few of all the great number of men are perfect. And if this creature be so marvellous, verily we must fear to treat of the conditions of the same, not only in words but even in thought, according to those words of *Ecclesiasticus*, "The wisdom of God, preceding all things, who hath searched out?" And those others where it saith, "Seek not out things that are too high for thee, and search not out things too hard for thee, but whatsoever things God hath commanded, think thereupon; and in his further works be not curious," that is anxious.[82]

3 I, then, who in this third section purposed to speak of certain conditions of such a being (insofar as in her body, by reason of the excellence of her soul, sensible beauty appeareth) timorously, and with no hardihood, purpose to begin to untie so great a knot, if not entirely yet at least in some measure.

4 I say, then, that after revealing the meaning of this section wherein this lady is commended under the aspect of her soul, we are to proceed and are to consider how I commend her under the aspect of the body, when I say, *Things are revealed in her aspect.*

5 And I say that in her aspect things appear which reveal of the pleasures (amongst the rest) of Paradise. The most noble thing, and that which is written down as the goal of all others, is to be satisfied, and this is being blessed; and this pleasure is verily (al-

---

82 *Ecclesiasticus* 1:3 and 3:22, respectively.

though in another way) in her aspect; for, by gazing upon her, folk are satisfied (so sweetly doth her beauty feed the eyes of those who look upon her), but in another fashion than by the satisfaction of Paradise, which is unbroken; for this may not come to any.

6 And since some might ask where this wondrous pleasure appears in her, I distinguish in her person two parts wherein human pleasure and displeasure are most apparent. Wherefore you are to know that in whatsoever part the soul doth most of her office, this she most fixedly purposes to adorn, and worketh most subtly upon it.

7 Whence we see that in the face of man, wherein she doth more of her office than in any other external part, she designeth so subtly that, by reason of her refining there to the utmost capacity of her material, no one face is like to any other; because the distinguishing potentiality of the matter, which is, in a way, unlike in every individual, is here reduced to actuality.

8 And inasmuch as the soul operates in the face chiefly in two places, because in these two places the three natures of the soul have some kind of jurisdiction, to wit, in the eyes and in the mouth, it chiefly adorns these, and there sets its whole purpose of beautifying, if it may. And in these two places I say that these pleasures appear, saying, *In her eyes and in her sweet smile.*[83]

9 Which two places, by a beautiful simile, may be called the balconies of the lady who dwelleth in the edifice of the body, to wit, the soul, because here, albeit in a measure veiled, she doth many times reveal herself. She revealeth herself in the eyes so manifestly that her present emotion may be recognized by whoso closely looketh there.

10 Wherefore, since there are six emotions proper to the human soul, whereof the Philosopher makes mention in his *Rhetoric*, to wit, grace, jealousy, pity, envy, love, and shame,[84] by none of these may the soul be impassioned without the semblance thereof appearing at the window of the eyes, unless it be shut within by great

---

83   *Par.* XVIII.19–21.

84   *Rhetoric* II.1.

exertion of power. Whence ere now certain have plucked out their eyes lest their inward shame should outwardly appear, as Statius the poet tells us of the Theban Oedipus when he says that "with external night he solved his convicted shame."[85]

11 It is revealed in the mouth, like a colour behind glass. And what is laughter save a coruscation of the delight of the soul, that is to say, a light appearing outwardly according as it exists within? And therefore it is fitting that a man, in order to show his soul moderate in merriment, should laugh in moderation, with a dignified severity, and with slight movement of his features, so that the lady who is then revealed, as said above, may appear modest and not dissolute.[86]

12 Wherefore the book *Of the Four Cardinal Virtues* bids us to observe this: "Let thy laughter be without cachinnation,"[87] that is to say, without clucking like a hen. Ah! wondrous laughter of my lady, whereof I speak, which is never perceived save by the eye!

13 And I say that love conveys these things to her there as to their proper place. And here love may be considered in two ways. Firstly the special love of the soul for these places, and secondly the universal love which disposes things to love and to be loved, and which ordains the soul to adorn these parts.

14 Then when I say, *They transcend our intellect*, I plead my excuse for seeming to utter but little(when I dwell upon it) of so great excellence of beauty; and I affirm that I say so little of it for two reasons. The one is that the things which appear in her aspect "transcend our intellect," to wit, the intellect of man; and I tell the manner of this transcending, which is after the fashion wherein the Sun transcends feeble vision, not only that wherein he transcends the sound and strong. The other is that the said intellect may not fixedly gaze on it, because the mind becomes intoxicated there, so that straightway after gazing it goes astray in all its activities.

---

85   *Thebaid* I.47–48.

86   *Par.* V.124–126, XVII.121–123.

87   Martin Dumiens, *Four Virtues.*

15 Then when I say, *Her beauty rains down flamelets of fire*, I have recourse to treating of its effect, since it is impossible to treat completely of itself. Wherefore you are to know that all those things that overcome our intellect, so that it cannot see what they are, are most suitably treated in their effects. Whence, treating thus of God, and of his sejunct substances, and of first matter, we may have a certain knowledge.

16 And therefore I say that, *Her beauty rains down flamelets of fire*, to wit, the ardour of love and of charity, ensouled by a gentle spirit, that is to say the ardour informed by a gentle spirit, to wit, right appetite, by the which and from the which springs the beginning of good thoughts. And it not only makes this but it unmakes and destroys its opposite, to wit, the innate vices which are chief foes to good thoughts.

17 And here we are to know that there are certain of the vices in a man whereto he is naturally disposed, as, for instance, some men in virtue of a choleric complexion are disposed to anger; and such vices are inborn or conatural. Others are vices of habit for which not complexion but habit is to blame; for instance intemperance, especially in wine. And these vices are to be escaped and overcome by good habit, whereby a man so becomes virtuous that his moderation needs no effort, as saith the Philosopher in the second of the *Ethics*.

18 But there is this difference between conatural passions and those of habit, that those of habit disappear entirely on the strength of good habit, because their source, to wit, the bad habit, is destroyed by its opposite; but the conatural ones, the source of which is in the nature of him who experiences the passion, though they may be much lightened by good habit, never entirely disappear so far as their first movement is concerned, but do completely disappear so far as their enduring is concerned, because habit is not an equipoise to the nature wherein is their source.

19 And therefore, that man deserves more praise who, though of bad natural disposition, corrects and rules himself contrary to the impulse of his nature, than he who, being good by natural disposition, retains himself in good conduct or recovers the way when he has lost it. Just as it is worthy of more praise to manage an intractable horse than another which is not vicious.

20 I say, then, that these flamelets which rain from her beauty, as has been said, shatter the innate (that is the conatural) vices to give to understand that her beauty has power to make a new nature in those who gaze upon it, which is a miraculous thing. And this confirms what is said above in the next preceding chapter when I say that she is the supporter of our faith.

21 Finally, when I say, *Whatsoever lady heareth her beauty*, under colour of an admonition I draw a conclusion as to the end whereto so great a beauty was made. And I say that whatever lady hears her beauty blamed for defect, is to gaze upon this most perfect example; wherein it is to be understood that this said example was made not only to improve the good but also to make a good thing out of an evil one.

22 And it adds in fine, *Of her was he thinking who set the universe in motion*, that is God, to give to understand that nature produced such an effect by divine determination. And thus ends all the second main section of this ode.

Chapter IX

1 The arrangement of the present treatise requires (now that two parts of this ode have first been explained according to my intention) that we proceed to the third, wherein I intend to clear the ode of an accusation that might have told against her. It is this, that before I came to compose this ode, thinking that this lady had become somewhat stern and haughty towards me, I made a little ballad wherein I called this lady proud and pitiless, which appears contrary to what is said of her here above.

2 And therefore I turn to the ode, and under colour of teaching her how she must excuse herself, I excuse her. And this is a figure (when inanimate things are addressed) which is called by the rhetoricians *prosopopæia*, and the poets very frequently employ it. *Ode, it seemeth that thy speech is counter,* and the rest.

3 Now the better to give the meaning of this to be understood I must divide it into three sections, for in the first is set forth the thing which needs excusing, then the excuse is proceeded with when I say, *Thou knowest that the heaven.* Finally, I address the ode as a person instructed as to what is to be done, when I say, *Thus plead thy excuse if thou have need.*

4 So I say first, "Thou ode who dost speak of this lady with so much praise, it seems that thou art contrary to a sister of thine." I say "sister" by similitude, for as a woman begotten by the same begetter is called sister, so may a man call a work that is done by the same doer a sister; for our doing is in a kind of way begetting. And I say why she seems counter to the other, saying, "Thou makest her humble, and the other made her proud," that is to say, haughty and disdainful, which is the same thing.

5 Having set forth this accusation, I go on to the excuse by means of an analogous instance, wherein sometimes the truth is at discord with the appearance, and, under sundry aspects, may be differently spoken of. I say, *Thou knowest that the heaven is ever shining and clear,* that is to say, it never loses its brightness, but for certain reasons it is sometimes permissible to speak of it as being darkened.

6 Where be it known that the proper objects of sight are colour and light, as Aristotle has it in the second *Of the Soul* and in the book *Of Sense and its Object.*[88] It is true that the other things are visible, but they are not the proper objects of sight, because some other sense perceives them, so that they cannot be called proper to sight, nor proper to touch; and such are shape, size, number, movement, rest, which we call "sensibles," and which we perceive with more than one sense. But colour and light are properly visible, because we apprehend them by sight alone, that is to say, with no other sense.

7 These visible things, both proper and common, insofar as they are visible, pass into the eye)I do not mean the things themselves,

---

88   *De anima* II.6–7 and *De sensu et sensato* I, respectively.

but their forms) through the diaphanous medium (not in reality but in intention), much as in transparent glass.[89]

8 And in the water which is in the pupil of the eye this passage which the visible form makes through the medium is completed, because this water is bounded, something like a mirror, which is glass with lead behind it; so it cannot pass any further on, but is arrested there after the fashion of a smitten ball. So that the form (which does not appear nor shine in the transparent medium) is arrested. And this is why an image is seen on leaded glass but not on other.

9 From this pupil the visual spirit, which extends continuously from it to the front part of the brain (where the sensitive power exists as in its fontal[90] principle) instantaneously, without any interval of time, makes a representation of it; and thus we see. Wherefore, in order that its vision may be true, that is to say such as the visible thing is in itself, the medium through which the form comes to the eye must be colourless, and so must the water of the pupil be; otherwise the visible form would be tainted with the colour of the medium and with that of the pupil.

10 And therefore they who desire to give some particular colour to the things in a mirror, interpose of that colour between the glass and the lead, so that the glass is embraced by it. It is true that Plato and other philosophers declared that our seeing was not due to the visible coming into our eye, but to the visual power going out to the visible. And this opinion is refuted as false by the Philosopher in that *Of Sense and its Object*.

11 Now that we have thus examined the mode of vision, it is easy to perceive that although the star is always equally clear and shining and experiences no mutation save that of local movement, as is proved in that *Of Heaven and Earth*, there may be many causes why it seems not clear and not shining, since it may so appear because of the medium which is continually changing.

---

89   *Purg.* XVIII.22–24.
90   Adjective of font.

12 This medium changes from abundance to paucity of light, as at the presence or absence of the Sun; and in his presence the medium, which is diaphanous, is so full of light that it overcomes the star and seems to be brighter than it. This medium also changes from subtle to gross, and from dry to moist, by reason of the vapours of earth which are continually rising. Which medium, by these changes, changes the image of the star which comes through it, its grossness affecting it in dimness, and its moisture or dryness affecting it in colour.

13 And it may also appear so by reason of the visual organ, that is the eye, which by reason of weakness or exhaustion may acquire a certain colour or a certain feebleness, as it often happens that the tunic of the pupil becoming violently blood-shot because of some disorder caused by illness, almost everything looks red, and therefore the star seems coloured thereby.

14 And, when the sight is enfeebled, a certain dispersion of the spirit takes place in it, so that things no longer seem knit together but sprawling, much as letters of our writing do on damp paper. And this is why many, when they have a mind to read, remove the writing to a distance from their eyes that the image may enter the more lightly and subtly; and thereby the letter remains more distinct in their sight.

15 And so the star too may seem blurred. And I experienced this in that same year wherein this ode was born; for greatly taxing my sight in eagerness of reading, I so weakened the visual spirits that all the stars appeared to me to be shadowed by a kind of halo.

16 And by long repose in dark and cool places, and cooling the body of the eye in clear water, I knit together again the disintegrated power, so as to return to my former good condition of sight. And thus we see that there are many causes (for the reasons noted) why the star may appear other than it really is.

Chapter X

1 Quitting this digression, which was necessary for the apprehension of the truth, I return to the matter in hand, and declare that as sometimes "our eyes call," that is judge, "the star" other than its real state is, so this little ballad considered this lady according to the appearance (discordant with the truth) that sprang from the infirmity of my mind which was impassioned by excessive longing.

2 And this I make clear when I say, "For the soul was in such terror, that methought dire" that which I saw in her presence; where be it known that the more closely the agent is united with the patient, so much the stronger is the passion, as may be understood by the opinion of the Philosopher in that *Of Generation.* Wherefore, the nearer the desired thing approaches to him who desires it, the greater is the desire; and the more the soul is impassioned, the more does it concentrate itself upon the appetitive part, and the more does it retreat from reason; so that, in such a state, a person does not judge as a man, but pretty nearly as some other animal, according to appearance only, not according to truth.

3 And this is why the semblance, which in truth was august, seemed to me "disdainful and cruel"; and it was in accordance with this judgment of sense that this little ballad spoke. And hereby it is given sufficiently to be understood that this ode considers this lady according to the truth, because of its discord with that other.

4 And not without reason do I say, *Where she perceiveth me,* and not "where I perceive her." But herein I would give to understand the great power that her eyes had over me, for even as though I had been diaphanous, their ray passed through me on every side. And here natural and supernatural reasons might be assigned, but let it suffice here to have said so much; elsewhere I shall discourse of it on more fitting occasion.

5 Then when I say, *Thus plead thy excuse if thou have need,* I enjoin upon the ode how to excuse itself (by the reasons assigned), where there is need, to wit, where any is in difficulty because of this contradiction; which is no other than to say that if any is in difficulty as concerns the contradiction between this ode and that little ballad, he is to consider the reason which has been told.

6 And this figure in rhetoric is worthy of much praise, and moreover is necessary; I mean when words are addressed to one person and intended for another; for admonition is ever laudable and necessary, yet it is not always suitable in every one's mouth.

7 Wherefore when a child is aware of a father's vice, and when a servant is conscious of a master's vice, and when a friend knows that his friend's shame would be increased or his honour depressed were he to admonish him, or knows that his friend is not patient but irritable under admonition, this figure is most beautiful and most profitable, and it may be called *disguising*.

8 And it resembles the action of the skilful warrior who attacks the fortress on one side to withdraw the defence from the other, for then the intention of the succour goes not to the same quarter as the battle.

9 And I enjoin upon her also to ask leave from this lady to speak of her. Where it may be understood that a man should not presume to praise another without rightly considering whether such is the pleasure of the person praised; for many a time he who thinks he is praising is in truth blaming, either through the fault of himself who speaks the praise, or of him who hears it.

10 Whence there is need of much discretion herein, which discretion is a kind of asking leave, after the fashion wherein I bid this ode ask it. And so ends all the literal meaning of this treatise; wherefore the arrangement of the work demands that, following up the truth, we proceed to the allegorical exposition.

Chapter XI

1 According as the order requires, returning again to the beginning, I declare that this lady is that lady of the intellect which is called Philosophy. But inasmuch as praises naturally produce a longing to

know the person praised, and since knowing a thing means understanding what it is, considered in itself and in all its causes (as saith the Philosopher in the beginning of the *Physics*), and inasmuch as the name does not expound this (although this is what it signifies, as the Philosopher says in the fourth of the *Metaphysics*, where it is asserted that the definition is that conception which the name signifies[91]) it is fitting at this point, before proceeding further in her praises, to show and to declare what it is that is called Philosophy, that is to say, what this name signifies.

2 And afterwards, when she herself has been explained, the present allegory will be more effectively treated. And first I will tell who first gave this name, and then I will proceed to its meaning.

3 I say then, that of old, in Italy, almost at the beginning of the foundation of Rome, which (as Paulus Orosius writes[92]) was 650 years, or a little more or less, before the Saviour came, about in the time of Numa Pompilius, second king of the Romans, there lived a most noble philosopher who was called Pythagoras. And that this was the time when he lived Titus Livius seems incidentally to indicate in the first part of his volume.[93]

4 And before him the followers after knowledge were not called philosophers but sages, as were those seven most ancient sages whose fame folk still preserve, the first of whom was Solon, the second Chilo, the third Periander, the fourth Thales, the fifth Cleobulus, the sixth Bias, the seventh Pittacus.

5 This Pythagoras, when asked whether he regarded himself as a sage, refused to appropriate the word to himself, and said that he was not a wise man but a lover of wisdom. And hence it afterwards came about that everyone who was devoted to wisdom was called a "lover of wisdom," that is a philosopher, for in Greek *philos* is as much as *amator* in Latin, and hence we say *philos* for *lover*, and *sophia*

---

91   *Physics* I.1 and *Metaphysics* IV.7, respectively.

92   *Histories* VII.iii.1.

93   "In placing Pythagoras at the time of Numa Pompilius (717–673 BC), D(ante) is relying on a mistaken reading of Livy (I.xviii.1–2)—the 'Titus Livius' mentioned here" (Frisardi).

for *wisdom*; wherefore *philos* and *sophia* are as much to say "lover of wisdom"; wherefore it may be noted that it is a name not of arrogance but of humility.

6 Hence is derived the word for the proper act of such an one, *philosophy*; as from "friend" is derived a word for the proper act of such, *friendship*. Whence may be seen, by considering the significance of the first and the second word, that "philosophy" is no other than "friendship to wisdom" or to knowledge; whence in a certain sense everyone may be called a philosopher, in virtue of the natural love for which begets in everyone the longing to know.

7 But since the essential passions are common to all, we do not speak of them under a word which singles out some particular participant in the essential thing. Thus we do not call John Martin's friend when we simply mean to indicate the natural friendship whereby we are all friends to all, but the friendship which has been generated over and above that which is natural, and which is proper and distinct in individual persons. Thus no man is called a philosopher in virtue of the common love.

8 Aristotle proposes, in the eighth of the *Ethics*, to call him a friend whose friendship is not hidden from the person loved, and to whom the person loved is also friendly, so that the good-will is on both sides;[94] and this must be in virtue of profit, or of delight, or of worthiness. And thus, in order that a man may be called a philosopher, there must be the love of wisdom which creates goodwill on the one side, and there must be the zeal and eagerness which begets goodwill on the other side also, so that intimacy and the manifestation of goodwill spring up between them. Wherefore a man cannot be called a philosopher without both love and zeal, for both the one be present.

9 And inasmuch as friendship contracted for delight or for profit is not real but only incidental friendship, as the *Ethics* shows,[95] so philosophy for delight or for profit is not real but only incidental philosophy. Wherefore we are not to call any man a real philos-

---

94 *Ethics* VIII.2.

95 *Ethics* VIII.3.

opher who is friendly with wisdom in some direction because of some certain delight; as are many who delight in composing odes, giving their zeal thereto, and who delight in the zealous study of rhetoric and music, but who flee and desert the other sciences, all of which are members of wisdom.

10 We are not to call him a real philosopher who is a friend of wisdom for profit, as are lawyers, physicians, and almost all the members of the religious orders, who do not study in order to know but in order to get money or office; and if anyone would give them that which it is their purpose to acquire, they would linger over their study no longer.

11 And as amongst the different kinds of friendship that which is for the sake of profit is least to be called friendship, so these, such as I speak of, have less share in the name of philosopher than any other folk. Wherefore, just as friendship contracted in virtue of worthiness is real and perfect and abiding, so is that philosophy real and perfect which is generated by worthiness alone, with no other respect, and by the excellence of the soul that feels this friendship, in virtue of right appetite and right reason.

12 So that here we may say that, just as there is real friendship between men when each one loves the other in entirety, so the real philosopher loves every part of wisdom, and wisdom every part of the philosopher, so as to draw him entirely to herself and allow him to dissipate no thought of his upon other things. Wherefore Wisdom herself says in the *Proverbs* of Solomon, "I love those that love me."[96]

13 And as real friendship, abstracted from the mind and considered only in itself, has as its subject the knowledge of the well-doing and has for form the attraction thereto, so philosophy considered in itself, apart from the soul, has as its subject understanding, and as its form an almost divine love of the thing understood. And as virtue is the efficient cause of real friendship, so truth is the efficient cause of philosophy.

---

96   Proverbs 8:17.

14 And as the goal of true friendship is the excellent delight which proceeds from intercourse according to what is proper to humanity, that is according to reason (as Aristotle seems to think in the ninth of the *Ethics*[97]), so the goal of philosophy is that most excellent delight which suffers no interruption nor defect, to wit, the true blessedness which is gained by the contemplation of the truth.

15 And thus it may be perceived who this my lady now is, in all her causes and in her constituent principle, and why she is called Philosophy, and who is the true philosopher and who the philosopher incidentally.

16–17 But since sometimes, in a certain fervour of mind, the source or goal of action and passion is called by the name of the action or passion itsel—as Vergil does in the second of the *Aeneid*, when he calls Aeneas, "O light"[98] (which was an act), "O hope of the Trojans" (which is a passion), though he was neither a light nor a hope, but was the source whence came to them the light of counsel, and was the object in whom reposed all the hope of their deliverance; and as Statius says in the fifth of the *Thebaid* when Hypsipyle says to Archemoros, "O thou comfort of my estate, and my lost fatherland, O glory of my service";[99] and as we constantly say, pointing to a friend, "see my friendship," and as a father says to his child, "my love"—by long wont, the sciences upon which philosophy plants her sight most fervently are called by her name, such as natural science, moral science, and metaphysic science; which last is called philosophy, because on her most necessarily and most fervently does she plant her vision. Whence may be seen how the sciences are called philosophy in a secondary sense.

18 Now that we have perceived how the primary is the real philosophy in her essence (which is the lady of whom I am speaking), and how her noble name is communicated by wont and use to the sciences, I shall proceed with her praises.

---

97   *Ethics* IX.9.

98   *Aeneid* II.281–283.

99   *Thebaid* V.608–611.

Chapter XII

1 In the first chapter of this treatise, the cause which moved me to compose this ode has been so fully explained that there is no occasion to discourse further of it, because it may easily be reduced to the exposition which has already been given. And, therefore, according to the divisions made, I will run through the literal meaning in quest of the other, translating the literal sense where necessary.

2 I say, *Love that discourses to me in my mind.* By "love" I mean the study which I devoted to acquiring the love of this lady. Where be it known that "study" may here be considered in two ways. There is one kind of study which brings a man to the habit of the art or the science, and there is another study which works in the habit when acquired, and plies it.

3 And this first it is that I here call love, which formed in my mind continuous, new, and most lofty ponderings on this lady, who has been indicated above; for this is the wont of study which is devoted to acquiring a friendship, because in the first place it ponders on the great significance of this friendship, while longing for the same.

4 This is that study and that affection which is wont to proceed the generating of friendship amongst men, when love is already born on the one side, and he who already loves longs and strives that it may spring up on the other side. For, as said above, philosophy is there when the soul and wisdom have become friends, so that each is entirely loved by the other, as in the fashion stated above.

5 Nor is there need of further discourse by way of the present exposition concerning this first verse, which was discoursed of as proem in the literal exposition; inasmuch as the understanding may very easily turn, by means of its first significance, to this its second.

6 Wherefore we are to proceed to the second verse which begins the treatise, in which I say, *The Sun seeth not, who circleth all the world.* Here you are to know that just as it is suitable to treat of an object of sense by means of a thing which is not an object of sense, so it is suitable to treat of an object of the intellect by means of a thing which is not an object of the intellect. And so, since in the literal exposition the discourse opened with the corporeal Sun, accessible to sense, we are now to discourse of the spiritual Sun, accessible to the intellect, that is God.

7 No object of sense in all the universe is more worthy to be made the symbol of God than the Sun, which enlightens, with the light of sense, itself first, and then all the celestial and elemental bodies; and in like manner God illuminates first himself with intellectual light and then the celestial and other creatures accessible to the intellect.[100]

8 The Sun quickens all things with his heat, and if he destroys certain things thereby, that is not of the intention of the cause but is an incidental effect; and in like manner God quickens all things in goodness, and if any of them be evil, it is not of the divine intention but must needs be in some way incidental to the progress of the effect intended.

9 For if God made both the good and the bad angels, he did not make them both by intention but only the good ones; then the wickedness of the bad ones followed, beside the intention, yet not so beside the intention but that God foreknew their wickedness. But so great an affection had he to produce spiritual creatures that the foreknowledge of some who must needs come to an ill end should not nor could not hinder God from this producing.

10 For nature would not be to praise if, well knowing that the blossoms of a tree must perish in some certain part, she were not to produce blossoms thereon, and because of the barren were to abstain from producing the fertile ones.

11 I say then, that God, who understandeth all (for his circling is his understanding), sees not so noble a thing as he sees when he looks upon the place where is this philosophy; for albeit God, looking upon himself, sees all things at once, yet inasmuch as the distinc-

---

100   *Inf.* I.13–18; *Par.* X.52–54, XXIII.28–30.

tion between things exists in him, after the fashion wherein the effect exists in the cause, he sees them distinct from one another.

12 He sees this most noble of all things absolutely, then, inasmuch as he sees her most perfectly in himself and in his essence. For if we call to mind what has been said above, philosophy is a loving exercise of wisdom, and this exists supremely in God, since in him is the highest wisdom and the highest love and the highest actuality, which may not be elsewhere save insofar as it proceeds from him.

13 The divine philosophy, then, is of the divine essence, because in him nought may be added to his essence; and she is most noble because the divine essence is most noble; and she is in him in perfect and true fashion, as though in eternal wedlock. In other intelligences she exists in a lesser way, as though a mistress, of whom no lover has complete enjoyment, but must satisfy his longing by gazing on her.

14 Wherefore it may be said that God sees not, that is to say understands not, anything so noble as her; and I say "anything" inasmuch as he sees and distinguishes the other things, as said above, since he sees himself as the cause of them all. Oh most noble and most excellent heart which is enamoured of the spouse of the Emperor of Heaven, and not only spouse but sister and most beloved daughter.

Chapter XIII

1 Now that we have seen it subtly declared at the beginning of her praises that, primarily considered, she exists in the divine substance, we are to go on and to consider how I declare that secondarily she exists in created intelligences.

2 I say then, *Every supernal intellect gazes upon her*, where we are to know that I say "supernal," bringing them into relation with God, who has been spoken of above; and hereby are excluded the intelligences that are in exile from the supernal fatherland, for they cannot philosophise because love is utterly quenched in them; and

to philosophise, as already said, there is need of love. Wherefore we perceive that the infernal Intelligences are bereft of the aspect of this most beauteous one; and inasmuch as she is the blessedness of the intellect, to be deprived of her is most bitter and full of all sadness.

3 Then when I say, *And such folk as are here enamoured*, I descend to explain how she also comes in a secondary sense, into the human intelligence; and with this human philosophy I then proceed in the treatise, commending her. I say, then, that the folk who are enamoured here, to wit, in this life, perceive her in their thoughts, not always but when love makes them feel of his peace. Wherein three things are to be observed which are touched upon in this passage.

4 The first is when it says, Such folk as here are enamoured, whereby a distinction seems to be made in the human race; and it must of necessity be made, for, as is clearly apparent, and as will be expressly explained in the next following treatise, an immense proportion of mankind lives more after sense than after reason. And those who live after sense cannot possibly be enamoured of her, for they cannot have any apprehension of her.

5 The second is where it says, *When love maketh them feel*, and the rest, where it seems that a distinction of time is made; and this too is necessary, because, albeit the sejunct intelligences gaze continuously upon this lady, the human intelligence may not do this, because human nature requires many things besides speculation (whereby the intellect and reason are fed) to sustain it. Wherefore our wisdom is sometimes only in habit and not in act. And this is not so with the other intelligences whom the intellectual nature by itself completes.

6 Wherefore, when our soul is not in the act of speculation, it cannot be truly said to be in company with philosophy except insofar as it has the habit thereof, and the potentiality of waking it; and therefore she is sometimes with the folk who are enamoured here, and sometimes is not with them.

7 The third is when it tells the hour when those folk are with her, that is when *Love maketh them feel of his peace*, which signifies no other than when man is in actual speculation; for study does not make aught of the peace of this lady felt, save in the act of speculation. And thus we see how this lady is primarily of God, and secondarily of the other sejunct intelligences by way of continuous contemplation, and afterwards of the human intelligence by way of discontinuous contemplation.

8 But the man who has her as his lady is always to be called a philosopher, although he is not always engaged in the distinguishing act of philosophy, because folk are chiefly to be named according to habit. Wherefore we call a man virtuous even when he is not doing a deed of virtue, because he has the virtuous habit, and we call a man eloquent even when he is not speaking, because of the habit of eloquence, that is to say, of speaking well. And concerning this philosophy, insofar as she is partaken by the human intelligence, the following commendations are to show how great a part of her goodness is conceded to human nature.

9 So I say next, *Her being so pleases him who gave it her*, from whom she flows as from her primal source, which doth ever attract the capacity of our nature and make it beautiful and virtuous. Whence, although certain attain to the habit of her, yet none so attain that it can be strictly called the habit, because the first study, namely that whereby the habit is begotten, can never perfectly acquire her.

10 And herein is perceived her distinctive praise, that whether perfect or imperfect she never forfeits the name of perfection. And because she is thus out of measure, it says that the soul of philosophy *Maketh it show forth in that which she doth guide*, that is to say that God ever sets of his light in her; where we must call to mind how it was said above that love is the form of philosophy, and therefore here it is called her soul.

11 Which love is manifested in the exercise of wisdom, which exercise brings with it wondrous beauties, to wit, content in every temporal state and scorn of all those things which others make their lords. Whereby it happens that the wretched others who behold this, pondering upon their defect, when the longing for perfection comes upon them, fall into labour of sighs; and this is what is meant by, *The eyes of those in whom she shines send messages thereof to the heart, filled with longings, which gather air and turn to sighs.*

Chapter XIV

1 As in the literal exposition, after the general praises, we descend to the special, first on the side of the soul, then on the side of the body, so now the text purposes, after the general commendations, to descend to the special ones. Wherefore, as was said above, philosophy here on earth has for her subject matter wisdom, and for her form love, and for the combination of the one and the other the exercise of speculation.

2 Wherefore in this verse, which begins as follows, *On her descendeth the divine power,* I purpose to commend love, which is a part of philosophy. Where be it known that for virtue to descend from one nature into another is nought else than to reduce the latter to her own likeness; just as we manifestly see that in natural agents, when their virtue descends upon things that receive it, they draw them to be so far like themselves as it is possible for them to come to be.

3 Whence we see that the Sun, when his ray descends down here, reduces things to the similitude of light insofar as by their dispositions they have the capacity for receiving light from his power. Thus I say that God reduces this love to his own similitude, in the degree wherein it is possible for it to liken itself to him. And the quality of this creating anew is set forth in saying, *As it doth upon an angel who beholdeth it.*

4 Where we are further to know that the prime agent—to wit, God—stamps his power upon some things after the manner of a direct ray, and upon others after the manner of a reflected splendour; for upon the intelligences the divine light rays without me-

dium, upon other things it is reflected by those intelligences which are first enlightened.[101]

5 But since we have here made mention of *light* and of *splendour*, for the sake of complete understanding I will explain the difference between these words, according to the opinion of Avicenna. I say that it is the custom of the philosophers to call the luminous principle *light*, insofar as it exists in the source from which it springs, and to call it a *ray*, insofar as it exists in the medium (between its source and the first body whereby it is arrested), and to call it *splendour* insofar as it is thrown back upon some other part which it illuminates.

6 I say, then, that the divine virtue draws this love to its own likeness without any intermediary. And this may be manifested chiefly herein, that as the divine love is eternal under every aspect, so, of necessity, it behoves its object to be eternal, so that the things which it loves must needs be eternal. And it is after this same fashion that this love makes us love, because wisdom, whereupon this love strikes, is eternal.

7 Wherefore it is written of her, "From the beginning, before the ages, was I created, and in the ages which are to come I shall not fail."[102] And in the *Proverbs* of Solomon wisdom herself says, "I was ordained from everlasting."[103] And in the beginning of the Gospel of John her eternity may be clearly noted; and hence it arises that where this love grows all other loves are darkened and almost quenched, inasmuch as its eternal object conquers and overcomes all other objects out of all proportion.

8 And this the most excellent philosophers openly revealed in their actions, whereby we know that they gave no heed to any other thing save wisdom. Thus Democritus, taking no heed of his own person, cut neither beard nor hair nor nails. Plato, caring not for temporal goods, took no heed to his royal dignity, for he was the son of a king. Aristotle, caring for no other friend, entered into

---

101   *Par.* I.1–3, XIII.52–60.

102   *Ecclesiasticus* 24:9.

103   Proverbs 8:23.

contention with his best friend save her—to wit, with the above-named Plato. And why do we speak of these, since we find others who despised their very lives for these thoughts, such as Zeno, Socrates, Seneca, and many others.

9 And so it is manifest that the divine virtue, in angelic fashion, descends upon men in this love; and to furnish experience of this, the text in sequence cries out, *And whatsoever gentle lady not believeth this, let her go with her and mark well,* and the rest. By "gentle lady" is understood a soul noble in intellect and free in the exercise of its own proper power, which is reason.

10 Wherefore other souls cannot be called ladies but handmaids, because they exist not for their own sake but for that of another, and the Philosopher says, in the second of the *Metaphysics,* that the thing is free which is there for its own sake and not for that of another.[104]

11 It says, *Let her go with her and mark well her gestures,* that is to say, Let her go in company with this love, and look upon that which she shall find within him; of which it treats in some part, saying, *Where she speaketh there cometh down,* that is to say, where philosophy is in act a "celestial thought" comes down, which argues that she is a more than human activity. It says "from heaven" to give to understand that not only she but the thoughts which are her friends are removed from base and earthly things.

12 Then, in sequence, it says how she confirms and kindles love, wheresoever she displays herself, with the "sweetness of her gestures," to wit, all her comely and tender semblance, free from all excess. And, in sequence, the more to persuade folk to be of her company, it says, *Gentle is that in lady which in her is found, and beauteous is so much only as is like to her.*

13 Further, it adds, *And affirm we may that to look on her gives help,* where be it known that the power to look upon this lady was granted to us in such ample measure, not only in order that we

---

104 *Metaphysics* I.2 (mistakenly referred to as "the second").

might see the countenance which she reveals to us, but that we may long to acquire the things which she keeps concealed.

14 Wherefore even as by her means much is perceived in its reason and in its sequence which without her appears a marvel, so by her means it becomes credible that every miracle may have its reason for a loftier intellect, and consequently may take place. Whence our excellent faith hath its origin, from which cometh the hope of that for which we long and which we foresee, and from this is born the activity of charity.

15 By which three virtues we rise to philosophize in that celestial Athens where the Stoics and Peripatetics and Epicureans, by the art of the eternal truth, harmoniously unite in one will.

Chapter XV

1 In the preceding chapter this glorious lady is commended according to one of her component parts, to wit, love. Now, in this chapter, wherein I purpose to expound that verse which begins, *Things are revealed in her aspects*, it behoves to treat in commendation of her other part, to wit, wisdom.

2 The text says, then, that in her countenance appear things *which show us of the joys of Paradise*, and it specifies the place of this appearance, to wit, in her eyes and in her smile. And here it is right to know that the eyes of wisdom are her demonstrations, whereby the truth is seen most certainly, and her smile is her persuasions, whereby the inner light of wisdom is revealed behind a certain veil; and in these two is felt that loftiest joy of blessedness which is the supreme good in Paradise.

3 This pleasure may not be in aught else here below save in looking upon these eyes and this smile. And the reason is this, that because everything by nature desires its own perfection, it may not without it be satisfied, which is being blessed; for however much it should have other things, without this it would still be left in a state of longing, in which it may not be with blessedness; inasmuch as blessedness is a perfect thing, and longing is a defective thing, for no one longs for what he has, but for what he has not, which is a manifest deficiency.

4 And in this look alone is acquired human perfection, that is the perfection of reason, whereon, as on its chiefest factor, all of our essence depends; and all our other activities, feelings, nutrition, and the rest exist for it alone, and it exists for itself and not for others. Therefore, if this be perfect so is that, to such a point that man, as man, sees his every longing as its goal, and so is blessed.

5 And therefore it says in the book of *Wisdom*, "unhappy is he who setteth at nought wisdom and teaching,"[105] which is the privation of being happy. It follows that by the habit of wisdom both being happy and being satisfied are attained, according to the teaching of the Philosopher. Wherefore we perceive that in her aspect there appear "of the things of Paradise," and so we read in the book of *Wisdom* already cited, in speaking of her, "she is the brightness of the eternal light, the spotless mirror of the majesty of God."[106]

6 Then when it says, *They transcend our intellect*, I plead my excuse, saying that I can speak but little of these things, because of their transcendency. Where be it known that in a certain sense these things dazzle our intellect, inasmuch as they affirm certain things to be which our intellect may not look upon—to wit, God and eternity and first matter; which are seen with the utmost certainty, and believed to be with absolute faith, and yet we can only understand what they are by process of negation. In this way we may approach to the knowledge of them, but no otherwise.

7 But here certain may encounter a great difficulty as to how wisdom can make a man blessed when she cannot perfectly reveal certain things to him; inasmuch as man's natural longing is to know, and without fulfilling his longing he may not be blessed.

8 Hereto the clear answer may be given that the natural longing in every case is measured by the possibilities of the thing longed

---

105 *Wisdom* 3:11.
106 *Wisdom* 7:26.

for; otherwise it would contradict itself, which is impossible; and nature would have created it in vain, which is also impossible.

9 It would contradict itself, for in longing for its perfection it would long for its imperfection, inasmuch as it would long to be ever longing, and never to fulfill its longing. And this is the error into which the accursed miser falls, perceiving not that he desires himself ever to be desiring, as he pursues the sum which it is impossible to reach. Also nature would have created it in vain, because it would not have been ordained to any end. And therefore human longing is measured in this life by that degree of knowledge which it is here possible to possess; and that point is never transgressed except by misapprehension, which is beside the intention of nature.

10 And in like manner is it measured in the angelic nature, and limited in quantity to that knowledge which each one's nature can apprehend. And this is why the saints envy not one another, because each one attains the goal of his longing, which longing is commensurate with the nature of his excellence. Whence, since it is impossible to our nature to know concerning God and to declare concerning certain things what they are, we have no natural longing to know this, and thus the difficulty is removed.

11 Then when I say, *Her beauty rains down flamelets of fire*, I descend to another pleasure of Paradise, to wit, the felicity (secondary to this primal felicity), which proceeds from her beauty. Where be it known that morality is the beauty of philosophy, for just as the beauty of the body results from the members, in proportion as they are duly ordered, so the beauty of wisdom, which, as said above, is the body of philosophy, results from the order of the moral virtues, which enable her to give pleasure that may be perceived by the senses.

12 And therefore I say that her beauty, to wit, morality, *rains down flamelets of fire*, that is to say, right appetite, which is begotten by the pleasure of moral teaching; which appetite actually removes us from even those vices which are natural to us, to say nothing of the others. And hence springs that felicity which Aristotle defines in the first of the *Ethics*, saying that it is "activity in accordance with virtue, in a perfect life."[107]

13 And when it says, *Wherefore, whatsoever lady heareth her beauty*, it proceeds with her praise. I cry out to folk to follow her, telling them what are her benefactions; namely, that by following her every one becomes good. Wherefore it says, "whatsoever lady" (that is, "whatsoever soul") perceives that her beauty is blamed, because it seems not such as it should seem, let her look upon this example.

14 Where be it known that the beauty of a soul is its ways, especially the virtues, which are sometimes made less beautiful and less pleasing by vanity or by pride, as we shall be able to see in the last treatise. And therefore I say that to escape this we are to look upon her; to wit, under that aspect wherein she is an example of humility, that is, in the part of her which is called moral philosophy. And I add that by gazing upon her, I mean wisdom, in that part, every vicious man will become upright and good. And therefore I say, *It is she who humbleth each perverse one*, that is, gently bends back whosoever hath been warped from the due order.

15 Finally, in supreme praise of wisdom, I say that she is mother of all origins whatever, saying that with her God began the universe, and specifically the movement of the heaven which generates all things, and from which every movement takes its beginning and its starting, saying, *Of her was he thinking who set the universe in motion*, that is to say, that she existed in the divine thought, which is intellect itself, when he made the universe. Whence it follows that she made it.

16 Wherefore, in the passage in *Proverbs*, Solomon says in the person of Wisdom, "When God prepared the heavens I was there, when he walled the abysses with a fixed law and with a fixed circuit, when he established the heaven above and suspended the fountains of water, when he fixed the limit for the sea and set a decree upon the waters that they might not pass their boundaries, when he laid

---

107　*Ethics* I.7.

down the foundations of the earth, I too was with him, ordering all things, and took my delight daily."[108]

17 Oh worse than dead, who flee from her friendship! Open your eyes and see that, before ye were, she loved you, preparing and ordering your progress; and, after ye were made, to direct you aright she came to you in your own likeness.

18 And if ye may not all come to look upon her herself, do honour to her in her friends, and follow their commandments, as who proclaim to you the will of this eternal empress. Close not your ears to Solomon who bids you thereto when he says that "the way of the righteous is a shining light that goes on and increases until the day of blessedness,"[109] following after them, gazing upon their doings, which should be a light to you on the path of this most brief life.

19 And here may be ended the real meaning of this present ode. But the final verse, which appears as a *tornata*, may be very easily brought down to this exposition by means of the literal one, save insofar as it says that, in that other poem, I call this lady "cruel and disdainful." Where be it known that at the beginning this philosophy appeared "cruel" to me, on the side of her body, that is wisdom; for she smiled not upon me, inasmuch as I did not apprehend her persuasions; and "scornful" because she turned not her eyes to me, that is to say, I could not perceive her demonstrations. And the fault of all this was on my side.

20 Whereby, and by what has been said in the literal meaning, the allegory of the *tornata* is manifest; so that it is time, in order to go further on, to make an end of this treatise.

---

108   Proverbs 8:27–30.
109   Proverbs 4:18.

Book IV

Le dolci rime d'amore

I

The sweet rhymes of love, which I was wont
to search out in my thoughts,
needs must I abandon; not that I have no hope
of a return to them.
But because the scornful and haughty gestures
which in my lady have appeared,
have closed the way to me of wonted speech.
And because meseems 'tis time for waiting,
down will I lay my tender style,
which I have held in treating of love,
and I will tell of the worth
whereby a man is truly gentle,
with harsh and subtle rhyme
refuting the judgment false and base
of such as would have it that of gentlehood
the principle is wealth,
and, at the outset, I call upon that Lord
who dwelleth in my lady's eyes,
so that of herself she is enamoured.

II

A certain one held empire who would have gentlehood,
according as he deemed,
to be the ancient possession of wealth,
with gracious manners.
And some other was there
of lighter wisdom,
who recast such saying,
and stripped it of its latter phrase,
methinks because he had it not.
After him go all they
who make folk gentle because of race
which has long abode in great wealth.
And so inured
is such false thought amongst us,

that folk call that man
a gentleman who can aver, 'I was
grandson or son of such a one of worth,'
though he himself be nought
But basest doth he seem, to whoso looks on truth,
who hath been shown the way and thereafter errs therefrom;
and he hits nigh to who should be a corpse yet walk the earth.

III

He who defines, 'Man is a living trunk,'
in the first place, speaks that which is not true,
and further, utters the falsehood in defective guise;
but haply sees no more.
In like fashion did he who held empire
err in definition,
for in the first place he lays down the false,
and on the other hand
proceeds defectively.
For riches cannot (as is held)
either give gentlehood or take away,
since in their nature they are base.
Further, who paints a figure,
unless himself can be it, can not set it down,
nor is an upright tower
made to lean by a river that flows far away.
That they be base and imperfect is apparent,
for how much soever gathered
they can give no quiet, but multiply care;
wherefore the mind that is upright and true
is not dismayed by their dispersion.

IV

Nor will they have it that a base man can become gentle,
nor that from a base father can descend
a family that ever can be held as gentle.
This is avowed by them.
Wherefore their argument appears to halt,
inasmuch as it lays down
that time is requisite to gentlehood,
defining it thereby.
Further it followeth from what I have above set down,

that we be all gentle or else simple,
or that man had not an origin:
but this I grant not,
neither do they, if they be Christians.
Wherefore to sound intellects
'tis manifest that what they say is vain,
and thus do I refute the same as false,
and therefrom dissociate me
And now I would declare how I regard it,
what is gentlehood and whence it comes;
and I will tell the tokens that a gentleman retains.

V

I affirm that every virtue in principle
cometh from one root,
I mean virtue that maketh man blessed in his doing.
This is (according as the Ethics say),
"a selective habit,
which abideth solely in the mean";
such are the words set down.
I affirm that nobility in its constituent essence
ever implies the goodness of its seat,
as baseness ever implies ill;
and virtue, in like fashion,
always carries the import of good;
wherefore in one same implication
the two agree, being to one effect.
Therefore the one needs must derive from the other
or both from the same third.
But if one signifies all that the other signifies,
and more as well, the derivation will rather be from it.
And let this which I have now declared be presupposed.

VI

Gentlehood is wherever there is virtue,
but not virtue where she is,
even as the heaven is wherever is the star,
but not conversely.
And we in women and in youthful age
perceive this saving thing,
insofar as they are deemed alive to shame,

which is diverse from virtue.
Therefore shall be evolved (like perse from black)
each several virtue out of her,
or their generic kind, as I have laid it down above.
Wherefore let no one vaunt himself
and say, 'I belong to her by race';
for they are well-nigh gods
who have such grace, apart from all the guilty;
for God alone presents it to the soul
which he sees within its person
take perfect stand; even as to some
the seed of blessedness draws nigh,
dispatched by God into the well-placed soul.

VII

The soul whom this excellence adorns,
holds it not concealed;
for, from the first when she weds the body,
she shews it forth till death.
Obedient, sweet, and alive to shame,
is she in the first age;
and adorns her person with beauty
with well-according parts.
In manhood she is temperate and brave,
full of love and courteous praises,
and delights only in deeds of loyalty.
And in old age
is prudent and just and hath a name for open-handedness,
rejoicing in herself to hear and to discourse of others' excellence.
Then in the fourth term of life
to God is re-espoused,
contemplating the end that she awaits,
and blesses the past seasons.
See now how many be they deceived!

TORNATA

Against the erring ones take thou thy way, my ode,
and when thou shalt be
in the region where our lady is,
keep not thy business hid from her.

> Thou mayst securely say to her,
> 'I go, discoursing of a friend of thine.'

Chapter I

[1] Love, according to the unanimous opinion of the sages who have discoursed of it, and as we see by continuous experience, is that which brings together and unites the lover to the person loved. Wherefore Pythagoras says, "In friendship many are made one."[110]

[2] And inasmuch as when things are united they naturally communicate their qualities to each other, insomuch that sometimes the one is completely transformed to the nature of the other, it comes to pass that the emotions of the loved person enter into the loving person, so that the love of the one is communicated to the other, and in like manner hatred and longing and every other passion. So that the friends of the one are loved by the other, and the enemies hated; wherefore in the Greek proverb it says, "All things should be common between friends."

[3] So when I became the friend of this lady, mentioned above in the real exposition, I began to love and to hate in accordance with her love and hatred. I began, therefore, to love those who follow the truth, and to hate those who follow error and falsity, even as does she.

[4] But inasmuch as everything is lovable in itself, and nought is to be hated save for the evil superinduced upon it, it is reasonable and right to hate not things but their badness, and to strive to sever it from them. And if any other is intent upon this, my most excellent lady is most intent; I mean upon severing from things the badness which is the cause of their being hated; for in her is all reason, and in her, as in its fountain, is the right.

[5] I, following her in deed as an emotion, to the best of my power, abominated and disprized the errors of men, to the infamy or blame not of the erring ones but of the errors; blaming which I

---

110   *De officiis* I.xvii.56.

thought to make them displeasing, and when they had become displeasing, to separate them from those who for their sake were hated by me.

6 Amongst which errors there was one that I chiefly reprehended, which, inasmuch as it is not only hurtful and perilous to those who are involved in it but even to the rest who reprehend it, I set about severing from them and condemning.

7 This is the error concerning human excellence, insofar as it is sown by nature in us, which ought to be called nobility; which error, by evil habit and lack of intellect, was so entrenched that the opinion of almost everyone had thereby been falsified; and from false opinion sprang false judgments, and from false judgments sprang unjust reverence and vilipending, whereby the good were held in base contempt, and the bad honoured and exalted. Which thing was the worst confusion in the world, as he may see who subtly considereth what may follow therefrom.

8 And inasmuch as this my lady a little estranged her tender looks from me (especially in those parts wherein I considered and searched out whether the prime matter of the elements was understood by God), therefore I abstained for a season from frequenting her countenance, and, as though sojourning away from her presence, I set about contemplating in thought the defect of men with respect to the aforesaid error.

9 And to avoid idleness, which is the chief enemy of this lady, and to quench that error which robs her of so many friends, I purposed to cry aloud to the folk who were going on the wrong path, in order that they might direct themselves on the right way; and I began an ode, the opening of which I said, *The sweet rhymes of love which I was wont*, wherein it is my purpose to bring back folk to the right way concerning the proper knowledge of real nobility, as may be seen by making acquaintance with its text, on the expounding of which I am now intent.

10 And inasmuch as in this ode I am intent on so needful a succour, it was not well to speak under any figure, but it behoved me to provide this medicine by the quick way, in order that health, the corruption of which was hurrying to so foul a death, might be quickly restored.

11 There will be no need, then, to disclose any allegory in expounding it, but only to explain the sense according to the letter. By my lady I still understand the same, of whom was the discourse in the preceding ode, to wit, that most virtuous light, philosophy, whose rays make the flowers bud, and bear as fruit that true nobility of man, concerning which the ode before us purposes to speak in full.

Chapter II

1 At the beginning of the exposition we have undertaken, the better to give to understand the meaning of the ode before us, it behoves us first to divide it into two parts; for in the first part the proem is spoken, in the second the treatise follows. And the second part begins at the beginning of the second verse, where it says, *A certain one held empire who would have gentlehood.*

2 The first part again may be comprised in three members. The first contains the reason why I depart from my accustomed speech; in the second I say what it is my intention to treat of; in the third I ask aid of that which may most aid me, namely the truth. The second member begins, *And because meseems 'tis time for waiting.* The third begins, *And at the outset I call upon that Lord.*

3 I say, then, that it behoves me to drop the sweet rhymes of love which my thoughts were wont to search out; and I assign the cause, when I say that it is not because I purpose to make no more rhyme of love, but because unwonted looks have appeared in my lady which have bereft me of matter for speaking of love at the present.

4 Where, be it known, the gestures of this lady are not here called scornful and haughty save according to appearance; even as in the tenth chapter of the preceding treatise may be seen how on another occasion I declare that the appearance was discordant from the reality; and how this may be (that one same thing may be sweet and may appear bitter, or be clear and appear obscure) can there be sufficiently perceived.

5 Next, when I say, *And because meseems 'tis time for waiting*, I tell, as already observed, whereof I purpose to treat. And here we are not to pass dryshod over what is implied in "time for waiting" (since that is the chief cause of my procedure), but are to consider how reasonable it is to await the right season in all our doings, and especially in our speech.

6 Time, as Aristotle says in the fourth of the *Physics*, is "the enumeration of movement in respect to before and after."[111] It is the enumeration of the movement of the heavens, which disposes things here below diversely to receive the several informing powers.

7 For the earth is one way disposed in the beginning of spring to receive into herself the power that informs grasses and flowers, and in another way in winter; and one season is otherwise disposed than another, with regard to receiving the seed. And in like manner our mind, insofar as it is based upon the composition of our body, which must needs follow the circulation of the heavens, is one way disposed at one time, and another at another.

8 Wherefore words, which are like the seed of activities, must be very discreetly retained and let go, both in order that they may be well received and brought to fruit, and in order that on their own side they fail not by sterility. And therefore forethought as to time must be taken, both for him who speaks and for him who is to hear; for if the speaker be disposed amiss, his words are often hurtful, and if the hearer is disposed amiss, words which are good are ill received. And therefore Solomon says in *Ecclesiastes*, "There is a time to speak, and there is a time to be silent."[112]

9 Wherefore I, feeling the disposition to discourse of love disturbed within me, for the reason which has been told in the preceding chapter, thought fit to wait on time, which brings with it the goal

---

111   *Physics* IV.11, 14.
112   Ecclesiastes 3:7.

of every longing, and comes of itself, as though with a gift, to those who grudge not the wait.

10 Wherefore says St. James the Apostle in his *Epistle* in the fifth chapter, "Behold, the husbandman waiteth for the precious fruit of the earth, patiently enduring until he receive the early and later."[113] For well-nigh all our troubles, if we come to look at their origins rightly, proceed in a way from not knowing how to handle time.

11 I say that since it seems well to wait, I will lay down, that is to say, I will let be, "my tender style," that is the tender fashion I have observed in discoursing of love, and I declare that, *I will tell of the worth* whereby man is truly "gentle." And whereas "worth" may be understood in sundry ways, here "worth" is taken as a capacity of nature, or an excellence given by her, as will be seen below.

12 And I promise to treat of this matter with subtle and harsh rhyme. For we are to know that rhyme can be understood in two ways, that is to say a larger and a narrower. In the narrow sense it means that harmony which it is the custom to make in the last syllable and the last but one. In the larger sense it means that whole way of discourse which, in regulated numbers and time, falls into rhymed consonants. And it is so that it is to be taken and understood in this proem.

13 And therefore it says "harsh" insofar as it refers to the sound of the composition, which to suit so weighty a subject should not be smooth; and it says "subtle" with reference to the meaning of the words, which proceed by subtle argument and disputation.

14 And I add, *Refuting the judgment false and base*, where there is a further promise to refute the judgment of folk filled with error; "false," that is remote from truth, and "base," that is established and confirmed by baseness of mind.

15 And heed must be given to this, that in this proem the promise is first to treat of the true and then to refute the false; and in the treatise the opposite is done; for first the false is refuted, and then

---

113   James 5:7.

the true is handled, which seems not to correspond to the promise. And therefore be it known that though both the one and the other be intended, the chief intention is to treat of the true; and to refute the false is so far intended as it conduces to making the truth more plainly appear.

16 And here the promise to treat of the truth comes first, as the main intent, which brings to the mind of the hearers the longing to hear; in the treatise the false is first refuted, in order that when wrong opinions have been dissipated, the truth may be more freely received. And this method was observed by the master of human reason, Aristotle, who always first fought with the opponents of the truth, and then, when they had been convicted, demonstrated the truth.

17 Finally, when I say, *And at the outset I call upon that Lord*, I summon truth to be with me, which is that Lord who dwelleth in the eyes— to wit, in the demonstrations—of philosophy. And verily the truth is Lord, for when espoused thereto the mind is *Lady*, and otherwise she is a servant without all liberty.

18 And it says, *So that of herself she is enamoured*, because philosophy, which, as was said in the preceding treatise, is "the loving exercise of wisdom," contemplates herself when the beauty of her eyes is revealed to herself. And what else is this but to say that the philosophizing soul not only contemplates the truth but also contemplates its own contemplation of the beauty thereof, turning upon itself and enamouring itself of itself by reason of the beauty of its direct contemplation? And thus ends what the text of the present treatise brings, by way of proem, in three members.[114]

Chapter III

1 Having inspected the meaning of the proem, the treatise is to follow; and the better to show it forth, it behoves to divide it into its chief parts which are three: for in the first, nobility is treated

---

114   *Par.* X.1–6, XXI.112–117, XXII.46–48, and XXXI.109–111.

according to the opinions of others; in the second, it is treated according to the true opinion; in the third, the speech is directed to the ode, by way of a certain adorning of what has been said.

2 The second part begins, *I affirm that every virtue in principle.* The third begins, *Against the erring ones take thou thy way, my ode.* And after these general sections, other divisions must needs be made, rightly to apprehend the meaning which is to be set forth.

3 And let none marvel if we proceed by means of many divisions; inasmuch as it is a great and lofty work that is now under our hands, and little investigated by authors; nor let them marvel that the treatise whereon I am now entering must needs be long and subtle, to unravel the text perfectly according to the meaning which it bears.

4 I say, then, that this first part is now to be divided into two: for in the first are laid down the opinions of others, in the second they are refuted; and this second part begins, *He who defines, "man is a living trunk".*

5 Again, what is still left as the first part has two members: the first is the definition of the opinion of the emperor; the second is the variation on his opinion by the vulgar herd, which is bare of all reason. This second member begins, *And some other was there of lighter wisdom.*

6 I say then, *A certain one held empire,* that is to say, such an one exercised the imperial office. And here be it known that Frederick of Swabia, the last emperor of the Romans (I say the last up to the present time, notwithstanding that Rudolf and Adolf and Albert have been elected since his death and that of his descendants), when asked what gentlehood was, answered that it was "ancient wealth and gracious manners."

7 And I say that, *Some other was there of lighter wisdom,* who, weighing and turning about this definition on every side, cut off the last clause—to wit, the "gracious manners"—and clung to the first—to wit, the "ancient wealth." And as the text seems to conjecture, it was haply because he himself had not fair manners, that, not

wishing to lose the name of gentlehood, he defined it according as it made for him, to wit, the possession of "ancient wealth."

8 And I declare that this opinion is that of almost every one, saying that after him went all those who held one gentle because he springs from a race that has long been rich; inasmuch as almost all bark out this.

9 These two opinions, although the one, as has been said, is utterly to be neglected, seem to have two weighty reasons to support them. The first is the Philosopher's declaration that what is the opinion of the majority cannot be absolutely false; the second is the most excellent authority of the imperial majesty.

10 And that the power of the truth which confutes all authority may be the better seen, I purpose to expound how supporting and weighty is each one of these reasons. And in the first place, we can have no knowledge concerning the imperial authority, unless its roots be found. And these we must expressly handle in a special chapter.

Chapter IV

1 The root foundation of the imperial majesty is in truth the necessity of human civility; which is ordained for a certain end, to wit, the life of felicity; to the which no man is sufficient to attain by himself without the aid of any, inasmuch as man hath need of many things which no one is able to provide alone. Wherefore the Philosopher saith that man is by nature a social animal.[115]

2 And as an individual man requires the companionship of home and household for his completeness, so likewise a household requires a district for its completeness, since otherwise it would suffer many defects which would be a hindrance to felicity. And since a district cannot satisfy itself in everything, needs must there be a city for its satisfaction. And further, the city requires for its arts

---

115 *Politics* I.2.

and for its defense to have mutual relations and brotherhood with the neighboring cities; wherefore the kingdom was instituted.

3 And inasmuch as the human mind rests not in the limited possession of land, but ever, as we see by experience, desires to acquire more territory, needs must discords and wars arise betwixt kingdom and kingdom. Which things are the tribulations of cities, and through the cities of districts, and through the districts of households, and through the households of man; and thus is felicity impeded.

4 Wherefore, to abolish these wars and their causes, needs must all the earth and whatsoever is given to the generations of man for her possession be a monarchy, that is one single princedom having one prince; who, possessing all things and not being able to desire more, shall keep the kings contented within the boundaries of their kingdoms, so that there shall be peace between them, in which peace the cities may have rest, and in this rest the districts may love one another, and in this love the households may receive whatsoever they need, and when they have received this, man may live in felicity, which is that whereto man was born.

5 And upon these arguments the words of the Philosopher may be brought to bear, which he utters in the *Politics*, that when diverse things are ordained for one end, one of them must be the ruler or guide, and all the rest must be ruled or guided by it.[116] Even as we see in a ship that the diverse offices and diverse ends of it are ordained to one single end, to wit, the making of the desired port by a prosperous voyage; wherein, like as each officer regulates his proper function to its proper end, there is one who considers all these ends and regulates them with a view to the final end; and he is the shipmaster whose voice all are bound to obey.[117]

6 And we see the same thing in religious orders, and in armies, and in all things which are ordained, as aforesaid, to some end. Whereby it may be manifestly seen that for the perfection of the universal religious orders of the human race it behoves that there should be

---

116   *Politics* I.5.

117   *Purg.* XVI.103–111, XXXIII.37–39.

one, as shipmaster, who, considering the diverse conditions of the world, and ordaining the diverse and necessary offices, should have the universal and indisputable office of commanding the whole.

7 And this office is called by pre-eminence empire, without any qualification, because it is the command of all the other commands. And hence he who is appointed to this office is called emperor because he is the commander who issues all these commands. And what he says is law to all, and he ought to be obeyed by all, and every other command draws its strength and authority from his. And thus it is manifest that the imperial majesty and authority is the loftiest in the fellowship of man.

8 But some might cavil and say that although the office of empire be necessary for the world, yet it follows not that reason requires the authority of the Roman prince is to be supreme (which is the point we have to make); but that the Roman power was acquired not by reason, nor by decree of universal consent, but by force, which seems to be the contrary of reason.

9 To this we may answer readily that the election of this supreme officer must needs proceed, in the first instance, from the council which maketh provision for all, to wit, from God; since the election would else not have been equal for all; since, before the above-said officer, there was no one giving his mind to the general good.

10 And because there never was, nor shall ever be, a nature more sweet in the exercise of lordship, more firm in its maintenance, nor more subtle in acquiring it than the nature of the Latin folk (as may be seen by experience), and especially that of the hallowed people in whom the high Trojan blood was infused, God chose that people for such office.

11 So we see that since it might not be attained without the greatest virtue, nor exercised without the greatest and most humane benignity, this was the people who was best disposed to it. Wherefore, at the beginning the Roman people got it not by force but by the divine providence which transcends all reason. And herein doth Vergil agree, in the first of the *Aeneid*, where, speaking in the person of

God, he says, "To them (to wit, to the Romans) I assign no limit of things nor of time. To them have I given empire without end."[118]

12 Force, then, was not the moving cause, as the caviller supposed, but was the instrumental cause, even as the blows of the hammer are the cause of the knife, whereas the mind of the smith is the efficient and moving cause. And thus not force but reason, and moreover divine reason, was the beginning of the Roman empire.

13 And that this is so may be seen by two most manifest reasons, which show that this city was imperial, and had special birth and special progress from God.[119]

14 But inasmuch as this may not be handled in the present chapter without excess of length, and long chapters are the foes of memory, I will make a further digression of another chapter to set forth the arguments indicated above. Nor will this be without profit and much delight.

Chapter V

1 It is no marvel if the divine providence, which utterly surpasses angelic and human perception, proceeds many times by ways hidden to us; inasmuch as even human operations many times conceal their purport from men themselves. But it is matter for great marvel if ever the working out of the eternal council proceeds so manifestly that our reason discerns it.

2 Wherefore, at the beginning of this chapter, I may speak with the mouth of Solomon, who saith in his *Proverbs*, in the person of wisdom, "Hearken! for I am to speak of great things."[120]

3 When the immeasurable divine goodness willed to reconform to itself the human creature (which was parted from God by the sin of the disobedience of the first man and thereby deformed), it

---

118   *Aeneid* I.276–279.

119   *Par.* VI.55–57.

120   Proverbs 8:2.

was appointed in the most lofty and united divine consistory of the Trinity that the Son of God should descend to earth to effect this harmony.[121]

4 And inasmuch as at his coming into the world it was meet that not only heaven but earth should be in its best disposition—and the best disposition of earth is when it is a monarchy, that is to say, when it is all subject to one prince, as aforesaid—therefore, that people and that city who were destined to bring this about (to wit, the glorious Rome) were ordained by the divine Providence.[122]

5 And because the abode wherein the celestial king must enter ought to be most clean and pure, there was likewise ordained a most holy family from the which, after many merits, should be born a woman supremely good amongst all the rest, who should be the treasure-house of the Son of God. And this family is that of David. And the triumph and honour of the human race, Mary to wit, was born from it.[123]

6 Wherefore it is written in Isaiah, "A rod shall spring out from the root of Jesse, and a flower shall spring up from his root."[124] And Jesse was the father of the above-said David. And it was all at the same point of time wherein David was born and Rome was born, that is to say Aeneas came into Italy from Troy, which was the origin of the most noble city of Rome, as testify the Scriptures. Whereby the divine election of the Roman Empire is manifest enough; to wit, by the birth of their holy city being at the same time as the root of the family of Mary.

7 And incidentally, we may note that since the heaven itself began to roll it ne'er was in better disposition than at the time when he who made it and who rules it came down below; as even now, by virtue of their arts, the mathematicians[125] may retrace.

---

121   *Par.* XXIII.37–39.

122   *Purg.* XVI.106–108.

123   *Par.* XXXIII.4–6.

124   Isaiah 11:1.

125   i.e. astronomers.

8 Nor was the world ever so perfectly disposed, nor shall be again, as then when it was guided by the voice of one sole prince and commander of the Roman people, as Luke the Evangelist beareth witness. And therefore there was universal peace which never was before nor shall be, and the ship of the human fellowship was speeding straight to the due port in tranquil voyage.

9 Oh ineffable and incomprehensible wisdom of God, which against thy coming into Syria didst make so great a preparation beforehand in heaven above and here in Italy; and oh most foolish and vilest brutes, pasturing in the semblance of men, who presume to discourse against our faith, and with your spinning and delving would fain know what God hath ordained with so great wisdom! Cursed be ye and your presumption and whoso believeth on you!

10 And, as has been said before at the end of the preceding chapter, not only had she a special birth from God but special progress; for briefly beginning from Romulus, who was her first father, until her most perfect age, that is to say the time of the aforesaid emperor, she advanced not by human but by divine activities.

11 For if we consider the seven kings who first governed her, Romulus, Numa, Tullus, Ancus, and the Tarquin kings, who were like the guardians and protectors of her childhood, we may find from the scriptures of the Roman histories, and especially from Titus Livius, that they were all of diverse nature according to the needs of the period of time which was proceeding in their day.

12 Then if we consider her more advanced youth, when she was emancipated from the guardianship of royalty by Brutus, the first consul, even until Caesar, the first supreme prince, we shall find that she was uplifted not by human but by divine citizens, into whom was inspired not human but divine love, in their love of her. And this could not nor might not be, save for some special end, purposed by God in so great an infusion of heaven.

13 And who shall say that it was without divine inspiration that Fabricius refused an almost infinite quantity of gold because he would not abandon his fatherland; that Curius, whom the Sam-

nites tried to corrupt, refused a huge mass of gold for love of his fatherland, saying that the Roman citizens desired to possess not gold but the possessors of the gold; that Mutius burnt his own hand because he had missed the blow whereby he had thought to deliver Rome?

14 Who shall say of Torquatus, who judged his own son to death for love of the public good, that he endured this without divine help? And the above-said Brutus, in like manner? Who shall say it of the Decii and of the Drusi, who laid down their life for their country? And of the captive Regulus, sent from Carthage to Rome to exchange the captive Carthaginians against himself and the other captive Romans, who shall say that when the legation had withdrawn, the advice he gave, for love of Rome, against himself, was prompted only by human nature?

15 Who shall say of Quintus Cincinnatus, who was appointed dictator and taken from the plough, and after his term of office laid it down of his own accord, and went back to his ploughing; who shall say of Camillus, banished and cast into exile, that he came to free Rome from her foes, and when he had freed her withdrew of his own will into exile so as not to offend the authority of the senate, without divine instigation?

16 Oh most hallowed bosom of Cato, who shall presume to speak of thee? Verily none can speak of thee more worthily than by keeping silence, and following the example of Jerome, who in his proem to the Bible, where he comes to tell of Paul, says that it were better to hold one's peace than to come short in speech.[126]

17 Of a surety it must be manifest, when we remember the life of these and of the other divine citizens, that not without some light of divine goodness, superadded to the excellence of their own nature, such marvels were done. And it must be manifest that these most excellent ones were instruments wherewith the divine providence proceeded in the Roman empire, wherein many a time the arm of God was seen to be present.

---

126   *Purg.* I.31–33, 76–81.

18 And did not God set his own hand to the battle in which the Albans fought with the Romans, at the beginning, for the headship of rule, when one only Roman held in his hands the freedom of Rome? Did not God interpose with his own hand when the Franks had taken all Rome and were seizing the capitol by stealth at night, and only the voice of a goose gave notice of it!

19 Did not God interpose with his own hand when in the war of Hannibal so many citizens had perished that three bushels of rings were carried off to Africa, and the Romans were ready to abandon their land had not that blessed Scipio, young as he was, undertaken his expedition into Africa for the deliverance of Rome? And did not God interpose with his own hand when a recent citizen, a small estate, Tully to wit, defended the liberty of Rome against so great a citizen as was Catiline? Yea, verily.

20 Wherefore we need demand no more in order to see that a special birth and special progress, thought out and ordained by God, was that of the holy city. And verily I am of firm opinion that the stones that are fixed in her walls are worthy of reverence, and the soil where she sits more worthy than man can preach or prove.

Chapter VI

1 Above, in the third chapter of this treatise, promise was given to discourse of the loftiness of the imperial authority and of the philosophic. And therefore, having discussed of the imperial authority, my digression must further proceed to the inspection of that of the Philosopher, according to the promise made.

2 And our first business here is to see what "authority" means, because there is more need of knowing it here than in the discourse concerning the imperial authority, which by reason of its majesty does not seem to be questioned.

3 Be it known, then, that "authority" is nought else than the act of an author. This word (to wit, *auctor*, without the third letter *c*) may spring from two principles; the one is that of a verb, dropped very much out of use in Latin, which signifies as much as "binding words together," to wit, *auieo*. And whoso regards it well, in its first form will clearly perceive that it shows its own meaning, for it is made of nought save the bonds of words, that is to say of the five vowels alone, which are the soul and juncture of every word; and it is composed of them in lithe manner, to figure the image of the tie.

4 For beginning with *A*, it turns thence to *U*, and then goes straight by *I* to *E*, whence it goes back and returns to *O*, so that truly they image forth this figure, which is the figure of a tie. And in as far as "author" is derived and descends from this verb, it is understood only of poets, who have bound their words with the art of music: and with this significance we are not at present concerned.

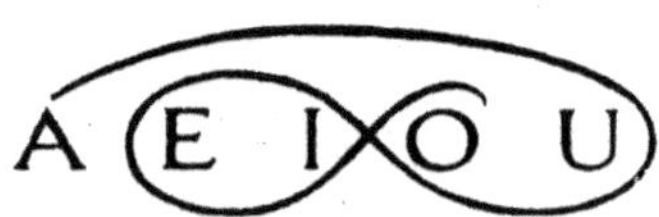

5 The other principle whence "author" descends, according to the testimony of Uguccione in the beginning of his *Derivations*, is a Greek word which is called "autentin," which is as much as to say in Latin, "worthy of faith and of obedience." Thus "author," so derived, is understood of every person worthy of being believed and obeyed. And hence comes that word of which we are treating, namely "authority"; whereby we may see that "authority" is as much as "utterance worthy of faith and of obedience."

6 It is manifest that Aristotle is most worthy of faith and of obedience. And that his words are the supreme and most lofty authority may thus be proved: amongst the workers and artificers of diverse arts and operations which are ordained for one final operation or art, the artificer or operator of that final art should be mainly obeyed and trusted by all, as he who alone considers the ultimate goal of all the other goals. Wherefore, the sword-maker and the rein and saddle-maker and the shield-maker should trust the cavalier, and so should all those trades which are ordained for the art of chivalry.

[7] And inasmuch as all human activities demand one goal, to wit, the goal of human life, whereto man is ordained as man, the master and artificer who explains and considers this should be mainly obeyed and trusted; and this is Aristotle: therefore he is most worthy of faith and of obedience.

[8] And to perceive how Aristotle is the master and leader of the human reason, inasmuch as he is intent upon its conclusive activity, it behoves us to know that this our goal, which each one naturally desires, was sought for in very ancient times by the sages. And inasmuch as they who desire this goal are so numerous, and the appetites differ in almost every single case, though there be one universal goal, yet was it right hard to discern it, as that wherein every human appetite would find direct repose.

[9] There were then certain very ancient philosophers, of whom the first and chief was Zeno, whose view and belief was that the goal of this human life is solely rigid integrity; that is to say, rigidly to pursue truth and justice without respect to aught; to show no grief, to show gladness at nothing, to have no sense of any emotion.

[10] And this is how they defined this integrity, "That which, apart from utility and apart from result, is, for its own sake, to be praised by reason." And they and their sect were called Stoics, and of them was that glorious Cato of whom I dared not to speak above.

[11] There were other philosophers whose view and belief was different from theirs; and of these the first and chief was a philosopher who was called Epicurus; who, seeing that every animal as soon as it is born, and as though directed by nature to the due goal, shuns pain and seeks pleasure, said that this our goal was voluptuary (I do not say "voluntary" but write it with a *p*), that is to say, delight without pain.

[12] And moreover, between delight and pain he placed no middle term, saying that "voluptuous" was no other than "without pain"; as Tully seems to recount in the first of the *Goal of Good*. And of these, who are called Epicureans after Epicurus, was Torquatus,

the noble Roman, descended from the blood of the glorious Torquatus of whom I made mention above.

13 There were others—and they took their rise from Socrates, and then from his successor Plato—who, looking more subtly and seeing and perceiving that in our activities we might and did err by excess and by defect, said that activity without excess and without defect, according to the standard of the mean selected by our choice, which is virtue, was that goal whereof we are at present discoursing. And they called it "virtuous activity."

14 These were called the Academicians (of whom were Plato and his nephew Speusippus), so called because of the place where Plato studied, to wit, the Academy; and they did not take their name from Socrates because in his philosophy nothing was affirmed.

15 But Aristotle, whose surname was Stagirites, and Xenocrates the Chaldeconian, his companion, by means of the almost divine intellect which nature had imparted to Aristotle, coming to knowledge of this goal pretty much by the method of Socrates and the Academicians, put the finishing touches on moral philosophy and brought it to perfection, especially Aristotle. And because Aristotle set the fashion of discoursing while walking backwards and forwards, they were called (I mean he and his companions) "Peripatetics," which is as much as to say "they who walk about."

16 And because the perfection of this moral science was brought to its limit by Aristotle, the name of the Academicians was quenched, and all they who learnt from this sect were called Peripatetics; and these yet hold sway over the world everywhere in teaching, and their doctrine may in a way be called the Catholic opinion; whereby it may be seen that Aristotle is he who directs and conducts folks to this goal; and this is what we wished to show.

17 Wherefore, to sum up, my main contention is now obvious, namely, that the authority of the supreme Philosopher, with whom we are now concerned, is in full and complete vigour. And it is not opposed to the imperial authority, but the latter without the former is perilous, and the former without the latter has a kind of weakness, not in itself but because of the disorderliness of men, so that when the one is bound up with the other they are most profitable and full of all vigour.

18 And therefore it is written in that of *Wisdom*, "Love the light of wisdom all ye who are before the peoples,"[127] which is to say, "Let the philosophical authority unite with imperial, for good and perfect rule."

19 Oh wretched ye who at the present rule! (and oh most wretched ye who are ruled!) for no philosophic authority unites with your government, neither by your proper study nor by the counsel of others, so that the word of *Ecclesiastes* applies to all, "Woe to thee, O land, whose king is a child and whose princes rise up early to feast";[128] and to no land may what follows be addressed, "Blessed is the land whose king is noble and whose princes eat in due season for necessity and not for luxury."[129]

20 Give heed who be at your sides, ye enemies of God, who have grasped the rods of the governments of Italy. It is to you, Charles and Frederick, kings, and to you others, chiefs and tyrants, that I am speaking. Behold who sit by your side to give counsel, and count how many times in the day this goal of human life is pointed out to you by your counsellors. Better were it for you to fly low like a swallow than like the kite to make the loftiest wheeling over vilest things.

Chapter VII

1 Since we have seen how the imperial and the philosophical authority, which seemed to support the opinions before us, are to be reverenced, we are now to return to the direct path of our contemplated progress.

---

127   *Wisdom* 6:23.

128   Ecclesiastes 10:16.

129   Ecclesiastes 10:17.

2 I say, then, that this last opinion of the vulgar has become so inured that without inspection of any argument everyone is called gentle who is son or grandson of any worthy man, although he himself be of nought. And this is where it says, *And so inured is such false thoughts among us, that folk call that man a gentleman who can aver: 'I was grandson or son of such an one of worth,' though he himself be nought.*

3 Wherefore be it noted that it is most perilous neglect to suffer a false opinion to gain footing; for just as grass multiplies in an uncultivated field and mounts up and overwhelms the ears of corn, so that when one looks from a distance the corn may not be seen, and the fruit is finally lost, so false opinion in the mind, if not chastised and corrected, grows and multiplies so that the ear of reason, to wit, the right opinion, is concealed and, as it were, buried and lost.

4 Oh, how great a thing have I undertaken in this ode, desiring now to cleanse so weedy a field as this of the common opinion, so long neglected of this tillage! Verily I purpose not to cleanse it throughout, but only in those parts where the ears of reason are not utterly suppressed; that is to say, I purpose to set right those in whom some glimmering of reason still survives, in virtue of their favoured nature; for of the rest no more heed is to be taken than of brute beasts, because it seems to me no less a miracle to bring a man back to reason when it has been utterly quenched than to bring back to life him who has been four days in the tomb.

5 When the evil state of this opinion of the people has been related, the ode, clean out of the order of the refutation, incontinently smites it as a hideous thing, crying, *But basest doth he seem to whoso looks on truth*, to give to understand its intolerable perniciousness, asserting that such as say so lie to the very uttermost; for he is not only base (that is ungentle) but the very basest, who is descended from good forebears but is himself bad. And I give an illustration from a way that has been pointed out.

6 Concerning which (to make it clear) I must put a question and answer it as follows: There is a plain with certain fields and footways—with hedges, ditches, boulders, logs, and well-nigh every kind of obstruction save on its narrow footways—and it has snowed so that the snow covers up everything, and gives it the same aspect all over, so that no trace of any path is to be seen.

7 A man comes from one side of the plain and desires to go to a house that is on the other side, and by his own ingenuity, that is, by his perception and the excellence of his wit, guided by himself alone, he goes by the direct path to the place he purposes, leaving the footprints of his steps behind him. After him comes another and wishes to go to the same house, and needs only to follow the footprints already left; and by his own fault that path which the other had contrived to find for himself, without guidance, this man loses, although he has guidance, and he twists about amongst the thorns and the ruins and reaches not the quarter where he should go.

8 Which of these should be called worthy? I answer: he who went before. And what should the second one be called? I answer: most base. Wherefore is he not called "not worthy," that is base? I answer: because he should be called "not worthy," that is base, who having no guidance should not journey rightly; but because this man had guidance his error and his fault cannot be exceeded, and therefore he is to be called not base but basest.

9 And thus he who is ennobled in race by his father or by some forebear and perseveres not therein is not only base but basest and worthy of all scorn and vituperation more than any other churl. And that men should be on their guard against this lowest baseness, Solomon, in the twenty-second chapter of the *Proverbs*, bids him who has had a worthy forebear: "Pass not the ancient boundaries which thy fathers set up,"[130] and earlier, in the fourth chapter of the said book, he declares: "The path of the just," that is of the worthy, "goeth forward as a shining light, and that of the wicked is darkened and they know not whither they plunge."[131]

10 And finally, when it says, *And he hits nigh to who should be a corpse yet walk the earth,* I say, to his further disgrace, that such a basest one is dead though he seem alive. And here be it known that a bad man

---

130   Proverbs 22:28.
131   Proverbs 4:18–19.

may rightly be called dead, and especially he who departs from the true path of his worthy forebear.

11 And this may be demonstrated thus: as Aristotle says in the second *Of the Soul*, life is the being of the thing that is alive, and since life is after many fashions (as in plants to vegetate, in animals to vegetate and feel, in men to vegetate, feel, move, and reason or understand), and things should be named from their most noble part, it is clear that life in animals (I mean brute animals) is feeling, and life in man is exercising the reason.

12 Therefore, if his life is the being of man, renouncing the exercise of reason is renouncing his existence, and so it is that he is dead. And does he not renounce the exercise of reason who gives himself no account of the goal of his life? And does not he renounce the exercise of his reason who gives himself no account of the path he ought to take? Assuredly he does, and this is most manifest in him who has the footprints before him and regards them not.

13 And therefore Solomon says in the fifth chapter of the *Proverbs*, "He shall die because he had no discipline; and in the multitude of his foolishness shall he be deceived";[132] that is to say, he is dead who does not become a disciple, and who follows not the master. And such an one is most base.

14 And of him some may say, "How is he dead and yet walks?" I answer that the man is dead but the beast survives. For, as says the Philosopher in the second *On the Soul*, the powers of the soul are graded, as the figure of the quadrangle is of higher grade than the triangle and the pentagon of higher grade than the quadrangle, thus the sensitive is of higher grade than the vegetative, and the intellectual of higher grade than the sensitive.[133]

15 And so, just as if you withdraw the last side of a pentagon you have a quadrangle left, but no longer a pentagon, so if you withdraw the last power of the soul, that is the reason, the man is no longer left, but something with a sensitive soul only; that is, a brute

---

132   Proverbs 5:23.
133   *De anima* II.3.

animal. And this is the meaning of the second verse of the ode we have in hand, wherein are laid down the opinions of others.

Chapter VIII

1 The fairest branch that rises from the root of reason is discrimination; for, as Thomas says in prologue to the *Ethics*, "to know the relation of one thing to another is the proper act of reason,"[134] and this is discrimination. One of the fairest and sweetest fruits of this branch is the reverence which the lesser owes to the greater.

2 Wherefore Tully, in the first *Of Offices*, speaking of the beauty which glows in integrity, says that reverence is part of it;[135] and as this reverence is a beautifying of integrity, so its opposite is a befouling and demeaning of the same, the which opposite may be called irreverence, or mutiny in our vernacular.

3 And therefore Tully himself, in the same place, says: "Carelessness to know what others think of him is the mark not only of an arrogant but of a profligate man;"[136] which is no other than to say that arrogance and profligacy consists in being without knowledge of oneself, which is the foundation of the standard of every kind of reverence.

4 Wherefore I, desiring to observe all reverence of speech, both to the prince and to the philosopher, while removing what is pernicious from the mind of certain, in order thereafter to let in upon it the light of truth, before proceeding to refute the opinions before us, shall make it clear that in refuting them I do not argue with irreverence either towards the imperial majesty or towards the Philosopher.

5 For were I to show myself lacking in reverence in any other part of all this book, it were not so foul a blot as if I were to do it in this treatise, wherein treating of nobility I am bound to show myself

---

134   Aquinas, *Ethics* I, lect. i.1.
135   *De officiis* I.xxvii.94–95.
136   *De officiis* I.xxviii.98–99.

noble and not churlish. And first I will show that I do not presume against the authority of the Philosopher, and then I will show that I do not presume against the imperial majesty.

6 I declare, then, that when the Philosopher says, "That which the majority think cannot be absolutely false,"[137] he does not mean to speak of outward or sensuous judgment but of inward or rational; for a sensuous judgment in accordance with the majority would often be most false, especially in the case of the objects common to more senses than one, wherein the sense is often deceived.

7 Thus we know that to the majority Sun appears to be a foot in diameter, which is most false, for according to the research and discovery which human reason, with its attendant arts, has made the diameter of the body of the Sun is five times as great as that of earth and half a time over. And since the diameter of the earth is 6,500 miles, the diameter of the Sun, which seems to sensuous judgment to measure a foot, is 35,750 miles.

8 And hereby it is evident that Aristotle did not mean sensuous judgment, and therefore, if I aim only at refuting this sensuous judgment, I am not going counter to the purport of the Philosopher, and therefore neither do I offend against the reverence due to him. And that it is the sensuous judgment which I purpose to refute is manifest.

9 For they who so judge, judge only by what they perceive of the things which fortune can give and take away; for when they see alliances and distinguished marriages and stupendous buildings and great possessions and mighty lordships, they suppose them to be the causes of nobleness, nay, they suppose them to be nobleness itself. Whereas if they judged by rational appearances, they would say the opposite, namely, that nobleness is the cause of these things, as will be seen below in this treatise.

10 And even as I speak not counter to the reverence of the Philosopher in refuting this (as is plain to see), so I speak not counter to the reverence of the empire; and I purpose to show why. But since

---

137   *Ethics* I.8.

we are arguing in the face of the adversary, the orator must take great heed in his speech lest the adversary draw matter therefrom to obscure the truth. I who am speaking in this treatise in the presence of so many adversaries cannot speak briefly. Wherefore, if my digressions are long, let no one marvel.

11 I say, then, that to show that I am not irreverent to the majesty of the empire we must first consider what reverence is. I say that reverence is no other than "the profession of due submission by patent sign"; and perceiving this, we must distinguish between the irreverent and the non-reverent. "Irreverent" implies privation, non-reverent implies negation. So irreverence is "withholding due submission by patent sign"; non-reverence is the not avowing of submission which is not due.

12 A man may repudiate a thing in two ways. One kind of repudiation clashes with the truth, when due profession is withheld, and this is properly disconfessing; in the other way a man may repudiate without coming into collision with the truth, when he will not confess that which is not; and this is properly denying; as for instance, for a man to repudiate the assertion that he is altogether mortal is to deny it in the proper sense of the word.

13 Wherefore, if I deny reverence to the Empire I am not irreverent. but I am non-reverent, for it is not contrary to reverence, inasmuch as it does not clash with it; even as "not being alive" does not clash with "life," but "being dead" clashes with it, for it is the privation of it; whence "being dead" is one thing, and "not being alive" is another, for "not being alive" pertains to stones.

14 And because death implies privation, which cannot be save in a subject of the habit in question, and stones are not subjects of life, therefore they should not be called "dead" but "not alive." In like manner I, who in this case owe no reverence to the Empire, am not irreverent in renouncing it, but am non-reverent, which is not mutiny nor a thing of blame.

15 Nay, reverence (if reverence it could be called) would be mutiny, for it would result in greater and more real irreverence, that is to say irreverence towards nature and towards truth, as will be seen below. Against this error, that master of the philosophers, Aristotle, guarded himself in the beginning of the *Ethics* when he says: "If we have two friends, and one of them is the truth, we must comply with the truth."[138]

16 But verily, since I have admitted that I am non-reverent, which is denying reverence, to wit, denying by patent signs submission that is not due, we must investigate how this act of mine is denying and not disconfessing; that is to say, how in this case I am not duly subject to the imperial majesty. And since the argument must needs be lengthy, I purpose to demonstrate it in a chapter of its own next following.

Chapter IX

1 To see how in this case, that is in refuting or confirming the emperor's opinion, I am not bound to submission to him, the argument conducted above in the fourth chapter of this treatise concerning the imperial office must be called to mind; to wit, that the imperial authority was invented for the perfection of human life, and that it is by right the regulator and ruler of all our doings, because, so far as our doings stretch, so far the imperial majesty has jurisdiction, and beyond these boundaries it does not extend.

2 But like as every art and office of man is confined to certain limits by the imperial office, so is this empire itself bounded by God within certain limits; nor need we marvel at this, for we see that the office and the art of nature is bounded in all its activities. For if we would take the universal nature of the whole, it has jurisdiction so far as the whole universe—I mean the heaven and the earth—extends; and this is up to a certain fixed boundary, as is proved in the third of the *Physics* and in the first *Of Heaven and Earth*.[139]

3 Therefore the jurisdiction of universal nature is bounded by certain limits, and by consequence so is the particular. Moreover,

---

138   *Ethics* I.6.

139   *Physics* III.5 and *De caelo* I.5–7, respectively.

he doth bound her who is bounded by nought, to wit, the prime excellence, which is God, who alone with infinite capaciousness comprehends infinitude.[140]

4 And to perceive the limits of our operations, be it known that those only are operations of ours which are subject to the reason and to the will; for albeit there are digestive operations in us, these are not human but natural.

5 And be it known that our reason is related to four kinds of operations, to be considered separately; for there are operations which it only considers and does not perform, nor can it accomplish any of them; for instance, things natural and super-natural, and mathematics; and operations which it considers and accomplishes by its own act, which are called rational, as are the arts of speech; and operations which it considers and accomplishes in material external to itself, as are the mechanical arts.

6 And all these operations, though their consideration is subject to our will, are not subject to our will in themselves, for however much we might wish that heavy things should rise upward by nature, they would not be able so to rise; and however much we might wish a syllogism with false premises to be a conclusive demonstration of the truth, it would not be one; and however much we might wish a house to sit as firmly when overhanging as when straight, it would not; because we are not, properly speaking, makers of these operations but their discoverers. It was another that ordained them, and a greater maker who made them.

7 There are also operations which our reason considers as they exist in the act of will, such as attacking and succouring, standing ground or fleeing in battle, abiding chaste or wantoning; and these are entirely subject to our will, and therefore we are considered good or bad on their account, because they are properly ours in their entirety; for, so far as our will can have its way, so far do operations that are really ours extend.[141]

---

140   *Purg.* XI.1–3.
141   *Purg.* XVIII.64–66.

8 And inasmuch as some equity is to be observed and some iniquity to be avoided in all these voluntary operations, and this equity may be missed for two reasons—either lack of knowing what it is or lack of will to pursue it—therefore was written reason invented, both to point it out and to enforce it. Wherefore Augustine says: "If it (equity) were known to men, and when known were observed, there would be no need of written reason."[142] And therefore it is written in the beginning of the *Old Digest*: "Written reason is the art of good and of equity."[143]

9 It is to write, to demonstrate, and to enforce this equity that the official is appointed of whom we are discoursing, to wit, the emperor; and to him we are subject to the extent of those operations, properly our own, of which we have spoken, and no further.

10 For this reason, in every art and in every trade the artificers and disciples are, and ought to be, subject to the chief and the master thereof in the respective trades and arts, outside of which the subjection is annulled, because the chieftaincy is annulled. Wherefore we may in some sort say of the emperor, if we wish to figure his office by an image, that he is the rider of the human will. And how that horse courses over the plain without the rider is manifest enough, and especially in the wretched Italy which, without any mediator at all, has been abandoned to her own direction.

11 And be it observed that the more special a thing is to any art or discipline, the more complete is the subjection therein; for if the cause be enhanced, so is the effect. Whence we are to know that there be some things so purely matter of art that nature is their instrument, such as rowing with the oar where the art makes an instrument of impulsion, which is a natural movement; or as in threshing... leaven, where the art makes an instrument of heat, which is a natural quality. And it is herein, most of all, that subjection is due to the chief and master of the art.

12 And there are things wherein the art is an instrument of nature, and these are arts in a lesser degree; and in them the artificers

---

142   See *De libero arbitrio* I.xv.31.
143   *Digesta* I.i.1.

are less subject to their chief, as in committing seed to the earth, wherein heed must be given to the will of nature; as in issuing from a port, wherein heed must be given to the natural disposition of the weather. And therefore we see that in these things there often arises contention amongst the artificers, and the superior asks counsel of the inferior.

13 There are other things which are not part of an art, but seem to have some relation to it, and as to this mistakes are often made. And in these things the learners are not subject to the artificer or master, nor are they bound to trust him, so far as the art goes. Thus fishing seems to have some connection with navigation, and knowledge of the virtues of herbs with agriculture, yet they have no common discipline, inasmuch as fishing comes under the art of venery and under its command, and the knowledge of the virtues of herbs under medicine or under some more general discipline.

14 In like manner, all these points which we have discussed with reference to the other arts may be noted with reference to the imperial art; for there are regulations in it which are pure arts, such as are the laws concerning matrimony, concerning slaves, concerning warfare, concerning the successors to titles; and as to these we are entirely subject to the emperor without any doubt or hesitation.

15 There are other laws which have, as it were, to follow the lead of nature, such as constituting a man of sufficient age for managing his own affairs, and herein we are not completely subject. There are many others which seem to have some relation to the imperial art; and herein those were and are deceived who believe that in such matters an imperial pronouncement carries authority. For instance, as to "manhood," we are not to accept any imperial judgment on the ground of its being the emperor's. So let us render to God that which is God's.

16 And accordingly we are not to trust nor accept the Emperor Nero, who said that manhood was beauty and strength of body, but him who should say that manhood is the apex of the natural life, and that would be the philosopher. It is therefore evident that defining "gentlehood" is not a part of the emperor's art, and if it

is not a part of his art, then in treating of it we are not subject to him, and if we are not subject we are not bound to reverence him therein, and this is exactly what we were in search of.

[17] Wherefore we may now with full freedom and with full courage of mind smite upon the breasts of the depraved opinions that are current on the earth, in order that the true opinion by this my victory may hold the field of the mind of those for whom it gives vigour to this light.

Chapter X

[1] Now that the opinions of others concerning nobility have been laid down, and it has been proved that I am free to refute them, I shall come to the discussion of that part of the ode which contains this refutation; and it begins, as said above: *He who defines: "Man is a living trunk"*. And so, be it known that the opinion of the emperor (although he set it down defectively) did in one phrase, to wit, where he said "gracious manners," really hit some part of the ways of nobleness, and therefore there is no thought of refuting it there.

[2] It is the other phrase, which is absolutely foreign to the nature of nobleness, that there is thought of refuting; for it seems to indicate two things when it speaks of ancient wealth, to wit, time and riches, which are utterly foreign to nobility, as I have already said, and as I shall prove below. And therefore the refutation falls into two parts. First, riches are rejected and then time is rejected as causes of nobleness. The second part begins: *Nor will they have it that a base man can become gentle*.

[3] Be it known that to reject "riches" is to refute not only that part of the emperor's opinion that indicates riches, but the whole of the opinion of the vulgar herd, which was based on riches alone. The first part is divided into two, for in the first it is asserted generally that the emperor was wrong in his definition of nobility; in the second is shown the reason why; and this second part begins: *For riches can not (as is held)*.

4 I say then, *He who defines: "Man is a living trunk"*, firstly speaks not the truth (that is to say, speaks false) insofar as he says "trunk," and then not the whole thing (that is to say, speaks it defectively), insofar as he says "living" and does not say "rational," which differentiates man from beasts.

5 Then I say that in like manner did he who "held empire" err in his definition; and I say not "emperor" but "who held empire," to indicate that, as said above, deciding this question is beside the imperial office. Then I say that he erred in like manner, because he laid down a false subject of nobility, namely, "ancient wealth," and then proceeded to a defective form (or differentiating principle), to wit, "gracious manners," which do not comprehend the whole formal principle of nobleness, but a very small part of it, as will be shown below.

6 And we are not to overlook (though the text says nought about it) that in this matter his honor the emperor not only erred in the phrases of his definition, but also in his mode of defining (although fame proclaims him to have been a great logician and clerk), for the definition of nobleness would be more suitably drawn from its effects than from its sources, inasmuch as it appears itself to have the character of a source, which cannot be made known by the things that precede it but by the things that follow from it.

7 Then when I say, *For riches can not (as is held)*, I show that they cannot cause nobleness, because they are base; and I show that they cannot take it away, because they are completely severed from nobleness. And I show that they are base by one very great and manifest defect that they have; and this I do when I say, *That they be base is apparent*, and the rest.

8 Finally I conclude, by virtue of what is said above, that the upright mind is not changed by their translation, which proves what was said above, viz., that they are severed from nobleness, because the effects of union do not follow. And here be it known that, as the Philosopher has it, whatever things produce anything, the latter must needs first exist perfectly in the being of the others. Wherefore he says in the seventh of the *Metaphysics*, "When one thing is generated by another, it is generated by it in virtue of existing in its being."[144]

9 Further, we are to know that everything which is destroyed, is destroyed because of some preceding change, and anything which is affected, must needs be some way connected with that change, as the Philosopher has it in the seventh of the *Physics* and in the first *Of Generation*.[145] These things laid down, I thus proceed and say that riches cannot (as folk suppose) confer nobility; and to show their still further remoteness from it, I add that they cannot take it away from him who has it.

10 "They cannot give it," inasmuch as they are naturally base, and by reason that baseness is contrary to nobility. And here baseness means degenerateness, which is opposed to nobleness, inasmuch as one contrary does not nor cannot produce the other, for the reason above stated, and all this is briefly appended to the text in the words: *Further, who paints a figure, unless himself can be it, can not set it down.*

11 Wherefore no painter could set down any figure, unless he had first in intention become such as the figure is to be. Further, they cannot "take it away," because they are remote from nobleness; and, for the reason stated above, whatsoever modifies or destroys anything must needs be connected with it.

12 And therefore it adds: *Nor is an upright tower made to lean by a river that flows far away*, which means to utter nought else than a parallel to what was said before, namely, that riches cannot take away nobleness, speaking as though this nobleness were an upright tower and as though riches were a river flowing far away from it.

Chapter XI

1 It now remains only to prove how riches are base, and how they are disconnected and remote from nobleness; and this is proved

---

144   *Metaphysics* VII.8.
145   *Physics* VII.2 and *De generatione* I.6, respectively.

in two clauses of the text, to which attention must now be given; and then when they have been expounded what I will have said will be evident, to wit, that riches are base and remote from nobleness, and thereby the arguments against riches urged above will be perfectly established.

2 I say then: *That they be base and imperfect is apparent.* And to prove that which it is my purpose to express, be it known that the baseness of a thing flows from its imperfection and its nobleness from its perfection, wherefore the more perfect a thing is the nobler is it in its nature, and the more imperfect the baser. And so if riches are imperfect it is clear that they are base.

3 And that they are imperfect the text briefly proves when it says: *For how much soever gathered, they can give no quiet, but multiply care.* Wherein is manifest not only their imperfection, but also that their condition is most imperfect, and therefore that they are most base. And to this Lucan testifies when he says, addressing them, "Without resistance did the laws perish; but ye riches, the basest part of things, stirred battle."[146]

4 Briefly, their imperfection may be seen clearly in three things: first, in their undiscerning advent; secondly, in their perilous growth; thirdly, in their hurtful possession. And before I prove this, a difficulty that seems to rise must be explained; for inasmuch as gold and gems have perfect form and act in their own being, it seems untrue to say that they are imperfect.

5 And therefore be it known that they themselves, in themselves considered, are perfect things—not riches, however, but gold and gems. But so far as they are designed for the possession of man, they are riches, and in this sense they are full of imperfection; for there is no inconsistency in one and the same thing under different aspects being both perfect and imperfect.

6 I say that their imperfection may be noted, firstly, in the want of discernment in their advent, wherein no distributive justice shines,

---

146 *Pharsalia* III.119–121.

but absolute iniquity almost always; which iniquity is the proper effect of imperfection.

7 For if we consider the ways in which they come, all may be gathered into three fashions; for either they came by pure fortune, as when without intention or hope they come by some unsought discovery; or they come by fortune supported by Reason, as by testaments or by mutual succession; or they come by fortune aiding reason, as in lawful or unlawful gains. By lawful I mean the earnings of art or trade or service; by unlawful I mean theft or plunder.

8 And in each of these three modes that iniquity of which I speak may be observed; for hidden wealth which is discovered or rediscovered oftener presents itself to the bad than to the good; and this is so obvious that it needs no proof. Indeed, I have seen the place on the ribs of mountain in Tuscany, called Falterona, where the basest churl of the whole countryside discovered, as he was digging, more than a bushel of santelénas of finest silver, which had been waiting for him maybe 1000 years or more.

9 And it was because he noted this want of equity that Aristotle declared that "the more subject a man is to understanding, the less subject he is to fortune."[147] And I affirm that inheritance by will or by succession oftener comes to the bad than to the good; and of this I will not bring any evidence, but let each man turn his eyes round his own neighborhood and he will perceive—that of which I speak not, so as to cast no smirch on any.

10 Would that it were God's pleasure that what the Provençal desired should come to pass, that "whoso is not heir of the excellence should lose the inheritance of the possessions." And I affirm that gain is precisely that which comes oftener to the bad than to the good; for illegitimate gains never come to the good at all, because they reject them.

11 What good man will ever seek gain by force or by fraud? It were impossible; for by the very choice of the unlawful undertaking he would cease to be good. And lawful gains rarely come to the good,

---

147 *Physics* II.5.

because, since much anxious care is needful thereto, and the anxious care of the good man is directed to weightier matters, rarely does the good man give sufficient attention thereto.

12 Wherefore it is clear that in every way the advent of these riches is iniquitous, and therefore our Lord called them iniquitous when he said, "Make to yourselves friends of the money of iniquity,"[148] inviting and encouraging men to liberality in benefactions which are the begetters of friends.

13 And how fair an exchange does he make who gives of these most imperfect things in order to have and to gain perfect things, such as are the hearts of worthy men! And this market is open every day. Verily this merchandise is unlike others, for when the thought is to purchase one man by benefaction, thousands are purchased by it.

14 And who has not Alexander in his heart even yet for his royal benefactions? Who has not the good King of Castile in his heart, or Saladin, or the good Marquess of Monferrato, or the good Count of Toulouse, or Bertram de Bourne, or Galleazzo of Montefeltro, when mention is made of their donations? Truly not only those who would gladly do the like, but they who would sooner die than do it, love their memory.

Chapter XII

1 As has been said, the imperfection of riches may be observed not only in their undiscerning advent, but pre-eminently in their perilous growth; and therefore the text makes mention only of that wherein the defect may be most eagerly perceived, saying of them that "how much soever gathered" they not only give no rest but create more thirst, so as to make folk still more defective and imperfect.

2 And here be it known that defective things may harbour their defects in such fashion that they appear not at first sight, the imperfection hiding under a pretext of perfection; or they may so har-

---

148 Luke 16:9.

bour them as completely to reveal them, so that the imperfection is recognized openly on the surface.

3 And those things which at first conceal their defects are the most dangerous, because, in many cases, we cannot be on our guard against them, as we see in the instance of a traitor who in appearance shows himself a friend, so that he begets in us a confidence in him, and beneath the pretext of friendship he hides the defect of enmity. And it is in this fashion that riches are dangerously imperfect in their growth; for, submitting certain things to us which they promise, they actually bring the contrary.

4 The false traitoresses ever promise (if it be well considered) to make him who gathers them full of satisfaction when they have been amassed up to a certain sum; and with this promise they lead the human will to the vice of avarice.[149] And this is why Boethius, in that of *Consolation*, calls them perilous, saying, "Ah me, who was he who first dug out the weights of hidden gold, and the stones that sought to hide themselves, those precious perils?"[150]

5 The false traitoresses promise (if it be well considered) to remove every thirst and every want and to bring satiety and sufficiency; for this is what they do at first to every man, confidently fixing this promise at a certain measure of their growth; and then, when they are amassed to that point, in place of satiety and of refreshment, they give and produce the thirst of a feverish bosom and not to be endured; and in the place of sufficiency they offer a new limit, that is to say, a greater quantity to long for; and together with it fear and great concern for what has already been acquired, so that verily they "give no quiet," but "multiply care," which, without them, was not there before.

6 And therefore says Tully, in that of the *Paradox* denouncing riches: "As to their money, and their splendid mansions, and their wealth, and their lordship, and the delights by which they are chiefly attracted, never in truth have I ranked them amongst things good or desirable; inasmuch as I saw for a certainty that in the abundance

---

149   Luke 16:9.
150   *Consolation* II, met. v, lines 27–30.

of these things men longed most for the very things wherein they abounded. For never is the thirst of cupidity filled nor sated. And not only are they tortured by the longing to increase their possessions, but they are also tortured by fear of losing them."[151]

7 And all these words are Tully's, and so they stand in that book which has been mentioned. And for further witness to this imperfection behold Boethius declaring in that of *Consolation*: "Though the goddess of riches should bestow as much as the sand rolled by the wind-tossed sea, or as many as the stars that shine, the human race will not cease to wail."[152]

8 And since it is fitting to gather yet more evidence to bring this to proof, let us pass by all that Solomon and his father cried out against them, all that Seneca, especially in writing to Lucilius, all that Horace, all that Juvenal, and briefly all that every writer, every poet, and all that the truthful divine scripture cries out against these false harlots, full of all defects; and that our faith may be drawn from our own eyes, let us give heed to the life of them who chase them, and see in what security they live when they have gathered of them, how content they are, how reposeful!

9 And what else, day by day, imperils and slays cities, countries, and single persons so much as the new amassing of wealth by any one? Which amassing reveals new longings, the goal of which may not be reached without wrong to some one. And what else is the one and the other Reason,[153] I mean the canonical and the civil, intended to cure so much as to make defence against the greed which grows as riches are amassed?

10 Verily the one and the other Reason manifests it sufficiently if we read their beginnings—I mean the beginning of their scripture. Oh how manifest, nay, rather how most manifest, is it that in their growth they are utterly imperfect, since nought save imperfection can spring from them when they are gathered together! And this it is that the text affirms.

---

151 *Paradoxa stoicorum* I.i.6.
152 *Consolation* II, met. ii, lines 1–8.
153 Here and in the following paragraph read "Law" (*ragione*).

11 But here by way of difficulty arises a question which we must not omit to ask and to answer. Some caviller against the truth might say that if riches are imperfect and therefore base because, as they are acquired the longing for them increases, by like reason knowledge should be imperfect and base, since in the acquiring of it the longing for it doth ever increase; wherefore Seneca says, "Had I one foot in the grave I should wish to learn."[154]

12 But it is not true that knowledge is made base by imperfection. Therefore, by the destruction of the consequent, the increase of longing does not produce baseness in knowledge. That knowledge is perfect is manifest from the Philosopher in the sixth of the *Ethics*, who says that "knowledge is a perfect account of things which are certain."[155]

13 To this question a brief answer must be given, but first we must see whether in the acquisition of knowledge the longing for it does so expand as is asserted in the question, and whether it is for a reason for which I assert that not only in the acquisition of knowledge and of wealth, but in every acquisition, human desire dilates, though in different ways.

14 Which reason is this, that the supreme longing of everything, and that first given to it by nature, is to return to its first principle. And inasmuch as God is the first principle of our souls, and hath made them like to himself, even as it is written, "Let us make man in our image and after our likeness,"[156] the soul itself most chiefly longs to return to him.[157]

15 And like a pilgrim who is traveling on a road where he hath never been before, who believes that every house which he sees from afar is the hostel, and finding that it is not directs his belief to another, and so from house to house until he comes to the hostel; even so our soul, so soon as it enters upon the new and never-yet-made journey of life, directs its eyes to the goal of its supreme

---

154 *Epistulae* LXXVI.3.

155 *Ethics* VI.3.

156 Genesis 1:26.

157 *Purg.* XVII.106–111.

good, and therefore whatever it sees that appears to have some good in it, it thinks to be it.[158]

16 And because its knowledge is at first imperfect, through having no experience or instruction, little goods appear great to it; and therefore it begins first from them in its longing. And so we see little children intensely longing for an apple, and then going on further, longing for a little bird, and then further on longing for fine clothes, and then a horse, and then a mistress, and then wealth, but not much, then much and then enormous. And this comes to pass because in none of these things does he find that for which he is ever searching, but believes he will find it further on.

17 Wherefore we may perceive that one desirable thing stands in front of the other before the eyes of our soul, something after the fashion of a pyramid, wherein the smallest part first covers all the rest, and is as it were the apex of the supreme object of longing, which is God, as it were the base of all the rest. Wherefore, the further we proceed from the apex toward the base, the greater do objects of our longing appear; and this is why in the process of acquisition the longings of men become more capacious one after the other.

18 But in truth we may lose this way in error, just as we may lose the paths of earth; for even as from one city to another there must needs be a best and straightest way, and another whichever recedes therefrom, to wit, the one which goes in the opposite direction, and many others, some departing less from it, and some approaching it less; so in human life are diverse paths, of which one is the truest and another the falsest, and certain less false and certain less true.

19 And even as we see that the path which goeth straightest to the city fulfilleth the longing and giveth rest after the toil, and that which goeth the contrary way never accomplisheth it, and may never give rest, so it cometh to pass in our life that he who taketh the right path reacheth the goal and hath rest, but he who goeth astray

---

158 *Inf.* I.1–3, XV.49–54; *Purg.* XXX.121–132.

never reacheth it, but with great toil of his mind ever gazeth before him with greedy eyes.

[20] Wherefore, although this discourse doth not fully answer the question raised above, yet doth it at least clear the way for the answer, for it maketh us perceive that every longing of ours dilateth not after one same fashion; but since this chapter is somewhat protracted, the answer to the question must be given in a new chapter, wherein will be ended the whole disputation which it is our present purpose to make against riches.

Chapter XIII

[1] In answer to the question I affirm that the desire of knowledge cannot be properly said to increase, although, as has been declared, it dilates in a certain fashion. For that which properly speaking increases is always one; the desire for knowledge is not always one, but is many; and when one ends another succeeds; so that, properly speaking, its dilating is not an increasing but a succession of great things to small.

[2] For if I desire to know the elements of natural things, the moment I know them this desire is completed and ended; and if I then desire to know what each of these elements is and how it exists, this is another new desire. Nor by the access of this am I bereft of the perfection to which the other led me; and this dilating is not the cause of imperfection but of greater perfection. But that of riches is properly an increasing, for it is always one only, so that here we can detect no succession of goals reached and perfections realized.

[3] And if the adversary should say that as the desire to know the elements of natural things is one and the desire to know what they are is another, so the desire for a hundred marks is one and the desire for a thousand another, I answer that it is not true; for a hundred is a part of a thousand and is related to it as part of a line to the whole line along which we proceed by one sole motion, and there is no succession there, nor perfected motion in any part.

4 But to know which are the elements of natural things and to know what each of them is, are not parts one of the other, but are related as different lines along which you cannot proceed by one motion, but when the motion of one is complete, the motion of the other succeeds.

5 And thus it appears that knowledge is not (as laid down in the question) to be considered imperfect because of the desire for knowledge, as riches are because of the desire for them; for in the desire for knowledge, desires are successfully accomplished and brought to perfection, and in the desire for riches it is not so; so that the question is solved and does not hold.

6 It is true that the opponent may still cavil and say that although many desires are satisfied in the acquisition of knowledge, yet we never accomplish the ultimate one, which is something like the imperfection of a desire which, remaining one and the same, never comes to an end.

7 Here again we answer that this counter assertion is not true, namely, that the ultimate desire is never accomplished, for our natural desires, as shown above in the third treatise, go down to a certain limit; and the desire of knowledge is a natural one, so that a certain limit satisfies it; although few, because of the ill path they take, complete the journey.

8 And he who understands the Commentator,[159] in the third *Of the Soul*, understands this from him; and therefore Aristotle in the tenth of the *Ethics*, speaking against the poet Simonides, says, "That man should draw himself to divine things the most he may";[160] wherein he shows that our power contemplates a certain limit. And in the first of the Ethics he says, "That the disciplined man requires to know the certainty of things in the degree wherein their nature admits of certainty";[161] wherein he shows that not only should a limit be contemplated on the side of the man who desires knowledge, but on the side of the desired object of knowledge.

---

159   Averroes, *Commentarium magnum in Aristotelis De anima*, 413b.16–19.

160   *Ethics* X.7 (see also Aquinas, *Summa Contra Gentiles* I.5).

161   *Ethics* I.3.

9 And that is why Paul says that, "We are not to know more than is fitting to know, but to know in measure."[162] So that in whatever way the desire for knowledge is taken, whether in general or in particular, it reaches perfection; and therefore perfect knowledge has a notable perfection; and its perfection is not lost by the desire for it, as in the case of accursed riches.

10 And how these be hurtful in their possession we are now briefly to show, for this is the third note of their imperfection. Their possession may be seen to be hurtful by two reasons; the one that it is the cause of evil, the other that it is the privation of good. It is the cause of evil, because by mere watchfulness it makes the possessor fearful and hateful.

11 How great is the terror of him who knows that he has wealth about him, as he journeys and as he stays, not only waking but sleeping, lest he lose not only his possessions but his life for his possessions' sake! Well do the wretched merchants know it who traverse the world, whom the very leaves which the wind tosses make to tremble when they are carrying their riches with them; and when they are without them, full of security, they shorten their way by song and discourse.

12 And therefore the Sage[163] says, "If the wayfarer had entered on his journey empty, he would sing in the face of the robbers."[164] And this is what Lucan means to say in the fifth book when he commends poverty for its security, saying, "Oh secure ease of the poor life, oh ye narrow homes and huts, oh wealth of the gods not yet understood! To what temples and to what fortifications could this ever chance, not to know any tumult of fear when the hand of Caesar knocks?"[165] And this Lucan says when he tells how Caesar came by night to the hut of the fisherman Amyclas, to cross the Adriatic Sea.

---

162   Romans 12:3.
163   Juvenal.
164   *Satires* X.22.
165   *Pharsalia* V.527–531.

13 And what hatred is that which every one bears to the possessor of wealth, whether through envy or through desire to seize the possessions! Verily it is so great that, many times the counter to the tenderness he owes, the son schemes the father's death. And of this the Latins have most great and manifest examples both in the region of the Po and in the region of the Tiber. And therefore Boethius, in the second of his *Consolation*, says, "Verily avarice makes men hated."[166]

14 Also their possession is the negation of good, for, when they are possessed, liberality is not practised, which is a virtue, and virtue is a perfect good and makes men illustrious and loved; which may not be achieved by possessing wealth, but by relinquishing the possession of it. Wherefore Boethius in the same book says, "Money is only good when, transferred to others by the practice of liberality, it is no longer possessed."[167] Wherefore the baseness of riches is manifest enough by reason of all their characteristics.

15 And so a man of right appetite and of true knowledge never loves them; and not loving them does not unite himself to them, but ever wishes them to be far removed from him, save as they be ordained to some necessary service. And this is reasonable because the perfect can never unite with the imperfect. And so we see that the curved line can never unite with the straight, and if there be any union, it is not of line with line, but of point with point.

16 And therefore it follows that the mind which is upright, to wit, in appetite, and true, to wit, in knowledge, is not undone by losing them, as the text lays down at the end of this section. And by this effect the text purposes to prove that they are a running stream remote from the upright tower of reason, or of nobleness, and thereby that these riches cannot take away nobleness from him who has it. And this is the method of disputing and refuting pursued in the present ode against riches.

---

166   *Consolation* II, pr. v.4.

167   *Consolation* II, pr. v.5.

Chapter XIV

1 The error of others having been refuted in that part wherein it rests upon wealth… in that part wherein it asserted time to be a cause of nobleness, saying "of ancient wealth"; and this refutation is conducted in that part which begins: *Nor will they have it that a base man can become gentle.*

2 And first this is refuted by an argument of the very ones who are in this error; then, for their greater confusion, this argument of theirs is itself also refuted, and this is done when it says: *Further, it followeth from what I have above set down.* Finally, the conclusion is reached that their error is manifest, and therefore it is time to turn to the truth, and this is done where it says: *Wherefore to sound intellects,* and the rest.

3 I say then: *Nor will they have it that a base man can become gentle,* and here be it known that it is the opinion of the erring ones that a man once a churl may never be called gentle; and a man who is son of a churl, in like manner may never be called gentle. And this shatters their own doctrine when they imply that time is required for nobleness, by inserting that word "ancient"; for it is impossible in the process of time to come to the moment that begets nobleness, according to this their argument (that has been rehearsed), which precludes a churl from being ever able to become gentle for ought that he may do or by any accident, and precludes the passage from a churl father to a gentle son.

4 For if the son of a churl is only a churl, then his son again is only the son of a churl, and therefore his son too is a churl; and so we shall never at all be able to find the point at which nobility begins by process of time.

5 And if the adversary, bent on making some defence, should say that nobility begins at the point of time when the base state of the ancestors is forgotten, I say that that is counter to them themselves; for of sheer necessity there would at that point be a transition from churlishness to gentleness, either of the same man from one into the other, or between father and son, which is contrary to what they lay down.

6 And if the adversary were stubbornly to defend his case by saying that they admit that this change can take place when the base state of the ancestors has fallen into oblivion, although the text takes no heed of this, it is right that the gloss should answer it. And therefore I answer thus, that from that contention of theirs follow four extreme absurdities, so that the argument cannot be good.

7 The first is that the better human nature became the harder and the slower would the generating of gentleness be, which is the greatest absurdity, inasmuch as a thing is the more mindful in proportion as it is better, and is a greater cause of good; and nobleness is counted amongst things that are good. And that this would be so is thus proved:

8 If gentleness or nobleness (by which I mean one and the same thing) were generated by oblivion, nobleness would be the sooner generated in proportion as men were more forgetful, for thereby all forgetfulness would come the quicker. Therefore the more forgetful men were the sooner would men become noble; and counterwise, the better memory they had the more slowly would they be ennobled.

9 The second is that this distinction between noble and base could not be made with respect to anything except men, which is highly absurd, inasmuch as we recognize in every kind of thing the features of nobleness or baseness, so that we often speak of a noble horse and a base one, and a noble falcon and a base one, and a noble pearl and a base one.

10 And that this distinction could not be made is thus proved: If oblivion of base ancestors is the cause of nobleness, then in cases where there has never been any baseness of ancestors there cannot be any oblivion of them (inasmuch as oblivion is the perishing of memory), so that in these aforesaid animals other than man, and plants and minerals, baseness and loftiness cannot be traced, since their nature holds them to one only and equal state, and in their

generation there can be no nobleness and so neither any baseness; inasmuch as these two are to be regarded as habit and privation, which are possibilities of one identical subject, and therefore in these things there can be no distinction between one and the other.

11 And if the adversary should choose to say that in other things nobleness means the excellence of the thing, but in men it means the memory of their base condition has perished, one would wish to answer not with words but with a dagger to such a stupidity as it would be to assign excellence as the cause of nobleness in other things, and oblivion as its principle in the case of men.

12 The third is that the thing generated would often come before the thing generating, which is utterly impossible; and this may be shown as follow: Let us suppose that Gherardo da Cammino had been the grandson of the basest churl that ever drank of the Sile or the Cagnano,[168] and that oblivion of his grandfather had not yet come about; who should dare to say that Gherardo da Cammino would have been a base man? And who would not agree with me and say that he was noble? Of a surety no one, howsoever presumptuous he might be; for noble he was, and so will his memory be for ever.

13 And if oblivion of his base ancestor had not come about (as is urged in the objection), and he had been great in nobility, and his nobleness had been thus openly perceived, as openly perceived it is, it would have existed in him before that which generated it had come about. And this is supremely impossible.

14 The fourth is that a man should be held noble when dead who was not noble when alive, than which there can be no greater absurdity; and that this would follow is shown thus: Let us suppose that in the age of Dardanus the memory of his base ancestors survived, and let us suppose in the age of Laomedon this memory had perished and oblivion had taken its place. According to the opinion we are attacking, Laomedon was gentle and Dardanus was a churl when they were alive. We, to whom the memory of their ancestors (I mean beyond Dardanus) has not come down, are we to say that

---

168   Two rivers in northern Italy; see also *Par.* IX.49.

Dardanus was a churl when he was alive and is noble now that he is dead?

15 And the report that Dardanus was the son of Jove is nothing counter to this, for it is a fable to which, in a philosophical discussion, we should give no heed. And, at any rate, if the adversary should choose to take his stand on the fable, verily that which the fable veils destroys all his arguments. And thus it is manifest that the argument which laid down oblivion as the cause of nobleness is false and erroneous.

Chapter XV

1 When the ode has disproved, on their own teaching, that time is demanded for nobleness, it straightway goes on to confound their aforesaid teaching itself, so that no rust may be left by their false arguments upon the mind which is disposed to the truth; and this it does when it says: *Further it followeth from what I have above set down.*

2 And here be it known that if a man cannot become gentle for a churl, and neither can a gentle son be born from a base father (as was laid down above in their opinion), one of two absurdities must follow: the one is that there is no nobleness; the other is that there has always been a multiplicity of men in the world, so that the human race is not descended from one single man. And this can be demonstrated.

3 If nobleness is not begotten anew (and it has been said above repeatedly that their opinion involves this, because it allows not its derivation from a base man to himself, nor from a base father to his son), a man is always such as he is born; and he is born such as his father; and so this transmission of one single condition has come down from the first parent; wherefore such as was the first generator, to wit, Adam, such must the whole human generation needs be, for from him to the moderns there is no room to find any change according to this argument.

4 Wherefore, if Adam himself was noble, we are all noble, and if he was base, we are all base, which is no other than to take away the distinction between these conditions, and so to take away the conditions themselves. And this is what the words *That we be all gentle or else simple* declare must follow from what has gone before.

5 And if this be not true, then of sheer necessity some folk must be reckoned noble and some reckoned base; and since the change from baseness to nobleness is ruled out, it follows that the human race is descended from diverse origins, that is to say, from one noble origin and one from base; and this is what the ode declares when it says: *Or that man had not an origin*, that is to say one sole origin (for it does not say *"origins"*); and this is most false according to the Philosopher, according to our faith which may not lie, according to the religion and ancient belief of the Gentiles.

6 For although the Philosopher does not lay down the succession from one first man, yet he will have it that there is one only essence in all men, the which diverse origins could not produce. And Plato has it that all men depend on one only "idea" and not on several, which is giving one sole origin to them. And without doubt Aristotle would laugh aloud if he heard folk making two species of the human race, like that of horses and of asses; for (with apologies to Aristotle) those who so think might at any rate be the asses.

7 That, judged by our faith (which is to be pursued absolutely), it would be most false is clear from Solomon, who, when he makes a distinction between all mankind and the brute animals, calls the former sons of Adam; and this he does when he says, "Who knows whether the spirits of the sons of Adam go up and those of the beasts go down?"[169]

8 And that it was false according to the Gentiles, behold the witness of Ovid in the first of his Metamorphoses, where he treats of the constitution of the world, according to the pagan belief, or that of the Gentiles, saying, "Man was born" (he does not say men); "man was born; whether the artificer of things made him of divine

---

169 Ecclesiastes 3:21.

seed, or whether the new-made earth, but lately darted from the noble ether, retained the seeds of the kindred heaven which, mingled with the water of the stream, the son of Iapetus (that is Prometheus) composed in the likeness of the gods who govern all."[170] Where he manifestly lays it down that the first man was only one.

9 And therefore the ode says: *But this I grant not*; that is that man had not an origin. And the ode adds: *Neither do they if they be Christians.* It says "Christians" and not "Philosophers" or "Gentiles," though their opinions too are against them; because the Christian doctrine is of greater vigour and crushes all cavil, thanks to the supreme light of heaven which illuminates it.

10 Then when I say: *Wherefore to sound intellects 'tis manifest that what they say is vain*, I draw the conclusion that their error is confounded; and I say that it is time for eyes to be opened to the truth. And this I tell when I say: *And now I would declare how I regard it.* I affirm, then, that it is plain to "sound intellects" by what has been said, that these utterances of theirs are vain, that is to say without the marrow of truth. And I say "sound" not without cause.

11 Wherefore be it known that our intellect may be spoken of as sound or sick; and I mean by "intellect" the noble part of our soul which may be indicated by the common term "mind."[171] Sound it may be called when not impeded in its activity by ill either of mind or of body; which activity consists in knowing what things are, as Aristotle says in the third *Of the Soul*.[172]

12 For, as to sickness of soul, I have perceived three terrible maladies in the mind of man. One is caused by boastfulness of nature, for many are so presumptuous that they suppose themselves to know everything; and therefore they affirm uncertain things as certain; the vice which Tully chiefly denounces in the first of the *Offices*, and Thomas in his *Against the Gentiles*, where he says, "Many are so presumptuous in character as to believe they can measure

---

170   *Metamorphoses* I.78–83.

171   *Inf.* IX.61–63.

172   *De anima* III.4.

all things with their intellect, considering everything true that approves itself to them, and everything false which does not."[173]

13 And hence it is that they never come at learning, believing that they are learned enough of themselves; they never ask questions, they never listen, but desire that questions should be asked of them, and before the question is well out they give a wrong answer. And of these Solomon says in the *Proverbs*, "Hast thou seen a man swift to answer? From him folly rather than correction is to be looked for."[174]

14 The second is caused by objectness of nature, for there are many so obstinate in their abasement that they cannot believe that anything can be known either by themselves or by any other; and such never search or argue for themselves, nor care at all what any other says. And against them Aristotle discourses in the first of the *Ethics*, saying, "That they are incompetent students of moral philosophy."[175] Ever like beasts do such live in grossness, without hope of any instruction.

15 The third is caused by frivolity of nature, for there are many of such frivolous fancy that they dash about whenever they argue, reaching their conclusion before they have formed their syllogism, and flying from this conclusion to another, and fancying all the time that they are arguing most subtly. And they start from no axioms and never really see any one thing truly in their imagination.

16 And of them the Philosopher says that we should take no heed nor have aught to do with them, saying in the first of the *Physics* that with him who denies the axioms it is not meet to dispute. And amongst such are many unlettered who would not know their A B C, and would fain discuss Geometry, Astrology, and Physics.

17 And by reason of sickness or defect of body the mind may be unsound, sometimes by defect of some principle from birth, as in the case of idiots; sometimes by disturbance of the brain, as in the

---

173   *De officiis* I.vi.18–19 and *Summa Contra Gentiles* I.5, respectively.

174   Proverbs 29:20.

175   *Ethics* I.4.

case of maniacs. And it is this malady of mind that the law contemplates when the *Infortiatum* says, "In him who makes a testament, soundness of mind, not of body, is required at the time in which the testament is made."[176]

18 Wherefore it is to those intellects which are not sick by malady of mind or body, but are free and unencumbered and sound with reference to the light of truth, that I say it is manifest that the opinion just spoken of is vain and without worth. Then it adds that I thus pronounce them false and vain and thus refute them; and this it does when it says: *And thus do I refute the same as false.* And afterwards I say that we are to proceed to demonstrate the truth, and I say that we are to demonstrate this, to wit, what gentlehood is, and how a man in whom it exists may be recognized; and I say this here: *And now I would declare how I regard it.*

Chapter XVI

1 "The king shall rejoice in God, and all those who swear by him shall be praised, because the mouth is shut of those who speak unjust things." These words I may verily here set forth, because every true king ought supremely to love the truth. Wherefore it is written in the book of *Wisdom,* "Love the light of wisdom, ye who are before the peoples,"[177] and the light of wisdom is truth itself. I say, then, that every king shall rejoice because that most false and pernicious opinion of mischievous and erring men, which they have hitherto unrighteously spoken concerning nobleness, has been refuted.

2 It is fitting to proceed to treat of the truth according to the division made above in the third chapter of the present treatise. This second part then, which begins: *I affirm that every virtue in principle,* proposes to determine about nobleness itself according to the truth. And this part is divided into two; for in the first the intention is to show what this nobleness is, and in the second how he in

---

176   *Digesta* XXVIII.i.2.
177   *Wisdom* 6:23.

whom it resides may be recognized. And this second part begins: *The soul which this excellence adorns.*

3 The first part has again two parts, for in the first certain things are investigated which are necessary for the comprehension of the definition of nobleness. In the second the definition itself is sought; and this second part begins: *Gentlehood is wherever there is virtue.*

4 To penetrate completely into the treatment we must first perceive two things: the one, what is understood by this word *nobleness*, simply considered without qualification; the other is, by what road we are to travel to find the above-named definition. I say, then, that if we would have regard to the common custom of speech, this word "nobleness" means the perfection in each thing of its proper nature.[178]

5 Wherefore it is not only predicated of man, but of all other things as well; for a man calls a stone noble, a plant noble, a horse noble, a falcon noble, whenever it appears perfect in its own nature. And therefore Solomon says in *Ecclesiastes*, "Blessed the land whose king is noble,"[179] which is to say no other than "whose king is perfect according to the perfection of mind and of body." And this he clearly shows by what he says before, when he says, "Woe unto thee, O land, whose king is a child,"[180] that is to say, not a perfect man; and a man is not a child simply in virtue of age, but in virtue of disorderly ways and defect of life, as the Philosopher instructs us in the first of the *Ethics.*

6 It is true that there are foolish ones who believe that by this word "noble" is meant "named and known by many," and they say that it comes from a verb which means "to know," to wit, *nosco.* And this is most false; for if this were so, those things which were most named and known in their kind would be the noblest in their kind; and so the obelisk of St. Peter would be the most noble stone in the world; and Asdente the cobbler of Parma would be nobler than any of his fellow-citizens; and Alboino della Scala would be more no-

---

178   *Purg.* XII.25–27; *Par.* VII.76–78.

179   Ecclesiastes 10:17.

180   Ecclesiastes 10:16.

ble than Guido da Castello of Reggio; whereas every one of these things is most false. And therefore it is most false that *noble* comes from *knowing*; but it comes from *not vile*, wherefore "noble" is as much as "not vile."

7 This perfection is what the Philosopher himself means in the seventh of the *Physics* when he says, "Everything is most perfect when it touches and reaches its own proper virtue; and it is then most perfect according to its nature. Wherefore the circle may be called perfect when it is really a circle";[181] that is to say, when it attains to its own proper virtue, then it exists in its full nature, and then it may be called a noble circle.

8 And this is when there is a point in it which is equally distant from the circumference. That circle which has the figure of an egg loses its virtue and is not noble; nor is that which has the figure of an almost full moon, because its nature is not perfect in it. And so it may be plainly seen that in general this word, to wit, "nobleness," expresses in all things the perfection of their nature. And this is the first thing we are in search of, the better to enter into the treatment of the section which we are about to expound.

9 Secondly, we were to see how we are able to travel in order to discover the definition of human nobleness, which is the scope of the present process. I say, then, that inasmuch as in those things which are of one species, as are all men, we cannot define their best perfection by essential principles, we must define and know it by the effects they manifest.

10 And so we read in the Gospel of St. Matthew when Christ says, "Beware of false prophets; by their fruits ye shall know them."[182] So the straight path leads us to look for this definition (which we are searching for) by way of the fruits; which are moral and intellectual virtues whereof this our nobleness is the seed, as shall be fully shown in the definition thereof. And these are the two things which it behoved us to perceive before proceeding to the rest, as said above in this chapter.

---

181   *Physics* VII.3.
182   Matthew 7:15–16.

Chapter XVII

1 Now when these two things are understood, which it seemed advantageous to understand before proceeding with this text, we are to go on to expound the text itself. It says, then, and begins: *I affirm that every virtue and principle cometh from one root, I mean virtue that maketh man blessed in his doing*; and it adds: *This is (according as the* Ethics *say) a selective habit*, setting forth the whole definition of moral virtue according as it is defined in the second of the *Ethics* by the Philosopher.

2 And the chief stress of this is on two things: the one is that every virtue comes from one principle; the other is that this "every virtue" means the moral virtues which are our subject; and this is manifest when it says: *That is (according as the* Ethics *say)*. Where be it known that our most proper fruits are the moral virtues, because in every direction they are in our power.

3 And they have been distinguished and enumerated diversely by diverse philosophers, but inasmuch as wherever the divine opinion of Aristotle has opened its mouth methinks that every other's opinion may be dropped, purposing to declare what they are, I will briefly pass through them in discourse according to his opinion.

4 These are the eleven virtues named by the said Philosopher.[183] The first is called Courage, which is weapon and rein to control rashness and timidity in things which bring destruction to our life. The second is Temperance, which is rule and rein to our gluttony and our excessive abstinence in things which preserve our life. The third is Liberality, which is the moderator of our giving and of our taking of temporal things.

5 The fourth is Munificence, which is the moderator of great expenditures, making the same and arresting them at a certain limit. The fifth is Magnanimity, which is moderator and acquirer of great honours and fame. The sixth is Love of Honor, which moderates and regulates us as to the honours of this world. The seventh is

---

183   For the following list see *Ethics* II.7.

Serenity, which moderates our wrath and our excessive patience in the face of external evils.

6 The eighth is Affability, which makes us pleasant in company. The ninth is called Truth, which moderates us in speech from vaunting ourselves beyond what we are, or depreciating ourselves beyond what we are. The tenth is called *Eutrapelia*,[184] which moderates us in sports, causing us to ply them in due measure. The eleventh is Justice, which disposes us to love and to do righteousness in all things.

7 And each of these virtues has two collateral foes, namely vices, the one in excess and the other in defect. And they themselves are the means between them; and they all spring from one principle, to wit, from the habit of our right selection. Wherefore it may be said generally of all of them that they are in an "elective habit consisting in the mean."[185]

8 And these are they which make a man blessed or happy in their operation, as saith the Philosopher in the first of the *Ethics* when he defines felicity, saying that "Felicity is action in accordance with virtue in a perfect life."[186] It is true that prudence, or sense, is set down by many as a moral virtue; but Aristotle enumerates her amongst the intellectual virtues, although she is the guide of the moral virtues and shows the way whereby they are combined, and without her they may not be.

9 But, be it known, in this life we may have two felicities, according to the two diverse paths, the good and the best, which lead us thereto; the one is the active life, and the other the contemplative. Which latter (although by the active life we arrive, as was said, at a good felicity) leads us to the best felicity and blessedness, as the Philosopher proves in the tenth of the *Ethics*.[187]

---

184   Good disposition.
185   *Inf.* XI.79–84.
186   *Ethics* I.7.
187   *Ethics* X.7.

10 And Christ affirms it with his mouth in the Gospel of Luke, speaking to Martha and answering her, "Martha, Martha, thou art anxious, and dost trouble thyself about many things; verily one only thing is needful," that is to say, the thing which thou art doing. And he adds, "Mary hath chosen the best part, which shall not be taken from her."[188] And Mary, as it is written before these words of the Gospel, sitting at the feet of Christ, showed no concern for the ministry of the house, but hearkened only to the words of the Saviour.

11 For if we were to expound this morally, our Lord meant therein to show that the contemplative life was the best, although the active life was good. This is manifest to whoso will apply his mind to the Gospel words. But some might say, arguing against me: Inasmuch as the felicity of the contemplative life is more excellent than that of the active, and the one and the other may be and is the fruit and end of nobility, why not proceed rather by way of the intellectual than by way of the moral virtues?

12 To this it may be answered briefly that in every discipline heed should be given to the capacity of the learner, and he should be led by that path which is easiest to him. Wherefore, inasmuch as the moral virtues seem to be and are more common and better known and more sought after than the other virtues, and more closely knit with outward manifestation, it was expedient and suitable to proceed by this path rather than by the other; for we should arrive equally well at a knowledge of bees by investigating the product of wax as the product of honey, though one and the other proceed from them.

Chapter XVIII

1 The preceding chapter brings us to define how every moral virtue rises out of one principle, that is to say a right and habitual selection; and that is what the present text implies up to that part which begins: *I affirm that nobility in its constituent essence.*

---

188   Luke 10:38–42.

2 In this part, then, we proceed, by way of probable inference, to learn that every virtue named above, taken severally or generally, proceeds from nobility, as effect from cause. And this is supported by a philosophical proposition which declares that when two things are found to agree in anything, they must both be reduced to some third thing, or one of them reduced to the other, as effect to cause; because one characteristic, primarily and essentially possessed, can only pertain to one thing, and if these two were not both the effect of some third, nor one the effect of the other, then both of them would possess this characteristic primarily and essentially, which is impossible.

3 It says, then, that nobility and virtue (such as we are discussing, namely moral virtue) agree in this, that the one and the other implies praise in him of whom it is asserted, and this when it says: *Wherefore in one same implication the two agree, being to one effect*; that is to say, the ascription of them to anyone implies praise of him and the belief that he is prized. And then it draws the conclusion on the strength of the above-noted proposition, and says that the one must needs proceed from the other, or both from a third; and adds that it is rather to be presumed that one comes from the other than that both come from a third, if it appears that the one implies as much as the other, and more yet. And this is what this line affirms: *But if one signifies all that the other signifies.*

4 Where you are to know that at this point the argument does not proceed by necessary demonstration (as though we should say, "if it is cold that begets water, and if we see the clouds," etc.), but expresses a fair and fitting induction; for if there are in us sundry things worthy of praise, and if there also is in us the principle whence praise of us flows, it is reasonable to reduce the former to the latter. And it is more reasonable to regard that which embraces several things as their principle than to regard them as its principle.

5 For the stem of the tree, which embraces all the other limbs, should be called the principle and cause of them, and not they of it. And thus nobleness, which comprehends every virtue (as cause comprehends effect), and many other praiseworthy activities of ours as well, ought so to be so regarded as that virtue should be reduced to it, rather than to some third thing that may be in us.

6 Finally, it says that what has now been expressed (to wit, that every moral virtue comes from one root, and moral virtue as above declared, agrees in one thing with nobility, so that the one must be reduced to the other or both to a third, and that if the one means all that which the other does and more, the latter proceeds from the former rather than from some other third) is all to be presupposed; that is to say, is ordered and prepared for what is further in view. And so ends this verse and this present section.

Chapter XIX

1 Now that in the preceding section three certain things have been decided, which were necessary in order to learn how we might define this excellent thing of which we are speaking, it behoves us to proceed to the following section, which begins: *Gentlehood is wherever there is virtue.*

2 And this must be reduced to two sections. In the first, a certain thing is proved which was touched upon, but left unproved, before. In the second, the conclusion is reached, and that definition which we are seeking is found. And this second part begins: *Therefore shall be evolved (like perse from black).*

3 To make the first section evident, we are to recall what was said above, that if nobleness has a larger scope and extent than virtue, virtue will rather proceed from it. Which thing, to wit, that nobility has a wider extent, is proved in this section; and it gives an illustration from the heaven, saying that wherever virtue is there is nobleness.

4 And here be it known that (according as is written in Reason and is held as the rule of Reason) those things which are obvious in themselves have no need of proof; and nothing is more obvious than that there is nobleness where there is virtue. And it is a matter

of common observation that everything after its own nature can be called noble.

5 It says then: *Even as the heaven is wherever is the star,* but this is not true conversely (viz., that wherever the heaven is there the star is also), just so there is nobleness wherever there is virtue, but not virtue wherever there is nobleness. And this with a fair and congruous illustration; for in truth it is a heaven in which many and diverse stars shine; the intellectual and the moral virtue shine in it; good dispositions given by nature shine in it, to wit, tenderness and religion, and the praiseworthy emotions, to wit, shame and compassion, and many others. There shine in it the excellencies of the body, to wit, beauty, strength, and, so to speak, unbroken health.

6 And so many are the stars that extend over this heaven that verily it is no matter for wonder if they make many and diverse fruits grow on human nobleness, so many are their natural characteristics and potentialities, comprised and united in one, simple substance; and in them, as in diverse branches, it bears diverse fruits. Nay, in very truth I dare to affirm that human nobleness, considered under the aspect of its many fruits, surpasses that of the angel, although the angelic be more divine in its unity.

7 Of this our nobleness, which fructifies in such and in so many fruits, the psalmist was aware when he composed that psalm which begins, "O Lord our God, how wonderful is thy name throughout the earth!"[189] where he extols man, as though marveling at the divine affection for the human creature, saying, "What is man that thou, God, visitest him? Thou hast made him but little less than the angels; with glory and with honour hast thou crowned him and set him over the works of thy hands."[190] Verily, then, it was a beauteous and congruous comparison of the heaven to human nobleness!

8 Then when it says: *And we in women and in youthful age,* it proves that which I say, showing that nobleness extends itself to a region where virtue does not. And it says that we *Perceive this saving thing* (which refers to nobleness, which is indeed a truly saving thing) to exist

---

189   Psalm 8:1.
190   Psalm 8:5–7.

where there is sensitiveness to shame, that is, fear of dishonour; as in women and in young folk, where shame is good and laudable; which shame is not a virtue but a certain estimable emotion.[191]

9 And it says: *And we in women and in youthful age, that is in young people;* because, according as the Philosopher hath it in the fourth of the *Ethics*, "Shame is not laudable nor becoming in old men nor in studious folk,"[192] because it behoves them to guard against those things which would cause them shame.

10 Of young people and of women not so much of this line of conduct is required, and therefore in them the fear of encountering disgrace through some fault is laudable, for it comes from nobleness. And their fear may be regarded as nobleness, just as impudence is baseness and ignobleness. Wherefore it is a good and most excellent sign of nobleness in children and those of unripe age when shame is painted in their faces after a fault, for then it is the fruit of true nobleness.

Chapter XX

1 When there follows next: *Therefore shall be evolved (as perse from black),* the text proceeds to that definition of nobility which we are seeking, and whereby we may perceive what this nobleness of which so many folks speak erroneously really is. It affirms then, drawing the conclusion from what has already been said, that every virtue, *or their generic kind,* namely the "elective habit consisting in the mean," will proceed from this, to wit, from nobleness.

2 And it takes an illustration from the colors, saying that as perse derives from black, so does it, namely virtue, derive from nobleness. Perse is a color mingled of purple and of black, but the black predominates, and it is called after it; and thus virtue is a thing combined of nobleness and emotion; but because the nobleness predominates over the other, virtue is called after it and is named goodness.

191 *Inf.* XVII.88–90.
192 *Ethics* IV.9.

3 And so it goes on to argue from what has been said, that no one, because he can say "I am of such and such a race," should believe that he has nobleness, unless these fruits are in him. And straightway it gives the reason, saying that those who have this "grace," to wit, this divine thing, are almost like gods, without taint of vice. And this gift can be given by none save God alone, with whom there is no selection of persons, as the divine Scriptures make manifest.[193]

4 Nor let any deem it too lofty an utterance when it says: *For they are well-nigh gods*: for, as argued above in the seventh chapter of the third treatise, just as there are men most base and bestial, so there are men most noble and divine. And Aristotle proves this in the seventh of the *Ethics* by the text of the poet Homer.[194]

5 Wherefore let not him of the Uberti of Florence, nor him of the Visconti of Milan, say, "Because I am of such a race I am noble"; for the divine seed falls not upon the race, that is the stock, but falls upon the several persons; and, as will be shown below, the stock does not ennoble the several persons, but the several persons ennoble the stock.

6 Then when it says: *For God alone presents it to the soul*, the discourse turns to the receptive being, that is the subject, whereon this divine gift descends—for it is in truth a divine gift—according to the word of the Apostle: "Every best gift and every perfect gift cometh from above, descending from the Father of Lights."[195]

7 It says, then, that God alone gives the grace to the soul of that man whom he sees perfectly balanced in his person and ready and disposed to receive this divine act. For, as the Philosopher says in the second *Of the Soul*, "Things must needs be in the right disposition for their agents in order to be acted on by them."[196] Wherefore if the soul takes not its perfect "stand," it is not so disposed as to receive this blessed and divine infusion; just as if a precious stone

---

193   *Purg.* VII.121–123.

194   *Ethics* VII.1.

195   James 1:7.

196   *De anima* II.2.

be ill-disposed, or imperfect, it cannot receive the celestial virtue, as said that noble Guido Guinizelli in an ode of his which begins, "To the gentle heart love repaireth ever."

8 It is possible, then, that the soul stands not well in the person through defect of complexion, and perhaps through defect of season; and in such as these this divine ray never glows. And such, whose soul is deprived of this light, may say that they are like valleys turned to the north, or caves beneath the earth, where the light of the Sun never descends unless thrown back from some other region whereon it shines.

9 Finally, it draws the conclusion and declares according to what has been said above (namely, that the virtues are the fruit of nobleness, which God implants in the mind that sits rightly), that there are some (namely, those who have understanding which are few) to whom, *the seed of blessedness draws nigh*. And it is evident that human nobleness is nought else than, *the seed of blessedness draws nigh, dispatched by God into the well-placed soul*, that is, the soul whose body is perfectly disposed in every part. For if the virtues are the fruit of nobleness, and if blessedness is the fruition of sweetness, it is manifest that this nobleness is the sower of blessedness, as has been said.

10 And if well considered, this definition embraces all the four causes, to wit, material, formal, efficient, and final; material, inasmuch as it says, "into the well-placed soul," which is the material and subject of nobleness; formal, inasmuch as it says, that it is "the seed"; efficient, inasmuch as it says, "dispatched by God into the soul"; final, inasmuch as it says, "of blessedness." And thus is defined this excellence of ours, which descends into us after the fashion of a supreme and spiritual virtue, as virtue into the stone from the noblest celestial body.

Chapter XXI

1 In order to understand the human excellence which is called nobleness, as the principle of all good in us, we are to elucidate, in this special chapter, how this excellence descends into us; and first in the natural way, and then in the theological, that is, the divine and spiritual way.

2 To begin with, we are to know that man is composed of soul and of body; but that which has been declared to resemble the seed of the divine virtue pertains to the soul. It is true that diverse reasonings have been held by philosophers concerning the difference of our souls; for Avicenna and Algazel would have it that they in themselves, and in their principle, were noble or base. Plato and others would have it that they proceeded from the stars and were noble, more or less, according to the nobleness of the star.

3 Pythagoras would have it that all were of like nobleness, and not only the human souls, but together with the human those of the brute animals and of the plants, and the forms of the minerals; and he said that all the difference was in the bodily forms. If each were to defend his own opinion, it might be that truth would be seen to exist in all of them. But inasmuch as on the surface they appear somewhat remote from the truth, it is better not to proceed by way of them, but by way of the opinion of Aristotle and of the Peripatetics.

4 And therefore I say that when the human seed falls into its receptacle, that is, into the matrix, it bears with it the virtue of the generative soul, and the virtue of heaven, and the virtue of the elements it combines, that is to say, its complexion; and it matures and disposes the material for the formative virtue which the soul of the generator gave.[197] And the formative virtue prepares the organs for the celestial virtue, which draws the soul from the potentiality of the seed into life.

5 And the moment it is produced, it receives from the virtue of the mover of the heaven the possible intellect, which potentially draws into itself all the universal forms, according as they exist in its Producer, but in a lesser degree in proportion as it is more removed from the prime Intelligence.

---

197 *Purg.* XXV.37–42.

⁶ Let no man marvel if I speak in such wise as seems hard to understand; for to me myself it seems a marvel how such a producing can be arrived at by argument and perceived by the intellect; and it is not a thing to expound in language—I mean in any language truly vernacular. Wherefore I would say like the Apostle, "Oh, height of the wealth of the wisdom of God, how incomprehensible are thy judgments, and thy ways past finding out!"[198]

⁷ And because the complexion of the seed may be more or less good, and the disposition of the sower may be more or less good, and the disposition of the heaven for the effect may be good, better, or best (since it varies by reason of the constellations which are continually changing), it comes to pass that from the human seed and from these virtues the soul is produced more or less pure. And according to its purity there descends into it the possible intellectual virtue, which has been spoken of, and in the way spoken of.

⁸ And if it chance that because of the purity of the receiving soul the intellectual virtue is well abstracted and absolved from every corporeal shade, the divine excellence is multiplied in it, as in a thing sufficient for its reception; and hence there is multiplication of this intelligence in the soul according as it may receive it. And this is that "seed of felicity" of which at present we are speaking.

⁹ And this harmonizes with the opinion of Tully in that *Of Old Age*, where, speaking in the person of Cato, he says, "Wherefore a celestial soul descended into us, coming down from the loftiest of habitations into a place which is counter to the divine nature and to eternity."[199] And in this such soul there exists its own proper virtue, and the intellectual virtue, and the divine, to wit, that influence of which we have just been speaking; wherefore it is written in the *Book Of Causes*, "Every noble soul has three activities, to wit, the animal, the intellectual, and the divine."[200]

¹⁰ And there are some of such opinion as to say that if all the preceding virtues were to accord in the production of a soul in their

---

198 Romans 11:33.

199 *De senectute* XXI.77.

200 *Book of Causes* III.1.

best disposition, that so much of the Deity would descend thereon that it would almost be another incarnate God; and this is almost all that can be said by way of natural science.

11 By way of theological science it may be said that when the supreme Deity, that is God, sees his creature prepared to receive of his benefaction, he commits to it as largely thereof as it is prepared to receive. And because these gifts come from the ineffable love, and the divine love is appropriated to the Holy Spirit, they are thence called gifts of the Holy Spirit.[201]

12 The which, as Isaiah the Prophet distinguishes them, are seven, to wit, wisdom, understanding, counsel, strength, knowledge, piety, and fear of God.[202] Oh, fair grain, and fair and marvellous seed! and oh, admirable and benign sower, who waitest only until human nature prepared the land for thee to sow! Oh, blessed they who fittingly cultivate such seed!

13 And here, be it known, that the first and noble shoot which sprouts from this seed to bear fruit, is mental appetite, which in Greek is called *hormen.* And if this be not well cultivated and kept straight by good habit, little avails the seed, and better would it be had it not been sown at all.

14 And therefore St. Augustine lays it down (and also Aristotle in the second of the *Ethics*) that man should accustom himself to well-doing and to restraining his passions, in order that this shoot that has been spoken of may grow strong by good habit and may be inured in its straightness, so that it may bear fruit, and from its fruit may issue the sweetness of human felicity.

Chapter XXII

1 It is enjoined by the moral philosophers who have spoken of benefactions that man ought to bestow thought and care on making the benefits he confers as useful as may be to the receiver.

---

201   *Par.* XXIX.64–66, XXXI.22–24.

202   Isaiah 11:2.

Wherefore I, desiring to be obedient to such command, purpose to render this my banquet in every one of its parts as useful as shall be possible to me.

2 And since it here occurs to me that there is place for some discourse of the sweetness of human felicity, I conceive that no more useful discourse can be made for those who know it not; for (as saith the Philosopher in the first of the *Ethics*, and Tully in that of the *Goal of Good* [203]) he makes ill progress toward the goal who does not see it. And in like manner he can advance but ill towards the sweetness who was not first aware of what it is.

3 Wherefore, inasmuch as it is our final solace, for which we live and accomplish whatsoever we do, it is most useful and necessary to perceive this goal in order to direct the bow of our activity towards it. And he is chiefly acceptable who points it out to those who see it not.

4 Letting be, then, the opinion on this matter which the philosopher Epicurus had, and that which Zeno had, I purpose to come at once to the true opinion of Aristotle and of the other Peripatetics. As said above, from the divine excellence sown and infused into us from the beginning of our generation there springs a shoot which the Greeks called *hormen*, that is natural appetite of the mind.

5 And as the grains which, when born, have at first an almost identical appearance while yet in the blade, and then, as they go forward, become unlike, so this natural appetite, which rises from the divine grace, first appears not unlike that which comes just from nature, stripped of aught else, and (like the blade of diverse grains) is almost identical with it. And this likeness is not confined to men, but extends to men and to beasts alike. And this appears herein that every animal, as soon as it is born, whether rational or brute, loves itself and fears and flees those which are counter to it, and hates them.

6 Then, as things proceed, there begins, as said above, to be unlikeness between them in the progress of this appetite, for one takes

---

203   *Ethics* I.1 and *De finibus* V.vi.15–16, respectively.

one path and another another. As saith the apostle, "Many run for the prize, but one is he who receives it,"[204] so these human appetites proceed from their starting point along diverse paths, and one only path is that which will lead us to our peace. And therefore letting be all others, our treatise is to hold after the one that begins aright.

7 I say, then, that from the beginning it loves itself, although without discrimination. Then it comes to distinguish the things which are most pleasant, and less and more detestable, and follows and flees in greater and less degree according as its consciousness distinguishes not only in other things which it loves secondarily, but just in itself which it loves primarily.

8 And recognizing in itself diverse parts, it loves those in itself most which are most noble. And since the mind is a more noble part of man than the body, it loves that more; and thus, loving itself primarily and other things for its own sake, and loving the better part of itself better, it is clear that it loves the mind better than the body or aught else; which mind it ought by nature to love more than aught else.

9 Wherefore, if the mind always delights in the exercise of the thing it loves (which is the fruition of love), exercise in that thing which it loves most is the most delightful. The exercise of our mind, then, is most delightful to us; and that which is most delightful to us constitutes our felicity and our blessedness, beyond which there is no delight, nor any equal to it, as may be seen by whoso well considers the preceding argument.

10 And let not any say that every appetite is mental, for here mind is taken only to mean that which has respect to the rational part, that is the will and the intellect. So that if anyone should choose to call the sensitive appetite mind, his objection would not and could not apply to the present matter; for none doubts that the rational appetite is more noble than the sensitive and therefore more to be loved; and so that is the thing of which we are now speaking.

---

204   1 Corinthians 9:24.

11 It is true that the exercise of our mind is twofold, to wit, practical and speculative (practical is as much to say operative); the one and the other most delightful, though that of contemplation be more so, as was declared above. The practical exercise of the mind consists in ourselves working virtuously, that is, in integrity, with prudence, with temperance, with courage, and with justice. The speculative exercise of the mind consists not in working ourselves at all, but in considering the works of God and of nature. And this and that exercise constitutes, as may be perceived, our blessedness and our supreme felicity. And this is the sweetness of the above-mentioned seed (as is now quite evident), whereto many times such seed attains not, by reason that it is ill cultivated and that its shoots go astray.

12 In like manner, by much correction and cultivation some portion of the outgrowth of this seed may be so led to a place where it did not originally fall as to come to this fruit. And this is, as it were, a kind of engrafting of another nature on a diverse root. And so there is none who can be excused; for if a man hath not this seed from his natural root, he may at least have it by way of engrafting. Would that, in fact, they were as many who had engrafted it on themselves as are they who have let themselves straggle away from the good root!

13 But, in truth, the one of these exercises is more full of blessedness than the other, to wit, the speculative, which, without any admixture, is the exercise of our most noble part, which, by reason of that fundamental love which has been spoken of, is chiefly to be loved, to wit, the intellect. And this part cannot, in this life, have its perfect exercise, which is to see God (who is the supreme object of the intellect), save insofar as the intellect considers him and contemplates him through his effects.[205]

14 And that we should supremely demand this blessedness and not the other (to wit, that of the act of life), the Gospel of Mark instructs us, if we would rightly consider it. Mark says that Mary Magdalene and James' Mary and Mary Salome went to find the

---

205   *Par.* I.4–9, XXXIII.58–66.

Saviour at the tomb, and found him not, but found a man dressed in white, who said to them, "Ye seek the Saviour, and I say unto you that he is not here. Nevertheless, fear ye not, but go and say to his disciples, and to Peter, that he will go before them in Galilee, and there ye shall see him as he said unto you."[206]

15 By these three ladies may be understood the three schools of the act of life, to wit, the Epicureans, the Stoics, and the Peripatetics, who go to the tomb, that is to the present world, which is the receptacle of corruptible things, and demand the Saviour, that is blessedness, and find not; but they find a man in white garments, who, according to the testimony of Matthew, and also of the others, was the angel of God. And therefore Matthew said, "The angel of God descended from the heaven and came and rolled away the stone and sat upon it; and his aspect was as lightning, and his garments were as snow."[207]

16 This angel is the nobleness of ours, which comes from God, as has been said, which speaks in our reason and declares to each one of these schools, that is to everyone who goes seeking blessedness in the act of life, that it is not there; but go your way and tell the disciples and Peter, that is those who go seeking it and those who have gone astray (as Peter did when he denied him), that he will go before them in Galilee; that is to say, that blessedness will go before them in Galilee, that is in speculation.

17 Galilee is as much as to say "whiteness," and whiteness is a color full of material light more than any other; and in like manner contemplation is fuller of spiritual light than aught else which is here below. And it says, "And will go before you," and does not say, "And will be with you," to give to understand that God is ever in advance of our contemplation; nor ever can we here come up with him who is our supreme blessedness. And it says, "And there ye will see him, as he said," that is, "And there ye will have of his sweetness, that is of felicity, as has been promised to you here,"

---

206   Mark 16:1–7.
207   Matthew 28:2–3.

that is to say, as it has been covenanted for you to have power to obtain.

18 And thus it appears that our blessedness, which is this felicity of which is the discourse, we can first find imperfect in the active life, that is in the activities of the moral virtues, and then perfectly, in a way, in the activities of the intellectual. The which two activities are the quickest and straightest ways to lead us to the supreme blessedness, which may not here be had, as appears by what has been said.

Chapter XXIII

1 Now that the definition of nobility has been adequately expounded and cleared, and has been illustrated in its divisions as far as possible, so that we can understand now what a noble man is, we are to proceed to the part of the text which begins: *The soul whom this excellence adorns*; wherein are shown the tokens whereby we may recognize the noble man that has been spoken of.

2 And this part is divided into two; the first affirms that this nobleness openly shines and glows through the whole life of the noble one; in the second, it is specifically indicated in its several lustres; and this second part begins: *Obedient, sweet, and alive to shame.*

3 Concerning the first part, be it known that this divine seed, of which we have spoken above, buds forth in our soul instantly, yielding itself in diverse fashions to every power of the soul, according to their needs. It buds, then, in the vegetative, in the sensitive, and in the rational, and branches out through the virtues of all of these, directing them to their perfections, and therein ever maintaining itself, until, together with that part of our soul which never dies, it returns to its most lofty and glorious sower, to heaven. And this it says in that first part which has been spoken of.

4 Then, when it says: *Obedient, sweet, and alive to shame*, and the rest, it sets forth that by which we may recognize the noble man, by apparent signs which are the working of this divine excellence. And this part may be divided into four, according as it works diversely in the four ages, to wit, in adolescence, in manhood, in age, and in decrepitude.

5 And the second part begins: *In manhood temperate and brave*; the third begins: *And in old age*; the fourth begins: *Then in the fourth term of life*. Such is the meaning of this part in general; concerning which it should be known that every effect, as effect, receives the likeness of its cause as far as it is possible to retain it.

6 Wherefore, inasmuch as our life (as said above), and also that of every creature that lives here below, is caused by heaven, and heaven displays itself to all such effects, not in its complete circle but in parts thereof, and thus its motion must needs be above them, and like an arch, as it were, embracing all lives as it mounts and descends (I say embracing these "lives" both of men and of other living things), they must needs be in a way likened to the image of an arch. Returning, then, to our own life alone, with which we are at present concerned, I affirm that it proceeds after the fashion of this arch, mounting and descending.

7 And be it known that this up-stretching arch would be equal in every case if the material of our seminal complexion did not impede the rule of human nature. But since the humid factor (which is the seat and the nutriment of the heat which constitutes our life) is less or more, and is of better quality, and has more duration, in one effect than in another, it comes to pass that the arch of life of one man is of less or greater stretch than that of another.

8 Death is sometimes violent or is hastened by incidental weakness; but only that which is commonly called "natural" constitutes the limit whereof the psalmist says, "Thou hast placed a boundary which may not be passed."[208] And inasmuch as the master of our life, Aristotle, was aware of this arch of which we are speaking, he seemed to maintain that our life was no other than a mounting and a descending, wherefore he says that wherein he treats of *Youth and Age*, that youth is no other than the growing of life.

---

208 Psalm 104:9.

[9] It is hard to say where the highest point of this arch is, because of the inequality spoken of above; but in the majority I take it to be somewhere between the thirtieth and the fortieth year. And I believe that in those of perfect nature it would be in the thirty-fifth year.

[10] And I am moved thereto by this argument that our Saviour Christ was of perfect nature, and it was his will to die in the thirty-fourth year of his age; for it was not fitting that the Divinity should thus abide in decrease. Nor is it to be believed that he would not abide in this our life up to the apex, inasmuch as he had been therein in the low estate of infancy.

[11] And this is manifested by the hour of the day of his death, for he desired to conform this to his life; wherefore Luke tells us it was about the sixth hour when he died, which is to say the apex of the day. Wherefore we may understand by this that about the thirty-fifth year of Christ was the apex of his age.

[12] However, it is not specially with reference to its central point that Scriptures divide this arch, but rather, according as the combinations of the contrary qualities which enter into our composition are four (to which, I mean to each combination, one section of our life seems to be appropriated), they divide it into four parts, which are called the four ages.

[13] The first is adolescence, which is appropriated to the hot and moist; the second is manhood, which is appropriated to the hot and dry; the third is age, which is appropriated to the cold and dry; the fourth is decrepitude, which is appropriated to the cold and moist, as Albert writes in the fourth of the *Meteorics*.

[14] And these parts occur in like manner in the year, in spring, in summer, in autumn, and in winter; and also in the day, that is up to tierce, then up to nones (omitting sext between these two, for an obvious reason), and then up till vespers, and from vespers onward. And therefore the Gentiles said that the car of the Sun had four horses, the first was called Eous, the second Pyroeis, the third

Aetheon, the fourth Phlegon (according as Ovid writes in the second of the *Metamorphoses*[209]), with reference to the parts of the day.

15 And briefly be it be known that, as said above in the sixth chapter of the third treatise, the church in distinguishing between the hours of the day makes use of the temporal hours, of which there are twelve in each day, long or short according to the measure of the Sun; and because the sixth hour, which is midday, is the most noble of the whole day, and the most virtuous, she approximates her offices thereto from each direction, that is to say before and after, as much as she may.

16 And therefore the office of the first part of the day, that is tierce, is called after its close, and that of the third part and of the fourth after their beginnings; and therefore we speak of "mid-tierce" before the bell rings for that division, and of mid-nones after the bell has rung for that division; and in like manner of mid-vespers. And therefore let every man know that the right nones ought always to be rung at the beginning of the seventh hour of the day; and let this suffice for the present digression.

Chapter XXIV

1 Returning to our purpose, I say that human life is divided into four ages. The first is called adolescence, that is, the "increasing" of life. The second is called "manhood," that is to say, the age of achievement, which may give perfection, and in this sense it is itself called perfect, because none can give aught save what he hath. The third is called old age. The fourth is called decrepitude, as said above.

2 As to the first, no one hesitates but every sage agrees that it lasts up to the twenty-fifth year; and because up to that time our soul is chiefly intent on conferring growth and beauty on the body, whence many and great changes take place in the person, the rational part cannot come to perfect discretion; wherefore Reason lays

---

209 *Metamorphoses* II.153–155.

down that before this age there are certain things a man may not do without a guardian of full age.

3 As for the second, which is truly the summit of our life, there is great diversity concerning the period to be taken; but passing over what philosophers and physicians have written about it, and having recourse to my own argumentation, I say that in the majority (on whom every judgment about a natural phenomenon may and should be based) this age lasts twenty years. And the argument which gives me this is that, if the apex of our arch is at thirty-five, the age under discussion should have as long a period of descent as it has of ascent; and this rising and descending may be likened to the sustained height of the arch wherein but slight bending is to be discerned.

4 We have it, then, that the prime of life is completed at the forty-fifth year. And as adolescence lasts twenty-five years, mounting up to the prime of life, so the descent, that is age, is a like period, succeeding to the prime of life; and so age ends at the seventieth year.

5 But inasmuch as adolescence (taking it as we have done above) does not begin at the beginning of life but some eight months after, and inasmuch as our nature is eager to rise and hangs back from descending (because the natural heat is reduced and has small power, and the humid is thickened, not in quantity but in quality, and so is less easily evaporated and consumed) it comes to pass that beyond old age there remains perhaps to the amount of ten years of our life, or a little more or a little less. And this period is called decrepitude.

6 Whence we have it of Plato—whom (both in the strength of his own nature, and because of the physiognomiscope which Socrates cast for him when he first saw him) we may believe to have had the most excellent nature—that he lived 82 years, as testifies Tully in that *Of Old Age*.[210] And I believe that if Christ had not been crucified and had lived out the space which his life had power to cover

---

210   *De senectute* V.13.

according to its nature, he would have been changed at the eighty-first year from mortal body to eternal.

7 Truly, as said above, these several ages may be longer or shorter, according to our complexion and composition, but however they may fall, I take it that the proportion laid down should be observed in them all, that is we must make the ages longer or shorter, according to the totality of the whole period of their natural life. Through all these ages this nobleness of which we are speaking manifests its effects diversely in the ennobled soul; and this is what this part about which I am at present writing purposes to show.

8 And here be it known that our nature, when good and straight, follows a seasonable procedure in us (as we see the nature of plants doing in them), and therefore different ways and different deportment are suitable at one age rather than at others, wherein the ennobled soul proceeds in due order, on one simple path, exercising its acts in their times and ages according as they are ordained for its ultimate fruit. And Tully agrees herein in that *Of Old Age*.[211]

9 And passing by the account which Vergil gives under a figure in the *Aeneid* of this changing progress of the ages, and passing by what Egidius the Eremite says in the first part of the *Regimen of Princes*, and passing by what Tully says of it in the first *Of Offices*, and following only that which reason may say of it herself, I say that this first age is the gate and path whereby we enter upon a good life.

10 And this entrance must of necessity have certain things which nature in her goodness, failing not in things necessary, giveth us; even as we see she giveth leaves to the vine to protect her fruit, and tendrils wherewith she supports and binds her weakness so as to sustain the weight of her fruit.[212]

11 Nature then, in her goodness, gives to this age four things needful for entrance into the city of the right life. The first is obedi-

---

211 *De senectute* II.5.
212 *Par.* VIII.112–114.

ence, the second is sweetness, the third sensitiveness to shame, the fourth is grace of body, as the text says in the first section.

12 You are to know, then, that like as he who was never in a city would not know how to keep the way without instruction from him who has practised it, so the adolescent who enters into the wandering wood of this life would not know how to keep the right path if it were not shown him by his elders. Nor would their indications avail if he were not obedient to their commandments, and therefore obedience was necessary for this age.

13 It is true that some might say, "Then can he be called obedient who shall give credence to evil commands, just as well as he who shall give credence to good ones?" I answer that this would not be obedience but transgression, for if the king command one path and the servant command another, the servant is not to be obeyed for that would be disobeying the king, and so would be transgression.

14 And therefore Solomon says when he purposes to correct his son (and this is his first injunction), "Hearken, my son, to the admonition of thy father,"[213] and then at once he warns him off from the evil counsel and instruction of others, saying, "Let not the sinners have power to allure thee with flatteries nor with delights, that thou go with them."[214] Wherefore, just as, so soon as he is born, the child cleaves to his mother's breast, in like manner, as soon as any light of the mind appears in him, he should turn to the correction of his father, and his father should teach him.

15 And let him see to it that he give him no example of himself in his works counter to his words of correction, for we see every son by nature look more to the prints of the paternal feet than to others. And therefore the law which provides for this affirms and commands that the person of the father should ever be regarded as holy and reverent by his sons. And thus we see that obedience was necessary in this age.

---

213   Proverbs 1:8.
214   Proverbs 1:10, 15.

16 And therefore Solomon writes in the *Proverbs* that "he who humbly and obediently endures fitting reprehension from the corrector shall be glorious,"[215] and he says "shall be" to give to understand that he is speaking to the adolescent who cannot be glorious at his present age.

17 And if any should cavil, in that this is said of the father and not of others, I say that all other obedience should be reduced to the father. Wherefore the Apostle says to the Colossians, "Children, obey your fathers in all things, for this is the will of God."[216] And if the father is not living, this obedience should be reduced to him who is left as father by the father's last will; and if the father die intestate, it should be reduced to him to whom Reason commits his guidance.

18 And next his masters and elders should be obeyed, to whom in a certain sense he seems to have been entrusted by the father or by him who holds the place of father. But since the present chapter has been long, on account of the profitable digressions which it contains, the other points are to be discussed in another chapter.

Chapter XXV

1 Not only is this well-natured soul obedient in adolescence, but it is also sweet, and this is the second thing which is necessary in this time of life for rightly entering the gate of manhood. It is necessary because we cannot have perfect life without friends, as Aristotle hath it in the eighth of the *Ethics*;[217] and the greater part of friendships appear to be sown in this first age, because therein man begins to be gracious or the opposite. The which grace is acquired by sweet conduct, to wit, gentle and courteous speech, gentle and courteous service and action.

---

215   Proverbs 13:18 and 15:31.

216   Colossians 3:20.

217   *Ethics* VIII.1.

2 And therefore says Solomon to his youthful son, "The scorners God scorns, and to the meek God will give grace."[218] And elsewhere he says, "Remove from thee the evil mouth, and let churlish mowings be far from thee."[219] Whereby it appeareth that this sweetness is necessary, as has been said.

3 And further the emotion of abashment is needful to this period of life, and therefore in this period the good and noble nature manifests it, as the text says. And since abashment is the most obvious token of nobleness in adolescence (for it is then supremely needful for the right foundation of our life, which is what the noble nature purposes), we must diligently speak thereof some little.

4 I say that by abashment I understand three emotions necessary for the right founding of our life. The first is bemazement; the second is pudicity;[220] the third is shame; although the common folk perceives not this distinction. And all these three are needful to this period of life for this reason: This period needs to be reverent and desirous of knowledge; this period needs to be restrained, so as not to transgress; this period needs to be penitent for error, so as not to become hardened in erring. And all of these make up the emotions mentioned above, which are vulgarly called abashment.

5 For bemazement is bewilderment of mind on seeing or hearing, or in any wise perceiving, great and wonderful things; for insofar as they appear great, they make him who perceives them reverent towards them, and insofar as they appear wonderful, they make him who perceives them desirous to have knowledge of them. And therefore the ancient kings contrived magnificent works of gold and gems and artful machinations in their mansions, that they who beheld them should be bemazed and therefore reverent, and should make question of the honourable conditions of the king.

6 And therefore says Statius, the sweet poet, in the first of the *Story of Thebes*,[221] that when Adrastus, king of the Argives, saw Polynices

---

218   Proverbs 3:24.

219   Proverbs 4:24.

220   Modesty.

221   *Thebaid* I.482ff.

clad in a lion's hide, and saw Tideus covered with the hide of a wild boar, and minded him of the answer which Apollo had given concerning his daughters, that he was bemazed, and therefore the more reverent and the more desirous to know.

7 Pudicity is a shrinking of the mind from foul things, with the fear of falling into them; as we see in virgins and in good women and in the adolescent, who are so modest that not only where they are urged or tempted to err, but where only a bare imagination of venereal pleasure can be found place, all are painted in the face with pale or with red colour.

8 Wherefore says the above-named poet in the first book *Of Thebes,*[222] just cited, that when Aceste, the nurse of Argia and of Deiphyle, daughters of king Adrastus, brought them before the eyes of their august father, in the presence of two strangers, to wit, Polynices and Tideus, the virgins became pale and red, and their eyes fled from every other regard and kept turned only to their father's face, as though secure.

9 Oh, how many faults does this pudicity restrain! How many unseemly acts and demands does it put to silence! How many unseemly desires does it rein back! How many evil temptations does it not abash—not only in the modest person's self, but in him who looks thereon! How many foul words does it hold back! For, as Tully says in the first *Of Offices,* "There is no foul act that is not foul to mention."[223] And accordingly a clean and noble man never so speaks that his words would be unseemly for a woman. Oh, how ill it becomes the man who goes in search of honour to speak of things which would be unseemly in the mouth of any woman!

10 Shame is fear of disgrace for a fault committed. And from this fear springs repentance for the fault, which has in itself a bitterness which is a chastisement against repeating the fault. Wherefore this same poet says in that same passage, that, when Polynices was questioned by king Adrastus of his origin, he hesitated before speaking for shame of the fault he had committed against his father, and

---

222   *Thebaid* I.527ff.
223   *De officiis* I.xxxv.127.

further for the faults of Oedipus his father, which seemed to leave their trace in the shame of the son. And he did not mention his father, but his ancestors and his land and his mother. And by all this it well appears that shame is necessary to this period of life.

11 And not only does the noble nature display obedience, sweetness, and abashment in this age, but it displays beauty and agility of body, as the text says when it declares: *And adorns the person.* And this "adorns" is a verb and not a noun; I mean a verb indicative, present tense, and third person. And here be it known that this effect also is necessary for the excellence of our life, for our soul must needs accomplish a great part of its doings by a bodily organ; and it accomplishes them well when the body is well ordained and disposed in its parts.

12 And when it is well ordained and disposed, then it is beauteous as a whole and in its parts; for the due order of our members conveys the pleasure of a certain wondrous harmony; and their right disposition, that is their health, throws over them a color lovely to behold.

13 And so, to say that the noble nature beautifies its body and makes it comely and alert, is to say not less than that it adjusts it to the perfection of order. And this, together with the other things that have been discoursed of, appears to be needful to adolescents; and these are the things which the noble soul, that is the noble nature, being, as said above, a thing sown by divine providence, designs for it in its first stage.

Chapter XXVI

1 Now that we have discoursed upon the first section of this part, which shows whereby we may recognize the noble man by outward tokens, we are to proceed to the second section thereof which begins: *In manhood temperate and brave.*

2 It says, then, that as the noble nature in adolescence shows itself to be obedient, sweet, and alive to shame, giving adornment to the person, so, in the prime of life, it is temperate and brave and loving and courteous and loyal, which five things appear and are necessary to our perfection insofar as has respect to ourselves.

3 And concerning this we are to know that everything which the noble nature prepares in the first period of life is provided and ordained by the foresight of universal nature, which ordains particular nature to her perfection. This perfection of ours may be considered in two ways.

4 It may be considered as having respect to ourselves, and this perfection should be reached in the prime of our life, which is its apex; or it may be considered as having respect to others. And since it is necessary first to be perfect and then to communicate perfection to others, this second perfection must needs be had after that age, to wit, in old age, as will be said below.

5 Here, then, must be called to mind the discourse contained above in the twenty-second chapter of this treatise concerning the appetite which is born in us from our beginning. This appetite never doth aught else save pursue and flee; and whensoever it pursues the right thing in the right degree and flees the right thing in the right degree, man is within the boundaries of his perfection.

6 But this appetite must needs be ridden by reason. For just as a horse let loose, however noble he may be by nature, does not conduct himself aright by himself without a good rider, so this "appetite," which is known as irritable and appetitive, however noble it may be, must needs obey reason, which guides it with rein and with spurs, like a good horseman.

7 The rein it uses when appetite is in pursuit (and this rein is called temperance, which shows the limit up to which the pursuit is to be carried); the spur it uses when appetite is fleeing to make it return to the place whence it seeks to flee (and this spur is called courage, or consciousness of greatness, which virtue shows us where to make a stand and fight).

8 And thus restrained, Vergil, our greatest poet, shows Aeneas to have been in that part of the *Aeneid* where this period of life is rep-

resented, which part embraces the fourth, the fifth, and the sixth books of the *Aeneid*. And how great a restraint was that, when having received from Dido so much solace, as will be discoursed of below in the seventh treatise, and experiencing such delight with her, he departed to follow a path honourable and praiseworthy and fruitful, as is written in the fourth of the *Aeneid*.

[9] How great spurring was that when the same Aeneas hardened himself to enter alone with the Sybil into Hell and search for the soul of his father Anchises, in the face of so many perils, as is shown in the sixth of the aforesaid story! Whereby it appears how in manhood it behoves us for our perfection to be temperate and brave. And this is what goodness of nature accomplishes and shows forth, as the text expressly says.

[10] Moreover, it is needful to this period of life, for its perfection, to be loving; because it behoves it to look back and fore, as being itself in the meridian circle. It behoves it to love its elders, from whom it has received being and sustenance and instruction, so that it may not seem ungrateful. It behoves it to love its juniors, so that, loving them, it may give them of its benefits, by whom, then, in its lessening prosperity it may itself be sustained and honoured.

[11] And this love the above-named poet shows that Aeneas had in the above-mentioned fifth book, when he left the aged Trojans in Sicily, commending them to Acestes, and released them from their toils;[224] and when in that place he instructed Ascanius, his son, with the other young people, in tournament. Whereby it appears that love is necessary to this period, as the text says.[225]

[12] Further, it is needful to this period of life to be courteous, for although it becomes every age to be of courteous ways, yet to this age, above all, it is needful to practise them, since, on the other hand, age cannot do so, because of its gravity and the severity which is demanded of it; and so still more in the decrepitude.

---

224   *Aeneid* V.700–718, 746–761.
225   *Aeneid* V.545–603.

13 And this courtesy that most lofty poet shows Aeneas to have had in the above-said sixth book, where he says that Aeneas, king as he was, to honour the corpse of the dead Misenus (who had been Hector's trumpeter, and had afterwards commended himself to him), girt himself and took the axe to help hew the wood for the fire which was to burn the dead body, as was their custom.[226] Wherefore it is clear that this quality is required in manhood,; and therefore the noble soul displays it in this age, as was said.

14 Further, it is needful to this period of life to be loyal. Loyalty is the following out and putting into action of that which the laws dictate; and this is especially fitting for one in the prime of life; for the adolescent, as has been said, because of his minority, deserves pardon on easy terms; the senior ought to be just, in virtue of his wider experience, and should follow the laws only insofar as his own right to judgment and the law are one and the same thing; and he should follow his own just mind, as it were, without any law; which the man in his prime cannot do. And let it suffice that he observes the law and delights in observing it, just as the above-said poet in the above-said fifth book declares that Aeneas did when he instituted the games in Sicily on the anniversary of his father's death; for he loyally gave to each one of the victors what he promised for the victory, as was their ancient usage, which was their law.

15 Wherefore it is manifest that to this period of life loyalty, courtesy, love, courage, and temperance are needful, as says the text which we are now discussing; and therefore the noble soul reveals them all.

Chapter XXVII

1 We have sufficiently inspected and considered the section of the text which sets forth the probity which the noble soul furnishes to manhood, wherefore it seems right to turn to the third part which begins: *And in old age*, wherein the text purposes to show those

---

226 *Aeneid* VI.166ff.

things which the noble nature reveals and must have in the third period, to wit, old age.

2 And it says that the noble soul in age is prudent, is just, is open-handed, and rejoices to tell of the goodness and excellence of others, and to hear of it; that is to say, is affable; and truly these four virtues are most fitting to this age. And to perceive this, be it known that, as Tully says in that *Of Old Age*, "Our life has a fixed course and a simple path, that of our right nature; and in every part of our life place is given for certain things."[227]

3 Wherefore, just as that is given to adolescence (as said above), whereby we may come to perfection and maturity, so too is given to manhood that perfection and that maturity themselves, so that the sweetness of its fruit may be profitable to itself and to others; for, as Aristotle says, "man is a civic animal,"[228] wherefore he is required not only to be useful to himself but also to others. And so we read of Cato that he did not think of himself as born for himself, but for his country and for all the world.

4 Wherefore, after our own proper perfection, which is acquired in manhood, that perfection should also come which enlightens not only ourselves but others, and man should open out like a rose that can no longer keep closed, and should spread abroad the perfume which has been generated within; and this should come about in that third period of life with which we are dealing.

5 It is fitting, then, to be prudent, that is wise; and to be so demands a good memory of things formerly seen, and good knowledge of things present, and good foresight of things to come. And, as the Philosopher says in the sixth of the *Ethics*, "it is impossible for a man to be wise unless he is good,"[229] and therefore a man is not to be called wise who proceeds by stratagems and deceits, but he is to be called astute; for as no one would call a man who had skill to strike the point of a knife into the pupil of the eye wise, so

---

227   *De senectute* X.33.

228   *Politics* I.2.

229   *Ethics* VI.13.

neither is he to be called wise who hath skill to do some evil thing, doing the which he ever injureth himself ere he injures another.

6 If it be rightly considered, from prudence come good counsels which lead the man himself and others to a right goal of human affairs and doings. And this is that gift which Solomon, when he saw himself set to govern the people, required of God, as is written in the third book of *Kings*.[230]

7 And a prudent man such as this waiteth not till someone saith to him, "Give me counsel"; but himself foreseeing, without being requested he giveth him counsel, like to the rose which not only giveth its perfume to him who cometh to it that he may have it but also to every one who passeth it by.

8 Here some physician or legist may say, "That I am to carry my counsel and to give it even to those that ask it not, and pluck no fruit of my art?" I answer, as our Lord saith, "I receive freely if it hath been freely given."[231]

9 I say, then, sir legist, that those counsels which have not respect to thy art, and which proceed only from that good wit which God gave thee (and this is the prudence whereof we are now discoursing), thou shouldst not sell to the children of him who gave it thee. Those which have respect to the art which thou hast purchased, these thou mayest sell, yet not so but that it is fitting from time to time to pay tithes and give to God, that is to those poor who have nought left save the divine grace.

10 It behoves this period of life also to be just, so that its judgments and its authority may be a light and a law to others. And because this singular virtue, to wit, justice, was seen by the ancient philosophers to be revealed perfectly in this period of life, they committed the guidance of the city to those who had reached this age; and therefore the college of the rulers was called the Senate.

230　*Par.* XIII.91–96.
231　Matthew 10:8.

11 Oh, my wretched, wretched country! What pity for thee constrains me whensoever I read, whensoever I write, of aught that hath respect to civil government! But since justice will be dealt with in the last treatise but one of this volume, let it suffice at present to have touched this little upon it.

12 It is also meet for this period of life to be generous; because a thing is most in season when it satisfies the due of its nature; nor can the due of generosity ever be so satisfied as at this period of life. For if we would rightly consider how Aristotle proceeds in the fourth of the *Ethics*, and Tully in that *Of Offices*, generosity must be in such time and place that the generous man injure not either himself or others![232]

13 Which thing may not be without prudence and without justice, which to have in perfection by the natural way before this age is impossible. Ah, ye ill-starred and ill-born, who disinherit widows and wards, who snatch from the most helpless, who rob and seize the rights of others and therefrom prepare feasts, make gifts of horses and arms, robes and money, wear gorgeous apparel, build marvellous edifices, and believe yourselves to be doing generously.

14 And what else is this than to take the cloth from the altar and cover therewith the robber and his table? No otherwise, ye tyrants, should your presence be scoffed at than the robber who should invite his guests to his house and should set upon the table the napkin he had stolen from the altar with the ecclesiastical signs yet on it, and should suppose that no one would perceive it.

15 Hearken, ye stubborn ones, to what Tully saith against you in the book *Of Offices*: "Verily there be many who, desiring to be conspicuous and famous, take from these to give to those, thinking to be held in esteem if they make folk wealthy by what means soever. But this is so counter to what ought to be that nought is more."[233]

16 Further, it becomes this period of life to be affable, that is to love to speak of good and to hear of it, because it is well to speak good

---

232   *Ethics* IV.1 and *De officiis* I.xiv.42–44, respectively.
233   *De officiis* I.xiv.43.

on those occasions when it will be hearkened to. And this period of life carries a shade of authority, whereby it seems that men hearken more to it than to any earlier age. And it seems that it ought to have more beautiful and fair news because of its long experience of life. Wherefore Tully says in that *Of Old Age*, in the person of the ancient Cato, "Upon me has grown both the desire and the enjoyment of conversation beyond what was my wont."[234]

17 And that all these four things are fitting to this period of life, Ovid instructs us in the seventh of the *Metamorphoses*, in the story where he tells how Cephalus of Athens came to King Aeacus for help in the war that Athens was waging with Crete. He shows that old Aeacus was prudent, when, having lost by pestilence, through corruption of the air, almost all his people, he wisely had recourse to God, and asked from him the restoration of his dead people; and by his wit, which held him to patience and made him turn to God, his people were restored to him greater than before.[235]

18 He shows that he was just when he says that he made partition to his new people and divided his desolated land. He shows that he was generous when he said to Cephalus, after his request for aid, "O Athens, ask not help from me, but take it; and consider not the forces which this island holds, and all this state of my possessions, yours doubtfully. We lack not power, nay, we have superfluity, and the foe is mighty; and the time for giving is right prosperous and without excuse."[236]

19 Ah, how many things are to note in this answer! But for one with a good understanding it is enough that it be set down here, just as Ovid sets it down. He shows that he was affable when he carefully tells and rehearses to Cephalus in a long discourse the story of the plague of his people and the restoration of them.

20 Wherefore it is manifest enough that four things are suitable to this age, because the noble nature manifests them in it, as the text says. And that the example which has been spoken of may be the

---

234   *De senectute* XIV.46.

235   *Metamorphoses* VII.455–662.

236   *Metamorphoses* VII.507–511.

more memorable, he says of King Aeacus that he was the father of Telamon, or Peleus, and of Phocus, of which Telamon sprang Ajax, and of Peleus, Achilles.

Chapter XXVIII

1 After the section now discoursed upon, we are to proceed to the last, that is to the one which begins: *Then in the fourth term of life*; whereby the text purposes to manifest that which the noble soul doth in her last age, to wit, decrepitude.

2 And it says that she does two things; the one, that she returns to God, as to that port whence she departed when she came to enter upon the sea of this life;[237] the other, is that she blesseth the voyage that she hath made, because it hath been straight and good and without the bitterness of tempest.

3 And here be it known that, as Tully says in that *Of Old Age*, "natural death is, as it were, our port and rest from our long voyage."[238] And even as the good sailor, when he draws near to the port, lowers his sails and gently with mild impulse enters into it, so ought we to lower the sails of our worldly activities and turn to God with all our purpose and heart, so that we may come to that port with all sweetness and with all peace.

4 And herein we have a noteworthy instruction in gentleness from our own nature, for at such an age death is not pain nor any bitterness; but as a ripe apple, lightly and without violence, drops from its branch, so our soul, without pain, parts from the body wherein it has been. Whence Aristotle in that *Of Youth and Age* says that "the death that takes place in old age hath no sadness."[239]

5 And as to him who cometh from a long journey, ere he enter the gate of his city, the citizens thereof come forth to meet him; so come, and so should come, to meet the noble soul those citizens of

---

237 *Par.* I.91–93, 139–141.

238 *De senectute* XIX.70–71.

239 *De iuventute et senectute* 17.

the eternal life. And this they bring about by their good deeds and contemplations; for when the soul has already been surrendered to God and abstracted from the affairs and thoughts of the world, it seems to see those whom it believes to be with God.

6 Hearken what Tully says in the person of the ancient Cato: "I uplift myself in the utmost yearning to see your fathers whom I loved; and not only them, but also those of whom I have heard speak."[240]

7 The noble soul, then, surrenders herself to God in this period and awaits the end of this life with great longing, and seems to herself to be leaving an hostel and returning to her own house, seems to be coming back from a journey and returning to her own city, seems to be coming from the sea and returning to the port. Oh, wretched and vile, who with hoisted sails rush into this port, and where ye ought to rest shatter yourselves in the full strength of the wind and lose yourselves in the very place to which ye have made so long a voyage!

8 Verily the knight Lancelot would not enter there with hoisted sails; nor our most noble Latin, Guido of Montefeltro. In truth, these noble ones lowered the sails of the activities of the world; for in their advanced age they gave themselves to religious orders, putting aside every mundane delight and activity.

9 And no one can excuse himself by the tie of marriage which holds him in advanced age; for not only they turn to a religious order who liken themselves in garment and in life to St. Benedict and to St. Augustine and to St. Francis and to St. Dominic, but to a good and true religious order may they also turn who abide in matrimony, for God would have nought of us in religion save the heart.

10 And therefore St. Paul says to the Romans, "Not he is a Jew who is so outwardly, nor is that circumcision which is manifested in the flesh; but he is a Jew who is so in secret, and circumcision of the heart, in spirit, not in letter, is circumcision; the praise whereof is not from men but from God."[241]

---

240   *De senectute* XXIII.82–83.
241   Romans 2:28–29.

11 And further, the noble soul at this age blesses the times past, and well may she bless them; because turning back her memory through them she is mindful of her righteous doings, without which she could not come to the port whereto she is drawing nigh, with so great wealth nor with so great pain.

12 And she doth as the good merchant when, as he draweth nigh to the port, he examineth how he hath prospered, and saith, "Had I not passed by such a way, this treasure I should not have, nor should I have wherewith to rejoice in my city to which I am drawing nigh"; and therefore he blesseth the way that he hath made.

13 And that these two things are suitable for this period of life, the great poet Lucan figures forth to us in the second of his *Pharsalia*, when he says that Marcia returned to Cato and begged him and prayed that he would take her back again; by which Marcia is understood the noble soul.[242]

14 And we may thus convert the figure to the truth: Marcia was a virgin, and in that state she signifies adolescence; then she came to Cato, and in that state she signifies manhood; then she produced sons, by which are signified those virtues which are declared above to be fitting in the prime of life; and she departed from Cato and married Hortensius, whereby it is signified that the prime of life departs and old age comes. She bore sons also to him, whereby are signified the virtues which are declared above to be fitting in old age.

15 Hortensius died, whereby is signified the end of old age; and Marcia, having become a widow (by which widowhood is signified decrepitude), returned at the beginning of her widowhood to Cato, whereby is signified that the noble soul at the beginning of decrepitude returns to God. And what earthly man was more worthy to signify God than Cato?[243] Verily none.

16 And what says Marcia to Cato? "Whilst blood was in me," that is prime manhood, "whilst the maternal power was in me," that is

---

242   *Pharsalia* II.326ff.
243   *Purg.* I.31–109.

to say age, for she is in truth the mother of those other virtues, as has been said above, "I," says Marcia, "did and accomplished all thy commands," that is to say that the soul abode with constancy in the civic activities. She says, "I took two husbands," that is, "I have been fruitful in two ages."

17 "Now," says Marcia, "that my womb is wearied and I am exhausted for bearing offspring, to thee I return, no longer being such as may be given to another spouse," that is to say, that the noble soul, knowing that she has no longer any womb for fruit, that is to say when her members feel that they have come to feeble state, returns to God, who hath no need of the corporeal members.

18 And Marcia says, "Grant me the treaties of the ancient couch, give me the name only of marriage," which is to say that the noble soul saith to God, "Now give me repose, O my Lord." She saith, "Grant me at least that in this so much life as remaineth I may be called thine." And Marcia saith, "Two reasons move me to say this: the one is that it may be said after me that I died as Cato's wife; the other is that it may be said after me that thou didst not expel me, but didst give me in marriage of good heart."[244]

19 By these two reasons the noble soul is moved, and desireth to depart from this life as the spouse of God, and desireth to show that God was gracious to his creature. Oh wretched and ill-born, who prefer to depart from this life under the title of Hortensius rather than of Cato, with whose name it is well to end that which it behoves us to discourse concerning the tokens of nobility, because in him nobility itself shows all its tokens in every age.

Chapter XXIX

1 Now that the text has been expounded, as also those tokens which appear in the noble man in every age whereby he may be recognized, and without which he may not be, any more than the Sun can be without light, or fire without heat, the text at the end of all

---

244 *Pharsalia* II.340–341, 345.

that has been related about nobleness cries out against the people that saith, "O ye who have hearkened to me, *See now how many be thus deceived*," to wit, these who believe themselves to be noble because they are of famous and ancient generations and descended from excellent fathers, though they have no nobleness in themselves.

2 And here rise two questions, whereto at the end of this treatise it is well to give heed. Sir Manfred da Vico, who has now the titles of Praetor and Prefect, might say, "Whatsoever I may be, I call to men's minds and represent my ancestors, who by their nobleness earned the office of the Prefecture, earned to set their hands to the crowning of the Empire, earned the reception of the rose from the Roman pastor. Therefore I ought to receive honour and reverence from the people." And this is the one question.

3 The other is that he of San Nazzaro of Pavia, and he of the Piscicelli of Naples, might say, "If nobleness were that which hath been said, to wit, a divine seed graciously placed in the human soul, and if no progeny or race hath a soul, as is manifest, no progeny or race could be called noble; and this is counter to the opinion of those who say that our families are the most noble in their cities."

4 To the first question, Juvenal answers in the eighth *Satire*, when he begins, as it were, to exclaim, "What avail these honours which remain from them of old, if he who would fain mantle him therein liveth ill? if he who discourses of his ancestors and sets forth their great and marvellous deeds is intent on wretched and vile doings? And yet," (says the same satirist), "who will call him noble because of his good family, who is himself unworthy of his good family? This is no other than to call a dwarf a giant."[245]

5 Then afterwards he says to such an one, "Between thee and a statue, made in memory of thy ancestor, there is nought to choose, save that its head is marble and thine is alive." But herein (speaking with submission) I agree not with the poet, for the statue of marble or of wood or of metal, left as a memorial of some worthy man, differeth much in its effect from its unworthy descendant.

---

245 *Satires* VIII.1–5, 9–12, 19–20, 30–32, 51–55.

6 Because the statue ever confirms the good opinion in those who have heard the fair fame of him whose the statue is, and begets it in others; whereas the worthless son or grandson does just the reverse; for he weakens the opinion of those who have heard good of his ancestry; for a thought will come to them and say, "It may not be that all which is said of this man's ancestors is true, since we see such a plant of their sowing." Wherefore he should receive not honour but dishonour who beareth ill witness of the good.

7 And therefore Tully saith that "the son of the worthy man should strive to bear good witness to his father."[246] Wherefore, in my judgment, even as he who defames a worthy man deserves to be shunned by folk and not hearkened to, so the vile man, descended from worthy ancestors, deserves to be expelled by all. And the good man should shut his eyes so as not to look upon this reproach which reproaches the goodness that remains only in memory. And let this suffice for the present for the first question which was mooted.

8 To the second question may be answered that a family in itself hath not a soul; and yet it is true that it is called noble, and, in a certain sense, so it is. Wherefore, be it known that every whole is composed of its parts; and there are some wholes which have one simple essence together with their parts; as in one man there is one essence of the whole and of each of its parts; and what is said to exist in the part, is said in the same sense to exist in the whole.

9 There are other wholes which have not a common essence with their parts, like a heap of grain; the essence of such is secondary, resulting from many grains which have true and primary essence in themselves. And the qualities of the parts are said to exist in such a whole, in the same secondary sense in which it has an essence. Wherefore, a heap is called white because the grains whereof the heap is composed are white.

10 In truth, this whiteness is rather in the grains, primarily, and comes out as the result in the whole heap secondarily; and thus in a

---

246   Citation unknown; see *De re publica* VI.xvi.16 and VI.xxiv.26.

secondary sense it may be called white. And it is in this sense that a family or a race can be called noble. Wherefore, be it known that as the white grains must preponderate to make a white heap, so to make a noble race the noble persons must preponderate in it. I say preponderate, that is, exceed in number, so that their goodness by its fame may overshadow and conceal the contrary which is in it.

11 And just as from a white heap of grain you might remove the wheat grain by grain, and grain by grain substitute red millet till the whole heap at last would change its colour, so out of a noble race the good might die one by one, and worthless be born into it until it should change its name, and should not deserve to be called noble but base. And let this suffice as answer to the second question.

Chapter XXX

1 As is set forth above in the third chapter of this treatise, this ode has three chief parts; wherefore, since two of them have been discoursed upon, whereof the first begins in the aforesaid chapter and the second in the sixteenth (so that the first is completed in thirteen and the second in fourteen chapters, not counting the proem of the treatise on the ode, which is comprised in two chapters), we are now in this thirtieth and last chapter to discuss briefly the third chief division, which was composed as the *tornata* of this ode, for a kind of adornment, and which begins: *Against the erring ones take thou thy way, my ode.*

2 And here, to begin with, be it known that every good workman on the completion of his work should ennoble and beautify it as much as he may, that it may leave his hands the more noted and the more precious. And this it is my purpose to do in this section, not that I am a good workman, but that I aspire after being such.

3 I say then: *Against the erring ones,* and the rest. This "Against the erring ones," etc., is a whole section, and it is the name of this ode, chosen after the example of the good brother Thomas of Aquino, who gave the name *Against the Gentiles* to a book of his which he made to the confusion of all those who depart from our faith.

4 I say then "take thou thy way" as though I should say "thou art now complete, and it is time no longer to stand still but to go, for thy emprise is great." *And when thou shalt be in the region where our lady is,* tell her thy business. Where, be it noted, that (as saith our Lord) pearls must not be cast before swine, because it does them no good and is loss to the pearls;[247] and (as saith the poet Aesop in the first *Fable*) a grain of corn is more profit to a cock than a pearl, and therefore he leaves the one and picks up the other.

5 And, considering this, I caution and command the ode to reveal its business where this lady, to wit, Philosophy, shall be found. And there shall this most noble lady be found where her treasure-house is to be found, to wit, the soul wherein she harbours. And this philosophy not only harbours in the sages but also, as was shown above in another treatise, wherever the love of her harbours. And to such I tell my ode to reveal its business, because to them its teaching will be profitable, and by them it will be received.

6 And I say to it: Declare to this lady, *I go discoursing of a friend of thine.* Truly nobility is a friend of hers, for so much doth the one love the other that nobleness ever demands her, and philosophy turns not her most sweet regards in any other direction. Oh how great and beauteous adornment is this which at the end of this ode is given to her, calling her the friend of her whose true abode is in the most secret place of the divine mind!

---

247   Matthew 7:6.

Inferno: Book One of the Divine Comedy, Dante Alighieri,
a blank verse translation by Joe Carlson

Purgatorio: Book Two of the Divine Comedy, Dante Alighieri,
a blank verse translation by Joe Carlson

Paradiso: Book Three of the Divine Comedy, Dante Alighieri,
a blank verse translation by Joe Carlson